DEVELOPING AND MAINTAINING VIDEO COLLECTIONS IN LIBRARIES

JAMES C. SCHOLTZ

ABC-CLIO

SANTA BARBARA, CALIFORNIA
OXFORD, ENGLAND

© 1989 by James C. Scholtz
All rights reserved. No part of this publication may be reproduced, stored in a retrieval system, or transmitted, in any form or by any means, electronic, mechanical, photocopying, recording, or otherwise, except for the inclusion of brief quotations in a review, without prior permission in writing from the publisher.

"Implementing a Video Packet Rotation System," by Randy Pitman, which appears on pages 170–177 of this volume, © 1989 Randy Pitman.

Library of Congress Cataloging-in-Publication Data

Scholtz, James C.
　Developing and maintaining video collections in libraries / James
　C. Scholtz.
　　　p.　　cm.
　Includes index.
　ISBN 0-87436-497-3
　1. Libraries—Special collections—Videocassettes.　2. Video tape recorders and recording—Library applications.　3. Libraries and television.　4. Videocassettes.　I. Title.
Z692.V52S36 1988　　　　　　　　　　　　　　　　　　　88-16871
026.02517'82—dc19　　　　　　　　　　　　　　　　　　　　　CIP

10　9　8　7　6　5　4　3　2　1

ABC-Clio, Inc.
Riviera Campus
2040 Alameda Padre Serra, Box 4397
Santa Barbara, California 93140-4397

Clio Press Ltd.
55 St. Thomas' Street
Oxford, OX1 1JG, England

This book is printed on acid-free paper ∞.

Manufactured in the United States of America

This book is dedicated to Irene Wood, *Booklist* nonprint editor. I thank her for her belief in my capabilities as a reviewer and author in the video field. I also dedicate it to the memory of my father. I would like to thank my family for putting up with me during the writing process.

LIST OF ILLUSTRATIONS   *xiii*
LIST OF TABLES   *xv*
PREFACE   *xvii*

INTRODUCTION 1

- THE MEDIA REVOLUTION   2
- HOW DOES VIDEO FIT IN?   4
- NOTES   5

1 THE VIDEO REVOLUTION: INDUSTRY, RETAILERS, AND LIBRARIES 7

- THE CONSUMER   7
  How Consumers Use Their VCRs   *7* • Hardware Purchasing Patterns   *8* • The Advent of Rentals   *10*

- THE RETAIL/RENTAL BUSINESS   12

    Rentals versus Sales   *12* • Selecting and Controlling Inventory   *13* • Methods of Security and Patron Access   *14* • What Types of Videos Are Being Stocked?   *16*

- THE LIBRARY SCENE   17

    Video Collections Nationwide   *18* • Problems for Librarians in the Video Age   *22*

- NOTES   23

2   STARTING THE COLLECTION   25

- STRATEGIC PLANNING—
  THE CHICKEN OR THE EGG   25

    Payoffs and Risks   *26* • Preplanning: A List of Essential Components   *27*

- GETTING STARTED   27

    The Patron Survey   *29* • Consultation   *31* • Conclusion   *31*

- SPECIFIC COMPONENTS
  OF COLLECTION PLANNING   31

    The Community Served and Its Needs   *31* • Collection Development   *32* • Materials Budget   *32* • Physical Needs for the Video Collection Area   *37* • Purchasing Equipment   *50* • Staffing and Workflow   *54* • Security Needs and Ease of Access   *55* • Acquisitions, Processing, Cataloging, and Collection Arrangement   *55* • Circulation and Use Policies and Procedures   *66*

CONTENTS ix

- CONCLUSION   67

- NOTES   68

3 COLLECTION DEVELOPMENT POLICY   69

- SPECIFIC COMPONENTS OF A
  COLLECTION DEVELOPMENT POLICY   71

  Description of Policy Factors   71

- A SAMPLE COLLECTION DEVELOPMENT
  POLICY   73

- SUMMARY   78

- NOTES   78

4 COLLECTION DEVELOPMENT GOALS AND EVALUATION AND SELECTION GUIDELINES   79

- IMPORTANT VARIABLES IN
  DETERMINING VIDEO COLLECTION GOALS   80

  Quality versus Demand 82 · Circulation as a Factor in Collection Development 85 · Circulation Statistics 85

- THE SIZE AND SHAPE
  OF THE INITIAL COLLECTION   87

  Popular Features versus Specialty Programs 87

- SELECTION AND EVALUATION STRATEGIES 88

  Evaluation Criteria *89* • Evaluating Review Sources *91* • Overview of the Function of Selection Aids *94* • A Select List of Video Reference Guides *95*

- THE *BILLBOARD* CHARTS:
  A TEST OF POPULARITY 103

- SUMMARY 105

- NOTES 109

5 | A GUIDE TO SELECTING AND MAINTAINING VIDEO EQUIPMENT 111

- BRIEF REVIEW OF
  VIDEO RECORDER TECHNOLOGY 112

  Beta versus VHS *114*

- MAGNETIC VIDEOTAPE 117

- SELECTING THE EQUIPMENT 118

- FEATURES AND FUNCTIONS
  OF VCRs AND EQUIPMENT 121

  VCRs: Portable and Tabletop *121* • Television and Receiver/Monitor *123* • Routing Connectors and Switches *125* • The Video Processor *126* • Broadcasting and Editing Equipment *126*

- VIDEOTAPE REPAIR AND MAINTENANCE 128

  How To Test, Clean, and Store Videotape *128* • How Long Will Videotape Last? *129* • Video Repair *131*

CONTENTS xi

- VCR MAINTENANCE   **134**

    Video Head Cleaners *135* • Typical Problems *135*

- CONCLUSION   **137**

- NOTES   **137**

6 | SPECIAL PROBLEMS CONCERNING VIDEO   139

- COPYRIGHT   **139**

    The Law *140* • The Issue of Public Performance *141* • Home Use, Fair Use, and Educational Use *143* • Potential Solutions *147* • The MPAA Warning Label and Library Usage *147* • Court Decisions *149* • At-Home Taping for Institutional Use *150* • Video Use Guidelines *150* • Source Material for Copyright Information *154*

- FEE-BASED VIDEOCASSETTE LOANS   **155**

- ACCESS BY MINORS   **157**

- WEEDING   **159**

- NOTES   **160**

7 | EXPLORING OPTIONAL PURCHASE PLANS   163

- CONSORTIUM PURCHASING   **163**

- VIDEO LEASING PLANS   164

    The Eastin-Phelan Programs *164* • The Videoplan Option *165*

- ROTATING COLLECTIONS: VIDEO CIRCUITS   166

- IMPLEMENTING A VIDEO PACKET ROTATION SYSTEM, by Randy Pitman, editor of *The Video Librarian*   170

    Selection *171* • Staff Support *173* • Pros and Cons *175* • A Tale of Two Systems *176* • Summary *177*

- NOTES   177

8 PREDICTING THE FUTURE   179

- THE SOFTWARE OUTLOOK   179

- VENDORS AND LIBRARIES   182

- THE HARDWARE SCENE   183

- SPECIAL OPTIONS AND COPYRIGHT   183

- SUMMARY   184

- NOTES   185

    APPENDIX: Freedom to View   187
    INDEX   189

ILLUSTRATIONS

FIGURES

2.1	Sample library patron questionnaire	*30*
2.2	Workplace design for a video area	*39*
2.3	Gaylord modular panel videocassette display unit	*42*
2.4	Track system display method	*43*
2.5	Diagrams for six-shelf home-built videocassette unit	*47*
2.6	Diagrams for 20-bin record display unit	*51*
2.7	Main entry catalog card for *Yellowstone in Winter*	*64*
4.1	Collection development process model	*81*
4.2	Sample video circulation statistics sheet	*86*
4.3	*Billboard*'s "Top Videocassettes Rental Hit Chart" for 17 August 1985 to 16 August 1986	*104*
4.4	*Billboard*'s "Top Videocassettes Sales Hit Chart" for 17 August 1985 to 16 August 1986	*105*
4.5	*Billboard*'s "Top Videocassettes Sales" chart for 28 March 1987	*106*
4.6	*Billboard*'s "Top Special Interest Videocassettes Sales" chart for 21 March 1987 (A) and for 28 March 1987 (B)	*107*

xiii

5.1	Azimuth recording and tracks on videotape	*113*
5.2	Illustrations of videotape paths	*116*
5.3	Videotape layered composition	*118*
5.4	Videotape manufacturers' tamper-proof screw heads	*132*
6.1	MPAA copyright warning notice	*142*
6.2	Letter from Warner Bros. Distributing concerning library use of home-use videocassettes	*145*

PHOTOS

2.1	Vid Pro Video Plak display system	*41*
2.2	Decatur Public Library (Illinois) video display area	*44*
2.3	Decatur Public Library (Illinois) record display units	*45*
5.1	Close-up of a VCR video drum	*114*

TABLES

1.1	Percentage of prerecorded video software dollar volume by configuration	9
1.2	Penetration of VCR units in U.S. homes	9
1.3	VSDA national averages for member stores	12
1.4	Percentage of prerecorded video software dollar volume in 1985	13
1.5	Percentage response for specialty video holdings for local/branch libraries	19
1.6	Percentage of video collection by genre for public libraries	20
2.1	Application of the McGrath budget formula	36
2.2	Index to *AACR II* cataloging rules for videos	63

PREFACE

Public librarians are becoming increasingly tangled in the home video web, and thus have a professional obligation to learn all they can about the concepts, social impact, technology, and utilization of the video medium so they can maximize its use within their respective libraries. The purpose of this book is to provide librarians with a how-to manual concerning video collection and service development that will give them all the basic tools necessary for establishing a new collection or redirecting an existing one. It contains up-to-date information on virtually all aspects of circulating video in libraries today. It is directed toward professional audiovisual librarians as well as the vast number of "nonprofessional" librarians operating in small libraries across the country. The library student aspiring to work in the audiovisual field, as well as the retail video marketing executive, may also find it useful. Topics covered include establishing a theoretical collection development rationale, setting goals, community/patron surveys, developing selection policies, specific problems, survey of current library practices, technical problems, and collection evaluation. It will provide a valuable "drawstring" resource, pulling together diverse current, topical information so that informed collection and service decisions can be made.

Although focusing primarily on public libraries, this book will cover specific problems encountered in library systems and school libraries as well. Particular emphasis will be placed on establishing goals and organizing a total program of collection development. Video holdings are particularly well suited to intensive collection management techniques because of their relatively small size compared to other library collections. Circulation, collection size, and subject/genre composition can be monitored and analyzed using either automated or manual systems.

Chapter organization follows a prescribed format: each chapter begins with a short introduction, then focuses on specific topics, usually concluding with a short review section to bring the entire chapter into perspective. The book is hierarchical in nature; each chapter uses the information presented in previous chapters as stepping stones. Documents, charts, and illustrations are included to further aid the reader's understanding and knowledge.

The scope is limited to the ½-inch videocassette; other specific formats such as the compact laser video disc, C, or 8mm are not discussed. However, most of the chapters are equally applicable regardless of format because the discussion is on a theoretical level. It is not the purpose of this volume to offer any new revelations; rather, it presents a commonsense guide for planning that will aid in maximizing the performance of any library's video collection. My successful practice within a medium-sized city library was incorporated with information from current periodicals, surveys, industry reports, and books in an attempt to meld theory and practice together to produce a timely, informative, and readily usable volume.

A special thanks to Randy Pitman, video coordinator at the Kitsap Regional Library in Bremerton, Washington, and editor of *Video Librarian*, for his segment on implementing a video packet rotation system.

James Scholtz

INTRODUCTION

The story of the video revolution reads like a Brothers Grimm fairy tale. On a particularly bright sunny morning in Anytown, USA, the residents awoke to find videocassettes available at their public library. When the library opened, vast throngs of people from every walk of life entered, and in a wink every video title was whisked from the shelves. Thus began the video revolution. Librarians reveled in the influx of new patrons and increases in circulation—a virtual panacea for those circulation declines when the library had "only books." Despite the revolution's auspicious beginnings, however, unforeseen problems and concerns lay ahead.

Later that day, the library was inundated with a group of hostile video rental store owners saying the library was "infringing on their turf." Also, several mothers complained about R-rated titles being available for their children to check out and watch at home. Patrons started making demands: "Get some newer titles." "Don't you have a list of all available titles?" "What do you mean, all the copies of *Rambo* are checked out?!" The library became a zoo, and the video revolution was in full swing.

This scenario dramatizes the point that video collections are not problem-free solutions for shrinking patronage and declining circulation. As with any collection, careful planning, materials selection, and evaluation must occur for it to be a success. Evidence has shown that a videocassette collection will substantially increase any library's circulation, but questions concerning the impact of, and need for, video within each community should be raised. Librarians exist to serve the information and entertainment needs of a diverse community. Those needs are realized in a variety of formats, such as books, serials, periodicals, phonorecords, cassettes, compact discs, computer software, and videocassettes.

The electronic age has brought us television, a form of mass communication that is unparalleled and that continues to have a profound impact on our lives. Video is an extension and product of that impact, combining television's excellent teaching capabilities with the added attraction of being totally user-directed. Never before in the history of television have we had the power to choose for ourselves exactly what we want to watch, when we want to watch it. This factor generates video's wide appeal. Video offers instruction and entertainment at our command; our choices are limited only by the availability of software. Film/video historian Michael Gitlin emphasizes that "the video revolution is here and libraries are cutting themselves out of a huge chunk of contemporary culture if they ignore it."[1] However, John W. Jones, director of the Neuse Regional Public Library (Kinston, North Carolina) cautions:

> Some speak of video as the new Messiah, others see the Phoenix rising from the ashes to devour the profession. Few seem to put video in context with the reality of the profession and the basic principles of good management. Video, simply put, is just another service and thus joins the family of services that many public libraries provide to the community. It is no more [and] no less. Therefore the decision to own or not to own ... should be made with the same consistency that the administration uses to establish a worth and value for any other service. In other words, the defense for having or not having video lies within the same frame of reference as does the philosophical reasoning for owning any other [types] of material.[2]

Today, some 40 million homes have videocassette recorders (VCRs), and a question often posed to librarians is When will video be included in the collection? It is extremely important, however, not to rush into any new service without a thorough knowledge of the subject and a predetermined plan of action.

THE MEDIA REVOLUTION

Public library involvement with new media activities (largely film) increased because of World War II. The war hurled the United States into a new era of literacy awareness. Thousands of men had to be

INTRODUCTION 3

quickly taught new skills, while training manuals had to be written to facilitate learning, simultaneously accommodating a wide range of reading levels. Media, in the form of slides, filmstrips, and especially films, became the most efficient vehicles for user-oriented, self-paced learning.

After the war, Bernard Berelson wrote,

> The American Public Library is a social invention designed for the preservation and dissemination of certain products of the nation and the community ... [designed] to provide ready and free access to books for all [and to be a] depository of knowledge, information, and entertainment, insofar as they are contained in library materials.[3]

The public library was becoming more responsive to popular demands, searching for more innovative and varied sources of information, and enlarging its services to encompass those new forms. As early as 1949, some forward-looking librarians sought to extend library services beyond traditional methods and materials. They realized that other forms of mass communication represented significant competition to public libraries. The far-reaching effect of new media upon the information environment of the library was being recognized.

The 1960s' "race for space" accelerated technology and brought an explosion of information. As technology progressed, videocassettes supplanted the open-reel tape medium. The importance of video as an instructional tool for individuals and small groups became widely accepted as it entered the school, college, and university arenas. Then, in the middle 1970s, the concept of home video was realized. Consumers could now time shift, or record real-time programs to watch later at their convenience. The time-shifting market strategy worked to a point, but no one could have conceived that the prerecorded videocassette industry would blossom into a multibillion-dollar industry. Today, families can watch what they want, when they want. However, there is still a catch—programming is now dependent upon the availability and commercial variety of prerecorded videocassettes.

Media, particularly 16mm films, began to take a foothold in educational and library circles when it was realized that many topics were much better served by a "how-to" approach incorporating motion rather than printed pages with still photographs and diagrams. But because of the large price attached to this medium and the specialized equipment needed to view it, film was treated only as a specialty item, not on the same plane as "standard" books. Media's equality as a standard information source was recognized in 1975 when the Audiovisual Committee of the Public Library Association (American Library Association) published *Guidelines for Audiovisual Materials and Services for Large Public Libraries,* which stated that

> audiovisual materials and services should have equal weight, concern, familiarity, and support of library administrators and staff as those of printed materials.[4]

During that same year, Lester Asheim spoke of the new media as "not in conflict with the library ideal but a contemporary expression of it, utilizing the new tools at hand to accomplish what is implicit in the traditional objectives."[5] Today, then, librarians have certain professional obligations to enter the new media age. The question for the future is not whether the public library will stock videocassettes; it is how to select and use them to their greatest potential within the library community.

HOW DOES VIDEO FIT IN?

Today we live in an electronic age. "Sesame Street" has just celebrated its twenty-fifth anniversary—more and more adults now only know a world that has been shaped and influenced by television. This is the primary reason why it is imperative for librarians to involve themselves with video. In spite of the fact that television has lessened communication within the family and adversely affected reading and writing skills among young people, it is the leading transmitter of information in our culture.[6]

Most librarians realize that some day they will have to enter the video world but are procrastinating, not because of a myopic viewpoint, but because of shrinking budgets, decreasing patronage, and apprehensiveness about video technology. Historically, the public library has been oriented toward the middle class, with a clientele that is a "self-selected [usually better-educated] minority with special characteristics."[7] In the past, new services and collections have not drawn many new patrons into the library. Normally, these new services are primarily, and consistently, used by the existing clientele. However, no other medium (except the phonorecord) has held the mass appeal and entrenched itself into society like the videocassette. Therefore, video may prove to be the exception to this rule.

Approximately 35 percent of U.S. homes with television now have at least one videocassette recorder, and that number is expected to increase to 75 percent by 1990.[8] The sales of VCRs have directly paralleled the early sales curve of color television sets. During 1986, 13.2 million VCRs were sold in the United States, and sales of slightly over 14 million are projected for 1987. Current figures indicate that 30 percent of the 15,000 U.S. public libraries have some type of circulating video collection, and over 80 percent of all public schools have at least one VCR.[9] The VCR is no longer an item purchased only by the wealthy; it can be found in homes of every economic class. This high video use, coupled with its overwhelming attraction, makes it feasible that new patrons may be drawn into a library just to check out videos. For libraries, this phenomenon increases the chances that circulation of traditional materials may also increase.

The home video revolution is new, and time will be needed to study, analyze, and recognize the value of videocassettes for the community library. The advantages as well as the disadvantages have to be weighed. Librarians need a realistic understanding of video technology and trends because, inevitably, it will be just one mode among many that will shape the future of information retrieval.

NOTES

1. Michael Gitlin, "Developing Video Collections: What Are the Alternatives?" *Film Library Quarterly* 15, No. 2–3 (1982): 5.
2. John W. Jones, "Regarding Videos, Be Consistent," *Librarian's Administrative Digest* 28 (October 1987): 61.
3. Bernard Berelson, *The Library's Public* (New York: Columbia University Press, 1949), 45.
4. James Brown, *New Media in Public Libraries* (Syracuse, NY: Jeffrey Norton, 1976), 3.
5. Lester Asheim, "39th Conference of the Graduate Library School" (Chicago: University of Chicago Press, 1975), 3.
6. Berelson, *The Library's Public*, xi.
7. Gitlin, "Developing Video Collections," 5.
8. Ray Serebrin, "Video in Public Libraries: A Guide for the Perplexed," *Library Journal* 119 (15 May 1987): 29.
9. Carol Emmens, "Video Collections & How to Build Them," *School Library Journal* 33 (September 1986): 43.

THE VIDEO REVOLUTION: INDUSTRY, RETAILERS, AND LIBRARIES

The video boom is hard to grasp in terms of numbers or dollars as it continues to grow by leaps and bounds. In terms of rentals and sales, retailers are just beginning to ask the question, How high is up? Everyone within the video industry is simultaneously delighted and confused by the extensive technological advances and the variety of hardware and software. The options opened to the public by home video technology are now so vast that the government is being asked to step in to regulate some aspects of the industry. A unique mixture of technological genius and marketing wizardry has combined to create a product that is as commonplace as toothpaste in today's society. All this for an industry that is less than ten years old. Of greater interest now, however, is what the future holds for producers, retailers, libraries, and consumers alike. In order to understand the video phenomenon and predict paths for the future, it is necessary to look at the expanding industry through the eyes of three factions: the consumer, the retail sales/rental business, and the library. This historical overview will provide a basis for analyzing and interpreting trends in terms of community wants and needs.

THE CONSUMER

☐ HOW CONSUMERS USE THEIR VCRs

To understand how people use their VCRs is to understand an important part of viewer values and behavior regarding communications. Librarians must obtain a feel for the consumer dynamics of VCR hardware and software consumption. Only then can they make educated decisions regarding video collections. When discussing the consumer, it is difficult to separate the influences of industry and marketing, for they are the entities that promote and entice buying. The consumer is both the initiating and sustaining force in determining a product's success.

The Electronic Industries Association reports that, in a survey conducted in 1986 that sampled 7,525 households with televisions in the United States, 35 percent owned a VCR. Owners averaged 9.3 hours per week playing tapes, with 6.1 hours of recording. The typical VCR is used around thirty times per month—40 percent of the time for recording and 60 percent for playback, with people watching what they have recorded more than once. Only 30 percent of playback time is used for rented or purchased videotapes. Seven out of ten VCR owners rent titles from video stores and average 35 rentals per year per person. Male heads of households were the heaviest users (49 percent), followed by female heads of households (37 percent). Other users accounted for 28 percent. First-time VCR buyers continue to dominate total sales, buying 83 percent of the machines sold in 1985.[1] These patterns show strong signs that VCRs are becoming integrated into home entertainment patterns. Wilkofsky Gruen Associates predicts that by 1995 videocassettes will become "the nation's leading entertainment medium."[2]

☐ HARDWARE PURCHASING PATTERNS

The U.S. home video market is dominated by two competing video systems—VHS (Video Home System) and Beta. RCA's magnetic disc and Pioneer's laser disc continue to have a small following, but, because of their read-only capacity, consumer interest has dwindled. The new 8mm and C formats are enjoying increased popularity, but it is doubtful that they will seize a major portion of the market, at least in the near future. Currently, the VHS format, developed by the Japanese Victor Corporation in 1976, holds approximately 90 percent of the home video market. The Beta format, developed by the Sony Corporation in 1975, now runs a poor second. The main reason for this trend was Sony's unwillingness to have anyone but themselves manufacture and distribute their product. Currently, many video rental stores are finding it difficult to get Beta software titles on demand because distributors are stocking them as special rather than regular items. Table 1.1 compares dollar volumes of four video systems for a two-year period.

VIDEO: INDUSTRY, RETAILERS, AND LIBRARIES 9

TABLE 1.1 Percentage of prerecorded video software dollar volume by configuration

VIDEO SYSTEM	1985	1984
VHS	83.7	76.1
Beta	14.6	14.5
Laser	0.5	4.9
CED	1.2	4.5

SOURCE: Video Software Dealer's Association, *1986 VSDA Annual Survey* (Cherry Hill, NJ: VSDA, 1986), 8.

According to *The Video Librarian*, since the conception of home video software about seven years ago, the video industry has consistently doubled its annual sales of both hardware and videocassettes. In 1986, sales totaled an enormous $3.3 billion. In 1983, 3.3 million VCRs were sold in the United States. That figure rose to 7.6 million in 1984, and in 1985, 11 million units were sold.[3] During 1987, approximately 14 million VCRs were expected to be sold, with an estimated 800,000 units being sold each month. A Market Opinion Research survey conducted in 1983 indicated that about 9 percent of U.S. television homes had a video recorder. VCR home penetration, shown in Table 1.2, is expected to reach 68.9 percent, or 63.9 million households, by the end of the decade.[4]

Changes in pricing were key factors in popularizing VCRs. The initial high prices of VCRs and VCR software combined to drive retailers into the rental business, a practice at first bitterly fought by Hollywood producers. When hardware first appeared, it retailed

TABLE 1.2 Penetration of VCR units in U.S. homes (in millions)

	NUMBER OF TVs	NUMBER OF VCRs	PERCENTAGE OF PENETRATION
1982	83.3	5.2	6.2
1984	86.0	14.0	16.0
1988 (est.)	92.7	35.0	38.0

SOURCE: Video Software Dealer's Association, *1985 VSDA Annual Survey* (Cherry Hill, NJ: VSDA, 1986), 2.

for approximately $1,500 per unit.[5] In 1981, the average price for a VCR was $728. Today's average VCR costs about $420, with a price range of $200 to $1,800. According to a recent issue of *Time*,

> VCRs are selling at nearly double the rate of a year ago [1984]. . . . "The interesting thing about the sales of VCRs" says David Rowe, *Video Store's* magazine editor, "is that they are not affected at all by seasonal variables." VCR sales are as strong in the slow months of retail sales as they are in the strong months.[6]

Currently, there is a manufacturing trend to phase out the midpriced models, giving the consumer a choice between the high-performance, multifunction models or the economy models. The rationale for this is that the consumer who wants hi-fi sound and integrated logic functions also prefers the other high-tech capabilities.

☐ THE ADVENT OF RENTALS

Most people originally purchased their VCRs for time-shift viewing. Today, prerecorded videocassettes have seized a large part of the market. In 1982, 3.5 million prerecorded videocassettes were sold; in 1983, 9.5 million; in 1984, 25 million; 50 million ($950 million worth) in 1985; and sales topped $1.6 billion in 1986. During 1987, sales were expected to reach $2.2 billion. In contrast, video rentals amounted to $3.65 billion in 1985 and $5.6 billion in 1986.[7]

In the beginning, feature films occupied the bulk of the available software, but as the audience and hardware grew, the need for more and different kinds of videocassettes was felt. The majority of the software industry was geared toward selling, but then some innovative retailers decided to rent the tapes instead, and suddenly a brand new, very profitable industry emerged. In 1980, the U.S. public rented 26 million tapes, and in 1984 they rented 304 million. According to Tim Baskerville, editor of *Video Marketing Newsletter*, retail videocassette sales for 1984 amounted to $575 million; rentals were almost twice that, totaling about $914 million. The industry had created a consumer who preferred to rent, rather than buy, software. In 1985, there were approximately 30,000 outlets handling the sales and rentals of videocassettes in the United States.[8] At first, locally owned stores dominated the scene. Then, chain stores, in an attempt to reduce overhead and maximize profit, usurped the market. Currently, there is a trend away from the retail outlet specialty store and into nontraditional outlets like bookstores, gas stations, and convenience and grocery stores.

According to a July 1985 survey conducted by the Fairfield Group, Inc., rental circulation was divided by type of video rented as follows:[9]

Hit movies	60%	Music videos	6%
Classic movies	18%	Adult movies	4%
Children's	10%	Instructional	2%

Librarians must be careful not to interpret these figures as absolute genre preferences. People can only rent what is offered by the stores, and the stores are out to make a profit. Therefore, demand for popular, ephemeral "blockbuster" movies is catered to. Although this results in very high circulation, it also promotes multiple-copy buying to satisfy immediate, high demand and creates a limited title variety per amount of money expended.

Before 1985, the majority of available video titles were feature films. Today, the *Video Source Book* lists approximately 50,000 available titles, 8,000 of which are "specialty" videos. The term *specialty video* is loosely applied to anything that is not a theatrical feature film. The label includes how-to and self-improvement tapes, information and education, music videos and performing arts tapes, children's videos, and television nostalgia packages. Features still dominate the market, but the slow steady trend is toward more specialty videos. Wilkofsky Gruen Associates projects that the feature/specialty ratio will go from today's 77/23 to 40/60 by 1995.[10] About 200 new movie titles are released each month, and most movies are available on tape less than one year from their release date in the theaters. It is amazing that it took only six years for Hollywood to release on video almost every film made in the past fifty years. But Hollywood is running out of movies to release, and this factor coupled with the prohibitive cost of acquiring major motion picture video rights has given the video industry additional incentives to find new program alternatives. Tom Hayworth, B. Dalton bookstore's divisional merchandise manager, feels that the two subjects people agree will work successfully for the videocassette medium are children's programming and do-it-yourself tapes.

The dynamics of consumer retail sales and rentals can be summed up as follows:

1. Although annual video sales have steadily increased, video rentals have also increased at a 3.5/1 ratio compared with sales. This indicates that consumers prefer to rent videotapes rather than to purchase them.
2. Although features comprise the bulk of the video rental business today, the reservoir of movies is rapidly drying up, and producers are moving to specialty videos.
3. Specialty programming is finding an increasing audience because VCR penetration into the home is on the rise.
4. This phenomenon will have a great impact on video collections in libraries within the next decade.[11]

THE RETAIL/RENTAL BUSINESS
☐ **RENTALS VERSUS SALES**

In most video outlets, the ratio of rentals to sales ranges from about 80 to 90 percent in favor of rentals. A recent survey found, "The ratio of sales to rentals went from 15.7/84.3 percent in 1984 to 22.8/77.2 percent in 1985, and is continuing in that direction."[12] Table 1.3 presents some characteristic national averages for Video Software Dealer's Association (VSDA) member stores and the changes from 1984 to 1985. Libraries might find these figures useful in planning video service—determining budget and average title selling price, loan fees, optimum collection size, and number of staff needed to run the service. A library video collection should be based on sound business strategies that include some degree of demand purchasing, inventory control and collection management, promotion, collec-

TABLE 1.3 VSDA national averages for member stores

AVERAGES	1985	1984
Prerecorded video sale transaction	$37.23	$42.66
Prerecorded video rental transaction	$2.66	N/A
Number of titles per store	1,968	1,578
Number of inventory units per store	2,589	2,321
Number of full-time employees	3	3.2
Number of part-time employees	4	3.0
Shrinkage/theft percentage per store	N/A	1.1%

SOURCE: Video Software Dealer's Association, *1985 VSDA Annual Survey* (Cherry Hill, NJ: VSDA, 1986), 1.

VIDEO: INDUSTRY, RETAILERS, AND LIBRARIES

tion arrangement/shelving, and staffing. Video retailers can be the best indicators of industry trends and forecasts and can be powerful allies in initiating industry changes.

☐ SELECTING AND CONTROLLING INVENTORY

The significance of the reversal of the sales-to-rental trend is twofold: the size of the market, which has made it profitable to produce exclusively for video, and the popularity of specialty programming. Most of the new productions are directed at lifestyle purchases such as cooking, hobbies, how-to, and fitness. The data in Table 1.4 compiled by the VSDA for their 1985 *Annual Survey* represent statistics provided by 40 percent of the members as of 1 February 1986.

Video stores are a cash business, and the cash flow looks good on paper but hides the real problem of too much inventory making too little money. It has become impossible to stock a store with all the popular titles. The average inventory has zoomed to almost 2,600 cassettes, up 400 from the 1984 average.[13] In December 1986, Megamovies, a New York–based rental chain, announced it would increase its flagship store holdings to 10,000 tapes, representing some 6,000 titles.[14] Ray Markman, president of Heritage Home Video in Chicago, says, "In the rental business, an $80 tape must be

TABLE 1.4 Percentage of prerecorded video software dollar volume in 1985

TYPE OF SOFTWARE	PERCENTAGE OF VIDEO DOLLAR
Action/adventure (features)	23.1
Comedy (features)	21.3
Drama (features)	15.2
Children's (features and specialty)	12.6
Science fiction (features)	9.3
Horror (features)	7.5
How-to (specialty)	4.8
Music video (specialty)	4.6
Foreign (features)	0.9
Sports (specialty)	0.7

SOURCE: Video Software Dealer's Association, *1985 VSDA Annual Survey* (Cherry Hill, NJ: VSDA, 1986), 1.

rented out 40 times (if the rental fee is $2) to pay for itself."[15] In 1987, the average cost of a videocassette was $37. During 1986, combined videocassette sales and rentals totaled $7.2 billion.[16] Today, the key question is, Will the small operations survive? Larger chain operators are cutting in on the smaller businesses because of their ability to stock a greater number and variety of titles. But these stores are also experiencing growing pains as the business expands into other nontraditional markets. The VSDA offers the following advice, which is applicable to libraries as well: (1) stock a broader range of titles; (2) stock specialty items that are unavailable elsewhere; (3) offer better and more in-depth customer service and assistance; and (4) react better (and more quickly) to local trends, popular movies, etc.[17]

☐ METHODS OF SECURITY AND PATRON ACCESS

Guarding against theft is another large concern for video retail stores. A variety of methods, including expensive electronic security devices, has been developed to improve security. Security measures run the gamut from simple ceiling mirrors and television cameras to locking entrance/exit gates that respond to magnetic-coded sensing strips on merchandise. Jim Ellis, president of a St. Louis, Missouri, video rental chain, Movies to Go, is skeptical about the success of electronic security because the cost of purchasing additional equipment, plus the added time of sensitizing/desensitizing the merchandise, only increases overhead and does not seem to outweigh the cost of replacing theft losses.[18]

The electronic antitheft system alluded to above is called Sensormatic. Similar in function to systems marketed by companies like Checkpoint and 3M, these systems are receiving mixed reviews in libraries. Checkpoint uses a 1½ x 1½ inch self-adhering foil label that, when sensitized, reflects radio waves into a security gate monitor as it passes through. The Tattle-tape and Whisper-tape systems developed by 3M utilize small magnetized strips instead of radio waves. The big problem is hiding the security label from the patron.

The librarian considering the question of security versus patron access must seek answers to several questions. Is the video display in a high-traffic/high-visibility area? If it is, it promotes easy patron access, but equally easy theft. Is there adequate staff to help patrons and aid in security? Can the display (and patrons) be easily seen from all staff work stations? Does the video area have only one entrance/exit or multiple access points? (Multiple access points are not advocated.) Have other local video stores had theft problems? Is the library placed in a part of the community conducive to theft? Has the staff been taught how to legally handle suspected thieves? Often, by redesigning the video area, theft can be minimized or eliminated with minimal expense.

Currently, the concept of open versus behind-the-counter display is being hotly debated. Bill Critchfield, Adventureland vice-president of corporate communications, says that 50 percent of Adventureland's 800-plus stores are now using open service, while the other 50 percent have traditional behind-the-counter service.[19] That is, the dummy boxes are displayed for patron perusal, but the actual merchandise is kept behind the counter with full clerk control.

Historically, the commercial cardboard video box has been used as a dummy, but video stores are now devising some innovative and space-saving methods of display. New York–based New Video is using a trademarked Videoflats display system. The Videoflat is a laminated, LP-sized jacket that contains the videocassette label, packaging notes, format information, and rental and sales prices. This idea saves space, allowing 1,500 individual titles to be displayed in a 6-foot browser bin.[20] Erol's, a 96-store chain of rental outlets headquartered in Springfield, Virginia, has always advocated open display of its rental stock without utilizing an electronic security system. Erol's vice-president of advertising and promotion, Ron Castell, emphasizes that

> having videocassettes behind the counter and empty boxes on the shelves is like having a can of corn on the shelf and going to the counter to ask for the corn. The advantages of having hands-on outweighs the negative of [theft]. You treat customers like second-class citizens when you worry about security.[21]

These new display methods are creating problems with inventory control and staffing. If the behind-the-counter service method is used, some sort of inventory count must be devised to keep track of the number of copies of any one title that is in or out. Multiple dummy boxes or pull cards with copy numbers are sometimes used. Many stores are looking into computerized inventory/ordering methods. All these methods require a one-to-one dummy to "live" title check. A growing, demanding, and video-wise public is developing, and retailers are finding that they must provide viewer service information such as, What's good? or, Who stars in what? Clerks must be versed in supplying plot synopses as well as broad title and subject availability. Often, it is not crucial that clerks know an answer, but rather how fast they can obtain an answer and the extent to which the answer satisfies the customer.

☐ WHAT TYPES OF VIDEOS ARE BEING STOCKED?

Not only are methods of doing business changing, but the mix of titles available is changing, too. Many stores are now stocking only one format, primarily VHS. Another trend seems to be the inclusion of specialty video in the stock of video rental stores. Specialty stock has often been limited to exercise and popular children's titles, but the variety is expanding. One of the biggest problems in selling specialty titles is the lack of prerelease public exposure of those titles. By the time a feature film is released on video, it has benefited from major television and print publicity and the public is craving it. Made-for-video productions are just now enjoying increased advertising and media coverage as a result, in part, of the celebrity status of the actors who have begun to star in them. B. Dalton's divisional merchandise manager, Tom Hayworth, feels that

> The future of videocassettes is not in the movies but in informational and educational material. The market is two or three years away, but the areas of potential will be in the lines such as how-to, home repair, cooking, sports, etc.[22]

Ron Castell, vice-president of Erol's, agrees, saying,

> We want to service the utility of the VCR, which we believe goes much further than just its ability to play back prerecorded entertainment. The VCR can be a teaching tool to convey a wide array of knowledge and information to consumers who know how and where to get it. Movies are cyclical; three months from now *Rambo* will be just another title and its rental potential will go way down. A video on car repairs will always be with us for a long time, though, because people will always have cars.[23]

Billboard magazine apparently agrees with the viability of specialty video because, starting with the 10 January 1986 issue, four new special-interest video sales charts covering recreational sports, health and fitness, hobbies and crafts, and business and educational video have been introduced. In an attempt to satisfy the more discerning customer, the New York metropolitan-based giant, Megamovies, is staffing stores with knowledgeable sales-oriented clerks who "talk movies" with customers. Megamovies is also analyzing and reacting to changing community interests and targeting different demographic groups. For example, they are offering over 1,000 children's titles stocked in a separate "Kid-vid" room complete with bean bag chairs and video monitors. In Huntington, New York, where there are lots of skiers, Megamovies carries many ski and travel videos. Megamovies also recognizes the need for the older classics and sponsors bimonthly, singles-oriented evening coffee klatch movie discussions.[24]

VCR permeation has reached a point where, even though specialty titles may be of interest to only a small local population, they will sell/circulate because that population is actually represented by hundreds of thousands of like-minded people in a viable and growing international market.

There are no clear-cut answers to the questions of security versus open service, what types of titles to stock, and how much service to provide. The librarian considering these questions must have a knowledge of the community, combined with a knowledge of available video software, plus an assessment of realistic goals in relation to the library's overall service philosophy and budgetary constraints.

THE LIBRARY SCENE

The New York Public Library's video collection at the Donnel Film Library was probably one of the first video collections in a public library. Since that time, many libraries have taken a plunge into video. This section will provide a brief overview of current library trends regarding videocassette collections and loan practices. It combines data from four different surveys: Wombat Productions, "Video and the Public Library" (1985); Professional Media Services, "Public Libraries and Videocassettes" (1984); and *Library Journal*'s (LJ) two surveys, "Videocassettes in Libraries" (1985) and "A Commitment to Cassettes" (1986).

☐ VIDEO COLLECTIONS NATIONWIDE

Wombat surveyed 260 state, regional, county, local and branch libraries nationwide and found that in 1985 83 percent of the regional centers (state and county libraries), and 73 percent of local/branch libraries currently had some type of circulating video collection. The regional centers indicated that 20 percent of their branches had video collections, with 36 percent more expected to have them in 1986. About 14 percent of the local/branch libraries that did not possess video collections planned to start them in 1986.[25] The American Library Association's survey, *Libraries in an Information Society: A Statistical Summary* (June 1987), indicated that 67.5 percent of public libraries serving populations of 25,000 or more held educational videocassettes and 69.9 percent held entertainment videos.[26] Market industry reports show a more conservative figure of around 51.3 percent for 1987, with an increase to 60.3 percent expected during 1988.[27]

The two *Library Journal* surveys indicated that video collections and composition varied widely from library to library. The size of title collections ranged from an average low of 45 to an average high of 2,600. Only 16 percent of these libraries had 400 titles or more.[28] The Wombat survey indicated majority clusters grouped around the low and high end ranges; 52 percent held less than 100 titles, while 22 percent held 300 titles or more.[29]

Most libraries serving populations under 25,000 do not have a full-time designated AV librarian, nor do they allocate space specifically for a video area. The video collection usually consists of a set of open or closed shelves or rotating wire racks.

According to Fred Philipp, president of Ingram Video, public libraries are spending an average of $8,200 on video acquisitions annually, up 5.1 percent from last year's average of $7,800. In 1986, 41.2 percent of libraries spent $1,500 or less on video. The vast majority, 70.5 percent, indicated that they expected to purchase less than 100 tapes per year. Only 5.2 percent expected to purchase more than 500 tapes annually, and only 8.6 percent of libraries possessed annual video budgets in excess of $20,000. Video budgets seem to correlate fairly closely with video collection size. The average annual budget (1986) among libraries possessing collections of 500 tapes was $22,500. Among libraries with fewer than 200 tapes, the average budget was $1,600.[30] *Library Journal*'s surveys indicated a slightly higher annual budget average of $13,000, with the range topping $70,000 at one library.[31]

Public libraries have widely varying plans for collection growth. The average projected increase in collection size was 42 percent, but the range went from a modest 14 percent to a high of 53 percent. About 40 percent indicated that they did not possess funding for the video collection.[32] Many of these libraries fund the collection by charging fees. The Neuse Regional Public Library in Kinston, North Carolina, has about 4,000 titles and charges $.25 per circulation with annual circulation exceeding 160,000. Revenue from this source now exceeds $42,000 per year.[33] Also, every library surveyed planned for collection growth even though its materials budget was not being increased.

Collection composition consisted of 79.3 percent entertainment (feature films, music videos) and 20.7 percent nonfiction or specialty videos. Multiple copies were purchased by 75 percent of the regional libraries and 45 percent of the local/branch libraries. The predominant choice was one to three copies (84 percent) of any title. The VHS format clearly dominated the scene with 94 percent; only 6 percent of the responding libraries wanted to own both VHS and Beta formats. Feature films were the most popular among library patrons by 61 percent. Of that number, 14 percent found children's equally popular.[34] Tables 1.5 and 1.6 illustrate relative video collection holdings for public libraries by genre and type.

TABLE 1.5 Percentage response for specialty video holdings for local/branch libraries*

TYPE OF HOLDING	PERCENTAGE RESPONSE
Travel	43.3
Sports	28.3
How-to	57.5
Health/physical fitness	43.3
Documentary/education	6.6
Science/nature	2.5
Literature	1.6
Children's	2.5
Cultural/performing arts	5.0
Business	.8
Language	2.5

*Percentages based on total number of respondents in each category rather than actual percentages of genre collection makeup.
SOURCE: Wombat Productions, *Video and the Public Library* (New York: Wombat, Spring 1985), 1.

TABLE 1.6 Percentage of video collection by genre for public libraries*

	1986	1987
Movies	48.3	43.1
Children's	33.5	34.9
Educational	8.6	11.1
How-to	7.5	9.9
Documentary	6.5	7.7
Exercise	4.2	4.1
Performance arts	3.7	4.6
Music	3.6	4.4

*Percentages represent actual collection composition averages. Totals exceed 100 percent because of category overlaps.
SOURCE: Data from Fred Philipps, president, Ingram Video, Nashville, Tennessee, interview with author, 4 December 1987.

Automated circulation systems can be successfully employed to identify popular genres and types of videos, thus aiding selection. Libraries not possessing automated systems can effectively use random samples, yielding similar results. Most libraries predominantly hold features; some purchase more copies of current top hits, while others purchase primarily classics. One method of assessing broad-based feature popularity is through the use of *Billboard* magazine's "Top Videocassettes" lists. *Billboard* publishes a weekly list of the 40 most popular videocassettes based on sales and rentals from a nationwide survey of video retailers.

The majority of libraries circulate video by using the closed-stack system without utilizing a magnetic security system. Commercial boxes are used as dummy displays. Only 29 percent of the libraries charged some sort of loan fee, with the most popular circulation period being one to three days. Standard fees were as low as $.50 per loan or as much as $3 for a 72-hour loan period. Lending periods were very similar across the country, and 61 percent offered either two- or three-day loans. Others made distinctions between work and nonwork days, or offered only overnight loans. Wombat's survey indicated that 31 percent of the local/branch libraries loaned titles for one day; 24 percent for two days; and 30 percent for three days. Those libraries that charged for video loans reported a wide variety of fee structures, but the overdue fines remained consistently high at $1 to $3 per day. Almost every library that responded indicated that they held the patron responsible for loss or damage. However, the same overwhelming majority reported little or no loss. Theft was found to be almost nonexistent. Loan and in-house use restrictions by age were noted in a surprising 83 percent of the libraries. The high circulation of videos exhibited by libraries seems to be independent of whether the library charges a fee or not.[35]

Librarians who have built popular, high-circulating collections have reported that the service has attracted new library users. Nearly 70 percent of the libraries responding to *LJ*'s survey felt that the availability of videocassettes in their libraries increased library patronage. Several libraries reported increases in new card registrations and observed changes in patron habits as occasional users tended to become frequent users. Some have speculated that these new users have become users of other library services as well, but there is no documentation to support these claims. The Cooperating Libraries of Central Maryland found that borrowers of video tended to be previous library users of a high education level between the ages of 30 and 39.[36] This high-education characteristic may be regional in nature, and currently contradicts the national trend. However, it does lend support to the theory that existing library patrons (primarily oriented toward the middle class) use libraries the most. It is also interesting to note that 35 percent of the libraries indicated that any one title in their collection circulated an average of 49 times or less; 33 percent indicated an average of 50 to 100 circulations per title.[37]

Perhaps as a consequence of the relatively small size of most video collections, many libraries indicated that they did not classify or catalog their collections. Those few that did catalog and/or classify their collections were equally divided in housing the cards in their main catalog or in a separate video catalog. About 50 percent reported having a title list available for patrons to take home. Over 70 percent of the surveyed libraries did their own cataloging, but more than half used a shortened form of cataloging information. The majority of libraries did not possess the equipment necessary to inspect/clean videocassettes; however, many of them realized the importance of this step.[38]

Most of the libraries regarded video jobber and distributor catalogs as their major selection and purchase tools. Video distributors were also the major source of acquisitions. Video reviews and individual producer catalogs, respectively, were next in line as sources for selections. A purchase discount seemed to be an important factor in selecting a distributor.

☐ PROBLEMS FOR LIBRARIANS IN THE VIDEO AGE

A host of new problems are also occurring with the increased community library usage and circulation of materials. The video revolution is both boom and bane to libraries. The video patron is often a totally different type of patron, sometimes difficult and demanding and not familiar with traditional library organization and procedures. The crush of high-volume circulation wears down an already slim staff. Providing adequate support and professional staff, budget allocation, and storage space, and deciding whether the library should purchase *Billboard*'s 40 "Top Videocassettes" were the main concerns of librarians. Acquisition can be a big problem: knowing where to go for what, getting the best price, finding a knowledgeable vendor/distributor, and getting the best service.

Many librarians are responding to the challenges that videocassette collections present. Most see it as a means to promote community use of the library, while also trying to complement, rather than compete with, retail video rental stores. For example, the Onondaga County Public Library (New York) has no popular films, choosing instead to emphasize subjects like "fly-fishing, volleyball, golf, and Shakespearean plays."[39] Both the Findlay-Handcock (Ohio) and the Comsewogue (New York) Public Libraries have collections exceeding 3,000 titles. The Decatur Public Library (Illinois) has a centralized collection of about 1,600 titles, which results in 3,800 to 4,000 circulations per month. Findlay-Handcock loans videocassettes for a five-day period; the Decatur Public Library loans them for an unusually long one-week period. Decatur's video circulation is about 100,000 per year, or approximately 600 per day. The Cleveland Public Library (Ohio) budgeted $95,000 in 1985 to increase the size of and decentralize its video collection.[40]

Professional library magazines and journals are filled with news items advertising individual libraries' circulation successes with video. However, nationwide there are wide variations in clientele size and makeup, collection size, circulation, genre and subject inclusion, and budgets of video collections. Librarians should realize that their collections may not perform as well as the collections cited in these periodicals. The key is to make a collection realize its maximum potential within a specific community. In order to accomplish this goal, a certain amount of community and library characteristic data must be gathered. From that data, a well-thought-out, predetermined, long-range service plan can be formulated.

NOTES

1. Peter P. Schillaci, "Video Trends: Past, Present, & Future," *Sightlines* 20 (Winter 1986/1987): 8.
2. Ibid.
3. Ray Serebrin, "Video in Public Libraries: A Guide for the Perplexed," *Library Journal* 119 (15 May 1987): 29.
4. Randy Pitman, "A Quick Overview of the Video Scene Today," *The Video Librarian* 1 (1 March 1988): 2.
5. Schillaci, "Video Trends," 8.
6. Linda Sunshine, "The Videocassette Business: Is There a VCR in Your Future?" *Publisher's Weekly* 227 (15 February 1985): 37.
7. "Prerecorded Cassette Rentals and Rental Sales, 1985–1986," *Ingram's Preface: Video for Bookstores*, March 1987, 1.
8. Sunshine, "Videocassette Business," 42.
9. Randy Pitman, "A Quick Overview of the Video Scene Today," *The Video Librarian* 1 (1 March 1986): 3.
10. Schillaci, "Video Trends," 8.
11. Sunshine, "Videocassette Business," 39.
12. Schillaci, "Video Trends," 8.
13. Ibid.
14. Jim Bessman, "Customer-Friendly Terminals Used," *Billboard*, 27 December 1986, 44.
15. Sunshine, "Videocassette Business," 43.
16. Ibid.
17. Ibid., 48.
18. Chris Morris, "New Display Alternatives Being Eyed," *Billboard*, 1 August 1986, 48.
19. Ibid.
20. Ibid.
21. Ibid.
22. Sunshine, "Videocassette Business," 37.
23. Ken Joy, "Summer Sales Boom Contradicts 'Dog Days' Consensus," *Billboard*, 30 August 1986, V83.
24. Bessman, "Customer-Friendly," 47.
25. Wombat Productions, *Video and the Public Library* (New York: Wombat Productions, Spring 1985), 1.
26. Mary Jo Lynch, *Libraries in an Information Society: A Statistical Summary* (Chicago: American Library Association, June 1987), 13.
27. Fred Philipp, president, Ingram Video, Nashville, Tennessee, interview with author, 4 December 1987.

28. Loretta L. Lettner, "An LJ Mini Survey: Videocassettes in Libraries," *Library Journal* 110 (15 November 1985): 35.
29. Wombat Productions, *Video*, 6.
30. Fred Philipp, president, Ingram Video, Nashville, Tennessee, interview with author, 4 December 1987.
31. Lettner, "An LJ Mini Survey," 37.
32. Ibid.
33. John W. Jones, "Regarding Videos, Be Consistent," *Librarian's Administrative Digest* 28 (October 1987): 61.
34. Lettner, "An LJ Mini Survey," 37.
35. Professional Media Services, "Public Libraries and Videocassettes," *In the Groove*, October 1983, 5.
36. Lettner, "An LJ Mini Survey," 37.
37. "Big Video Circulation at Ohio Library," *Library Journal* 110 (15 November 1985): 20.
38. Susan Avallone and Bette Lee Fox, "A Commitment to Cassettes," *Library Journal* 111 (1 November 1986): 35–36.
39. "'Nonfiction' Videotapes at Onondaga County, NY," *Library Journal* 110 (15 April 1985): 14.
40. "Big Video Circulation at Ohio Library," *Library Journal* 110 (15 November 1985): 16; "Cleveland Public Library Boosts Spending for Videos," *Library Journal* 110 (1 March 1985): 26.

2 STARTING THE COLLECTION

STRATEGIC PLANNING—THE CHICKEN OR THE EGG

Starting any new service or collection is a little bit like asking, Which comes first—the chicken or the egg? A certain amount of strategic planning must lay the decision-making groundwork before a new service is implemented. A strategic plan is the single most important element in establishing a successful new service. Existing resources such as space, staff, physical facilities, and budget must be assessed and placed in perspective with community demands. A new service can be undertaken as an experimental endeavor. However, care should be taken before starting out because, once provided, it is extremely difficult to discontinue it without a negative impact on public relations.

As Barbara Tolliver observes, "Strategic planning is the process of establishing goals and objectives and developing strategies to accomplish them."[1] Once formulated, the plan must then be monitored, evaluated, and adjusted according to the institution's perceived function and purpose within the community. A plan should assess the community's needs and the extent to which the library can realistically satisfy those needs; otherwise there is a substantial risk of overpromising and ultimately disillusioning the staff and the public. The librarian must gather and synthesize a great deal of information in this stage. After all the data have been analyzed, the results may indicate that the service should not, or cannot, be undertaken by the library at this time because of certain restrictions or limitations. Librarians must avoid new technology fever—*all* aspects of the library are ultimately tied to satisfying community wants and needs.

A well-developed strategic plan should consist of the following organizational elements:

1. Assessment of community needs
2. Evaluation of current library services and resources
3. Determination of the library's role within the community
4. Establishment of goals, measurable objectives, and priorities
5. Development and evaluation of strategies for implementation of change (plan of action)
6. Implementation of those strategies, i.e., establishing goal target dates
7. Monitoring and evaluation of progress toward the goals[2]

There is an old axiom stating that the plan is less important than the planning. In other words, it is the planning process that pays off.

Today, videocassettes are becoming entrenched in U.S. society, and it would be hard to question their popularity or viability as part of a library collection. Yet despite the changing video scene, many librarians continue to buy on demand, giving no thought to the shape, coverage depth, or purpose of the collection as it grows. They also expand services and facilities without first obtaining the necessary community needs data. Currently, libraries can muddle through quite well using a nonplanning expansion strategy. However, the time is near when this lack of planning may lead to ineffectual collections because of the changing video environment. A formal needs assessment does not have to be extensive, but librarians must know a few vital characteristics about their community's video demands. With this information, informed decisions that plan for today as well as tomorrow can be made. All libraries, no matter how big or small, can benefit from strategic planning.

☐ PAYOFFS AND RISKS

The ultimate payoff of planning for any new service should be a more efficient, community-responsive, well-used service. Planning should result in a better match of services to the needs of the community. This is not to say that changes are always necessary. There are often risks associated with making changes, and some librarians are hesitant because of this factor. Planning does not remove risk; it attempts to identify and assess risk and offer implementation options. Risks can be effectively minimized, making

STARTING THE COLLECTION

the process painless, if librarians avoid the following planning pitfalls: (1) collection of too little data; (2) lack of planning preparation; (3) getting too tied up with gathering statistics and analyzing data; and (4) being subjective rather than objective.[3]

☐ PREPLANNING: A LIST OF ESSENTIAL COMPONENTS

It is recommended that, in developing a strategic plan, a systems analysis approach be followed. This approach requires a listing of all the components that either affect or are affected by the new service. These components are then analyzed in an effort to determine the shape and viability of that service. Preplanning serves several functions that aid in establishing long- and short-term goals, specific objectives, collection and service priorities, the evaluation process, and effective use of library resources. Regardless of the type of library, these components should be examined in preplanning:

- Purpose of the library (mission)
- Specific community served and its needs
- Overall collection development for a five-year period
- Budget (five-year projected)
- Facility needs: space, equipment, storage, shelving, and display
- Staffing and workflow
- Security needs
- Acquisitions, processing, cataloging, and collection arrangement
- Circulation and use policies/procedures: in-house use, returns, damage evaluation, fines, and overdues
- Perceived trends in video marketing and technology
- Evaluation process.[4]

These components will be discussed at length later in this chapter.

GETTING STARTED

The AV librarian should seek to discover how community members satisfy their viewing needs. Do they buy or rent tapes? How many local rental and retail video outlets are there? What types of programming do those outlets possess, and what types are most popular? Is there an unfulfilled need for other types of programming? Is video hardware widely available, and is it selling? Does the community support theaters? What types of cable channels are offered and supported? Are there overlapping video services provided by other libraries, schools, or colleges in the area? Preliminary to any serious video planning a library should conduct a short survey among current patrons to answer four questions: What percentage of current patrons now owns a VCR? How many plan to purchase a VCR in the next year? What is the predominant video format within the community? What percentage of library patrons currently uses existing local video rental outlets?[5]

The next step is to formulate a series of questions addressing physical space needs, storage, acquisition procedures, collection development, collection size, patron access, circulation procedures, and damage assessment.

- Where will the collection be placed?
- How will the titles/volumes be stored, displayed, and arranged?
- Will security be a problem? What are the antitheft options?
- Will the titles be cataloged and classified? Will there be card catalog access and by using what access points (subject/genre headings)?
- What vendors/distributors should be used, and what type of ordering and tracking procedures should be followed?
- What materials selection sources are available, and how much money should be set aside to purchase those titles?
- Where are videocassette processing supplies available (such as Amaray cases and various labels)?
- Who on the staff will handle selection? Will extra staff be needed for patron assistance, circulation, reshelving and checking videos?
- Is in-house carrel viewing being considered, including equipment specifications and funding?
- What circulation guidelines should be set, including methods, loan periods, rental fees, overdue and damage fines?
- What provisions will be necessary for assessing patron damage by inspection and cleaning of videocassettes?
- Are branches or rotating collections being considered? (If so, all of the above questions must be considered on an individual branch basis.)

☐ THE PATRON SURVEY

Once the above questions have been considered, the librarian should enlarge upon that information by using a patron survey as an aid in establishing a base or core collection. Studies indicate that the majority of new library services are used primarily and consistently by existing, rather than new, patrons. Although it seems as though video in libraries deviates from this rule, the survey should be directed toward current library patrons rather than the broader-based community. All questions should be structured so as to be succinct and closed-ended. Essay questions are inappropriate. Short, multiple-choice questions should be used, thereby minimizing subjective variables. For the most part, future-tense questions such as, Would you use . . . if . . .? should be avoided because of the tendency to answer questions based on expectations rather than actual truth. Also, the entire questionnaire should be kept as short as possible.

Specifically, the questionnaire should elicit responses to the following concerns: format needs, feature and nonfiction genre/subject needs, and possible loan period and fee preferences. The best method of obtaining responses is to set up a manned station at the entrance and ask patrons to fill out the questionnaires as they come in. By performing this task during a peak operating week and alternating station times, a more representative cross-section sample will result. A sample patron questionnaire is shown in Figure 2.1.

Any library service is ultimately judged by the extent to which it satisfies the needs of its clientele. This statement conceals two problems of immense complexity. First, what are the user needs in terms of provided services and materials, and how can they be accurately described at all? Second, to what extent is it possible to assess and quantify the effectiveness of a library service in attending to these needs? Librarians have attempted to draw distinctions between needs and wants and desires, attaching greater importance to the former. Patron needs are usually expressed in three different ways: overtly expressed needs, unexpressed needs, and unactivated needs.[6] Many patrons ask direct questions to staff concerning specific titles or collection subject areas—these are expressed needs. Unexpressed needs are those needs that have not been overtly expressed or interpreted in terms of specific library solutions. Many of these needs are displayed by minority clientele groups and the nonpatron community. Unactivated needs are initiated by the library to satisfy some currently unperceived but forthcoming patron desires. Buying the bestsellers in anticipation of need is a lower

1. Do you currently own a VCR? ___ yes ___ no
2. What type is it? ___ Beta ___ VHS ___ other (specify)
3. If no to #1, are you planning to purchase a VCR within the next six months?
4. Do you currently rent videos from a local video store? How often?
   ___ daily ___ weekly ___ monthly ___ occasionally
5. What types of feature videos are you most interested in seeing? (Check top 5, 1–5 decreasing level of interest.)

current hits	___	dramas	___
film classics	___	horror	___
comedies	___	sci-fi/fantasy	___
westerns	___	romance/drama	___
children's	___	war	___
musicals	___	mystery/suspense	___

   other (specify) _____

6. What types of specialty films are you most interested in seeing?

children's folk/fairytales	___	music videos	___
travel	___	history	___
science	___	war documentaries	___
crafts and hobbies	___	religious	___
sports and exercise	___	plays/theatre	___
nature/hunting/fishing	___	how-to	___
cooking	___	opera	___
business/motivational	___	other	___

7. Do you currently borrow any videos from other library systems or local libraries? ___ yes ___ no
   Please name. _____

FIGURE 2.1 SAMPLE LIBRARY PATRON QUESTIONNAIRE. This questionnaire is designed to assess videocassette ownership, interests, and use by current library patrons.

form of an unactivated need. Holding cooking classes in the library while purchasing (and advertising) cookery videocassettes is another example of stimulating and selling an unactivated need.

☐ CONSULTATION

Essentially, the questionnaire is designed to identify the aforementioned needs. Once armed with this information, the librarian should seek the aid of three other sources: (1) library legal counsel; (2) other libraries with existing video collections within close proximity (and possibly of similar size); and (3) local video rental stores. The national Video Software Dealer's Association (VSDA) can be contacted to find the regional office in your area if no local stores exist (VSDA, 100B-F Astoria Boulevard, Cherry Hill, NJ 08003; (609) 424-7117). These contacts will prove to be invaluable because they will help negate feelings of competition, provide extra information concerning all aspects of video, and aid in establishing further avenues of cooperation, such as cooperative purchasing, interlibrary loans, and public relations.

☐ CONCLUSION

The importance of seeking answers to the collection and service questions discussed earlier cannot be stressed enough. All libraries should have short- and long-range collection goals covering a five-year period. In this manner, all aspects of library administration are directed toward satisfying specific goals. Documenting the entire process is equally important, thereby avoiding similar mistakes in the future. Although librarians can learn from one another, it is important to realize that every library is somewhat unique. Most often, copycat collections do not work well; library collections and procedures must be tailored for individual community situations.

SPECIFIC COMPONENTS OF COLLECTION PLANNING
☐ THE COMMUNITY SERVED AND ITS NEEDS

A library's sole function is to serve the information and recreational needs of the community regardless of the media available. However, each community's information network will dictate the types of services provided by the library. A successful library video collection extends and complements other video collections in the community rather than relying upon direct competition and duplication of service.

As David Spiller notes, "It is important to ascertain the scope of the community to be served as regards age, occupation, ethnic composition, ability, interests, and projected informational needs."[7] Obviously, the informational needs of a high school, or a white-collar, middle-aged community would differ from those of a retirement community. The needs assessment and patron survey are specifically designed to provide information concerning identification of these needs.

☐ COLLECTION DEVELOPMENT

The collection development policy will be discussed at length in chapters 3 and 4. A general overview is presented here. A collection development policy is essentially a long-range planning document that addresses current and future information needs that are realized through the purchase of library materials. In this manner, library goals are synthesized into the materials selection and inclusion process. The librarian needs to know how broadly and to what extent the collection should be developed. Generally speaking, a public library video collection is small but must meet the general interest needs of patrons. A community college or school collection must be geared for specific curriculum needs. The librarian must decide how much collection detail is needed. Because an eclectic collection equilibrium is never reached, this component undergoes constant revision. It is necessary to know the characteristics of various types of information in order to determine which formats are best suited for effective communication of that information. Some subjects are better suited for video presentation than others. It is imperative that a library have a well-defined collection development policy that outlines video selection principles because it provides a solid foundation from which to build and evaluate specific collections.

☐ MATERIALS BUDGET

Depending upon the library, the video budget may include allocations for more than just materials. A budget entry should be specifically designated for videocassettes, but the overall budget must include total operational costs for the video collection. The video budget must be an integral part of the library's materials collection. Alternatively, these costs may be distributed throughout various other departmental budgets. Line items such as staff, protective cases, new equipment and repair, shelving, and security system costs as well as acquisitions, processing, and cataloging costs must be estimated and projected for the current year and the next four years (for a five-year long-range plan). All the strategic planning elements addressed in this book have budgetary ramifications, but this section will describe the materials (video purchases) only.

There is always a question as to the allocation of money for various material formats and the budget percentages allotted to them. Home videocassette prices have been dropping consistently since 1983. Today, the average price of a home video ($37) is only slightly higher than that of an academic book ($26.25).[8] Line-item materials budgets often consist of simple multiplication (e.g., a library wants to purchase 600 video titles during the fiscal year, 600 × $37 (average price) = $22,200). Budget changes are most often a simple percentage increase/decrease based upon last year's figure adjusted for price changes. Budgeting via a formula is advocated because it may provide a more logical and equitable distribution of available funds. This formula concept is based in part upon the zero-based and program-planning budget systems. Previous yearly figures are not necessarily used as budget starting points as the budget is based upon planned programs, priorities, and institutional goals. A well-thought-out budget formula plan can be quite flexible and adaptive to change.

One such formula approach is based upon previous performance (circulation) within subject/genre categories and is a true demand-oriented budget allocation system. However, programs (as dollar percentages) can be built into the system. Titles are broken down into narrow, similar-subject and genre categories. The yearly circulation of each category is divided by the collection's circulation total, yielding a percentage. This percentage is multiplied by the total allocated dollar amount, giving the new budget for each category. The librarian can divide the category total by the average cost of a videocassette and thus arrive at an approximate number of items to be purchased in that category.

The McGrath formula is another demand-oriented budget allocation model.[9] There is no magic minimum number of titles/volumes that a library must obtain in order to achieve an eclectic collection. Collection excellence must be measured using a local satisfaction scale that measures "complete" and "incomplete" collections by the number of filled and unfilled information/title requests and their respective increase or decrease during a specified time period. The McGrath formula is founded on two premises: (1) Demand dictates what the library buys; demand, in turn, is determined by use of the library (circulation). What is used is what people want, and this information aids in predicting future use patterns. (2) Two variables, the number of videos circulated and the average cost of a videocassette within each category, are the essential ingredients of the formula. The category framework should be by subjects, possibly within the Dewey decimal classification system.[10]

The formula's steps are outlined in the following pages utilizing sample statistics. If circulation statistics are kept by a computerized system, categorization procedures are simplified. If a circulation system such as CLSI is utilized, various video format subjects and genres are given statistical codes. Then, the monthly circulation totals can be fed into a microcomputer spreadsheet to extrapolate current statistics and predict future trends. The use of a manual circulation system makes subject/genre statistics more difficult to obtain on a title/circulation basis. Random sampling is the best method for obtaining a better picture of video circulation and subject/genre popularity when manual circulation systems are used.

Table 2.1 outlines the steps for utilizing the McGrath formula for a video collection costing $6,000. For this example, it is assumed that the library has done all the necessary research, surveys, and goal preparation so that the $6,000 total is in line with the expected goals of the library. Table 2.1 illustrates the application of the McGrath budget formula to devise a percent/cost relationship in videocassette purchasing by genres and subjects.

Steps in using the McGrath formula:

STEP 1. Determine total yearly circulation (B) within individual categories (i.e., subject/genre breakdowns such as romance, horror, 300s, 700s, etc.). The categories can be as broad or as narrow as needed but the more specific the better.

STEP 2. Average cost (E) for any category can be computed in several ways. It is highly recommended that librarians keep track of purchases by subject/genre categories because this information can be used in a variety of ways. In this manner, a true average can be obtained. The mode (most frequently appearing number) is actually the best representation of the dollar price. The easiest way to calculate average cost is to divide each category total dollar amount spent (D) by the number of volumes purchased (C). Example: $1,000/50 (vols.) = $20.

STEP 3. To calculate cost/use (F), multiply each average cost (E) by its corresponding circulation (B). This is represented in dollars.

STEP 4. Divide each cost/use figure (F) by the cost/use total (I); the quotient is the percent cost/use (G).

STEP 5. Each percentage in (G) is multiplied by the total allocation (J); the result represents the dollar allocation for that category.

The formula shown in Table 2.1 is rigid in mathematical structure, but its application can be extremely flexible. Since it does utilize a preconceived budget dollar amount to arrive at category allocations, it is not a true program-based budget. Additional program objective percentages must be built into each category to reflect program-based budgeting. If it is desired that one or more categories should be strengthened, then the percentage budget allocations should be adjusted to reflect that specific collection objective.

Materials budgets should not be taken off the bottom of the total budget after other items have been taken care of—they should be allocated based on specific goals and needs. Program and zero-based budgeting techniques are specifically designed to assist in allocating monies based upon changing institutional goals. This author advocates using a budgetary process that combines line-item and program budgeting. Existing collections can effectively use line-item budgeting as long as programs and services stay the same. New and redirected collections should use a combined method (such as the McGrath formula) because there has been no cost history from which to draw upon. Service goals and collection objectives must be described in terms of measurable objectives, all of which must be costed out. In this manner, options can be explored in relation to their overall viability versus cost. As John Rutledge and Luke Swindler state, the budget should

> not be viewed as a criterion for selection but rather as an influence upon the relative extent to which selection criteria are acted upon. Those items that the library must have, should have, or could have—do not change in response to

TABLE 2.1 Application of the McGrath budget formula

GENRE/ DEWEY (A)	TOTAL YEARLY CIRC. (B)	NO. OF VOLS. (C)	COST (D)	AVERAGE COST/VOL. (E) D/C = E	COST/USE (F) B × E = F	PERCENT COST/USE (G) F/I = G	ALLOCATION (H) J × G = H
Comedy	500	50	$1,000	$20	$10,000	23	$1,380
100	75	10	$ 700	$70	$ 5,250	12	$ 720
500	200	20	$1,200	$60	$12,000	28	$1,680
700	400	25	$1,000	$40	$16,000	37	$2,220
					$43,250 (I)		$6,000 (J)

SOURCE: William E. McGrath, "A Pragmatic Book Allocation Formula for Academic and Public Libraries with a Test for Its Effectiveness," *Library Resources and Technical Services* 19 (Fall 1975): 361.

budgetary limitations; they remain the same whether money is available or not. Librarians must be able to determine relative priorities among a group of expensive titles.[11]

Obviously, if budgets were unlimited, selection would not be a problem; the library would just buy *everything* and there would be no need for a skilled librarian. However, this is not very practical. The budget should not be considered something ugly that impedes the development of the collection. Normally, budgetary constraints provide impetus for fiscal responsibility and eclectic selection.

☐ PHYSICAL NEEDS FOR THE VIDEO COLLECTION AREA

This section will discuss space utilization, traffic flow, design, equipment needs, and storage, shelving, and display options. Collection arrangement and display will be discussed in terms of space allocation. All library materials take up space. Space allocations should be made considering a five-year expansion plan. The amount of space used depends upon six factors: current collection size, anticipated growth (size), amount of circulation versus storage space, type of display/storage used (open dummy storage; behind-the-counter staff access requires more space), in-house equipment use, and traffic patterns.

Figure 2.2 diagrams one possible utilization of space for a video area. The purpose of this diagram is to serve as an aid in improving staff workflow and visibility, mainly by reducing barriers and enhancing the movement of people and/or work. This area uses low, double-aisle shelving with wide aisles, perimeter wall shelving, a display area, viewing carrels, service desk with fairly equal distance between all points, and a separate circulation desk. One entrance/exit enhances security. Low shelving and the service desk's location maximize visual security and aid patron contact. Dotted lines represent staff travel distances and visibility reference points, while the solid lines indicate patron lines of travel.

Because libraries differ in physical size, layout, and collection space/shelving requirements, no square footage requirements are indicated in the diagram. As a rule of thumb, most video stores allow 1,000 to 2,000 square feet for circulation and storage/display functions for 5,000 videos. In a library, a video area may be a separate room, combined with the total AV department, subdivided within the children's and adult departments, or just set aside from the main area. It should be clearly marked VIDEOCASSETTES. The following factors should be considered before diagramming a space utilization plan for any library video collection area:

1. Both patrons and staff must be able to access materials easily; the shelving arrangement must be attractively and logically oriented with browsing in mind.
2. Adequate space should be allowed for five years of anticipated growth.
3. One entrance/exit should be present. The collection area should be placed prominently in the front of the library to facilitate browsing, marketing, and the one-stop concept.
4. Viewing carrels should be placed in private areas but should be easily accessible by patrons and staff.
5. The circulation/return desk should be located near the entrance/exit. The librarian's viewer advisory station should be centrally located.
6. Diagonally staggered, double-sided, low aisle shelving should be used in large space areas. Perimeter shelving can also be used. This will maximize space usage while facilitating staff lines of sight for patron assistance and security. Aisle width between double-sided shelving should be 4 to 6 feet.
7. Adequate space at aisle ends should be given so that displays may be set up.

Shelving and Display Options
There are four optional methods in circulation/display shelving, each of which has advantages and disadvantages.

1. *Locked cases with staff/key access only.* This option utilizes space more effectively, and the glass/Plexiglas doors permit browsing. Most commercial cases do not use a frontal display; rather, they display spines. Additional staff must be available to unlock cases. Generic, plastic protective cases of uniform size could be used rather than the commercial boxes. Cases with the three-sided wraparound sleeve are desirable because the commercial box can be disassembled and inserted into the sleeve.

2. *Unlocked cases, dummy display with behind-the-counter access.* This option uses two sets of shelving: one for display, another for circulation. From the aspect of the initial equipment needed, this option requires more shelving/space. It also places the circulation workload directly upon the circulation staff. The dummies facilitate

STARTING THE COLLECTION   **39**

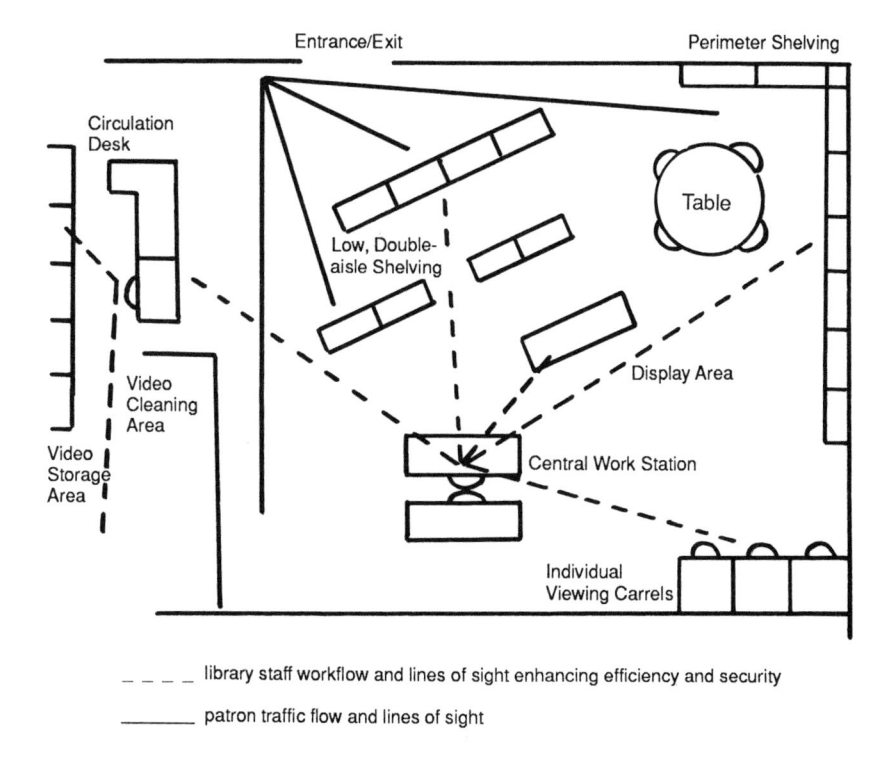

[Diagram: Workplace design showing Entrance/Exit at top, Perimeter Shelving along right wall, Circulation Desk at upper left, Low Double-aisle Shelving in center, Table with chairs at upper right, Display Area, Video Cleaning Area and Video Storage Area at left, Central Work Station in middle-lower area, and Individual Viewing Carrels along bottom right.]

– – – – library staff workflow and lines of sight enhancing efficiency and security

———— patron traffic flow and lines of sight

FIGURE 2.2 WORKPLACE DESIGN FOR A VIDEO AREA.

browsing, but they should be arranged in the case on a one-to-one relationship with the actual items. A patron makes a selection, takes the dummy to the circulation desk, and exchanges it for the actual item. The dummy is then shelved behind the counter in place of the actual title until its return. Individual title copies must be labeled.

   3. *Utilizing Videoflats or Video Browser Paks.* Commercial video packaging is displayed in a flat, record-album-like format that can be shelved in record bins instead of designing or purchasing special shelving. Item access is the same as described in option 2 above. The cost for a Videoflat is about $.60 to $1, while that of a Video Browser Pak is $.80 (1988 prices). Since the commercial box is inserted into the display, generic boxes must be purchased to house the actual videocassette (cost range $.60 to $2.25, 1988 prices). The advantage to this display option is that the library may not have to purchase additional shelving for the Videoflats if they have some old record

bins. Also, space is saved (about 30 titles can be displayed in a 12-inch-wide by 20-inch-deep bin, compared to a 3-foot-by-6-inch shelf for the same number of titles in boxes). Browsing seems to be enhanced by using this method because of the stylish look of the displays; however, crowding around the browsing bins may create a traffic flow pattern. Disadvantages stem from the additional staff/ processing time for preparing the Videoflats and the extra cost of materials.

4. *Open patron-access shelving without using security devices* such as 3M's Whisper-tape or Tattle-tape or the Checkpoint system. Open patron access uses space and staff most efficiently. It is recommended that there be only one entrance/exit for the video area to aid in security (perhaps a turnstile gate). This option also frees library staff for more important functions than unlocking video cases.

Commercial Sources and Costs

Shelving, as well as other products, can be obtained from a variety of sources such as video jobbers and library/video store supply houses. Listed below are some well-known product distributors. (Free catalogs are available upon request.)

Demco, Inc., Box 7488, Madison, WI 53707

Gaylord Brothers, Box 4901, Syracuse, NY 13221; (800) 448-6160 (see Figure 2.3)

Highsmith Co., P.O. Box 800, Highway 106 East, Fort Atkinson, WI 53538; (800) 558-3313

Video Store Shopper, 15759 Strathern Street, Van Nuys, CA 91406; (800) 325-6875

Mr. Video, 5550 Fulton Avenue, Van Nuys, CA 91401; (800) 432-4336, (818) 789-7238

Video Store Services, 4315 North Ravenswood Avenue, Chicago, IL 60613; (800) 654-7718, (312) 929-7718 in IL

Shelving comes in a variety of types depending upon needs, but basically it should provide a method of convenient display and/or storage. Librarians may opt for combining display and storage in one unit or separate the two functions. This fundamental decision, often based upon security, or space needs, will govern the types of shelving utilized. Most often, except for special displays, the shelving units should be consistent in type and structure. Videocassette shelving ranges the gamut from free-standing units (double- or single-sided), pegboard folding units, and rail wall-mount displays

STARTING THE COLLECTION 41

PHOTO 2.1 VID PRO VIDEO PLAK DISPLAY SYSTEM. This system uses tracks to display facsimiles of commercial videocassette boxes (plaks). Tracks come in 4-foot lengths and can be assembled in a variety of ways. Each track holds 11 plaks. (Vid Pro, 991 Matcheson Boulevard, Unit 2, Mississauga, Ontario L4W2V3; distributed by Ingram Video, 347 Reedwood Drive, Nashville, TN 37217.) (Photo courtesy of Vid Pro.)

to cassette leaves and rotating racks. The selection of commercially available shelving is limitless, with budget funds and space being the only constraints. Photo 2.1, Figure 2.3, and Figure 2.4 illustrate some commercially available shelving and display units.

A Canadian-based firm, Vid Pro, has developed an innovative, space-saving video display unit that can be easily adapted for wall, aisle, or rotating display. The Vid Pro Video Plak display system (Photo 2.1) maximizes space utilization and creates a uniform, neat appearance, taking up less space than the conventional method of video box display. The display consists of "plaks" and "tracks."

Exact, four-color, 4-inch-by-½-inch photographic reproductions of the commercially supplied original boxes are enclosed in a flat vinyl "plak." These plaks are anchored to a track system that is attached to any surface such as a pegboard or wall. Small inventory control tags are attached via an overlaid track and are used on a one-to-one correlation for additional copies. Patrons take a title/copy tag to the

FIGURE 2.3 GAYLORD MODULAR PANEL VIDEOCASSETTE DISPLAY UNIT. This unit is an example of unique shelving. The tower displays 60 videos, while the pockets hold 36 videocassettes per side, and modules can be grouped together. These modules are especially effective for utilizing corner or pillar space.

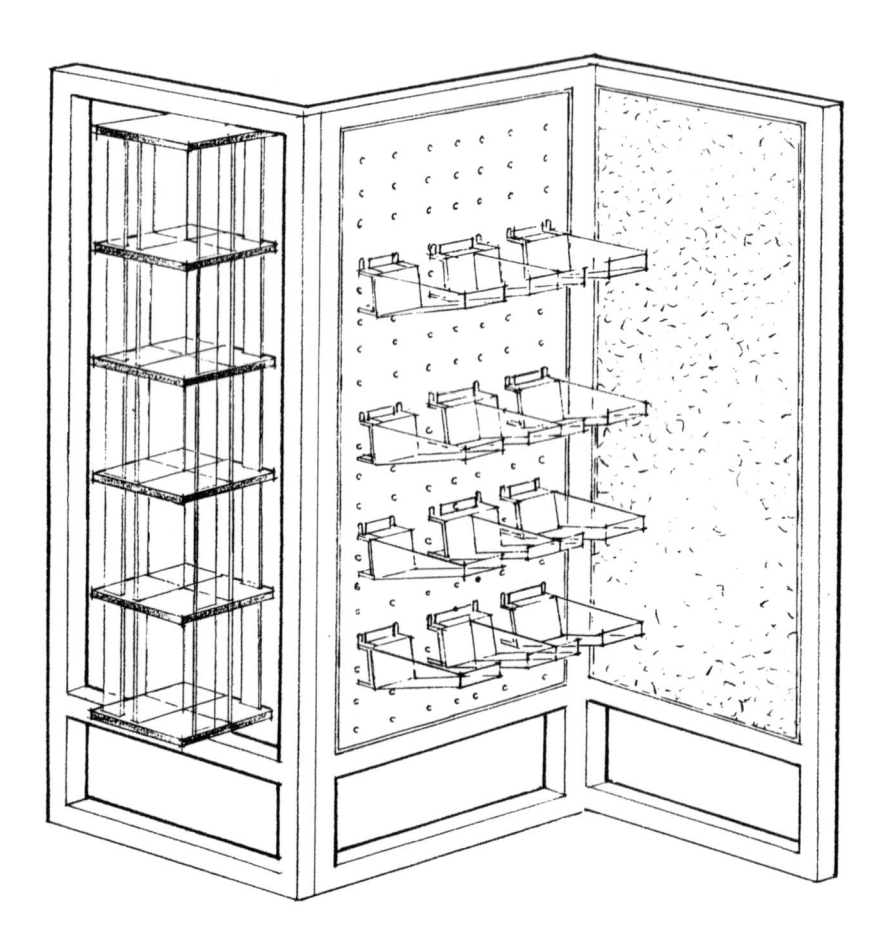

STARTING THE COLLECTION   **43**

circulation desk to check out the video. Tracks are available in 4-foot lengths housing 11 plaks per section. Plaks are approximately $4 each. Tracks are $5 each per 4-foot section. Fixture prices vary according to the style and quantity. This system is a cost-effective method to utilize space but is hampered by commercial availability of plaks. Information about the system can be obtained by writing to Ingram Video or directly to Vid Pro, 991 Matcheson Boulevard, Unit 2, Mississauga, Ontario L4W2V3.

Home-Built versus Commercial Equipment

1. *Locked cases with staff access only.* This build-your-own option has particular appeal if the library has its own skilled maintenance staff. Many times, a local carpenter or school shop/building trades class may build them for the library for a moderate cost. The Decatur Public Library (Illinois) has saved a considerable amount of money by building their own shelves and record bins. (See Photos 2.2 and 2.3.) The materials cost for a five-shelf, double-sided unit housing approximately 300 to 360 videocassettes would be about $325: about $125 for the plywood and $200 for the glass/Plexiglas sliding doors and rail mechanisms (1986 prices). Miscellaneous supplies include nails, screws, and paint. Keyed ratchet locks, such

FIGURE 2.4   TRACK SYSTEM DISPLAY METHOD.   This system displays the commercial box in an upright position. Many video stores utilize this display method (available from Video Store Shopper, 15759 Strathern Street, Van Nuys, CA 91406; and from Mr. Video, 5550 Fulton Avenue, Van Nuys, CA 91401).

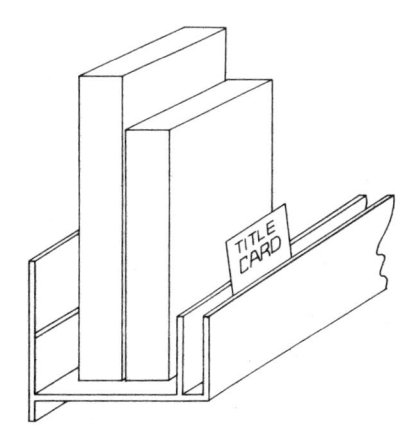

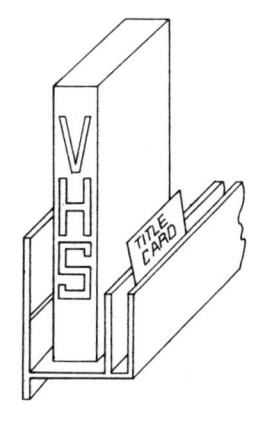

as those used on trophy cases, can be used for security. Commercially available videocassette shelving ranges in cost from $300 to $700. One single-sided model housing 180 to 210 videos, offered by Highsmith, costs about $300. ALPS, Inc., P.O. Box 31723, Raleigh, NC 27612, offers wall-mounted, double-sided leaf display racks; each leaf holds approximately 38 to 67 boxes. The wall units sell for about $175 to $225, while the carousel units sell for $220 to $735 (1986 prices).

2. *Unlocked cases, dummy display with behind-the-counter access.* Metal or wood shelving could be used. The shelving housing the dummies for patron browsing should be attractive. Videocassette dummies can be displayed frontally or showing the case spines. Side display utilizes space more efficiently, but frontal display is

PHOTO 2.2 DECATUR PUBLIC LIBRARY (ILLINOIS) VIDEO DISPLAY AREA. Generic Amaray boxes are displayed in locked, home-built, six-shelf double-sided units. Each unit holds about 300 to 360 videocassettes. Patron access is provided by library staff.

STARTING THE COLLECTION 45

more attractive. The home-built units described in Figure 2.5 can be used without the glass doors for this type of display, making the total cost about $125. Commercial shelving is available for about $180 to $300. Shelving, such as simple wall shelving, must also be provided for behind-the-counter storage.

3. *Utilizing Videoflat dummy displays.* Commercial packaging is displayed in an LP format shelved in record bins. The commercial video box is cut up, backed with cardboard to provide rigidity (if necessary), and inserted into a protective, clear Mylar archival envelope and sealed with archival tape. Both Demco and Gaylord offer the archival envelopes with approximate prices for single-fold, top-insert style ranging from $.33 to $1 per unit. Based on the Videoflat concept, Chicago One Stop, Inc., 509 East Illinois, Suite

PHOTO 2.3 DECATUR PUBLIC LIBRARY (ILLINOIS) RECORD DISPLAY UNITS. These attractive, home-built, 20-bin double-sided units hold approximately 500 to 600 LP albums; they are perfectly suited to hold Videoflats as well.

301, Chicago, IL 60611, and Demco offer a clear Mylar top-insert envelope (called a Video Browser Pak) measuring 12 by 8 inches that can accommodate the flattened commercial video packaging. Prices are approximately $.80 per unit.

The advantage of using the Videoflat display concept is that existing phonorecord shelving can be used. Also, more titles can be displayed and browsed within a smaller area. Record display/storage units can be purchased commercially for anywhere from $175 to $675. Individual plastic record tubs can be purchased for as little as $30. The Decatur Public Library found that it could build record bins in-house for much less than it could purchase them commercially. They are double-sided with 5 bins on the top and bottom of each side for a total of 20 bins. Total capacity would be approximately 500 to 600 Videoflats in an area of about 18 square feet (3 feet by 6 feet). The diagrams for the record bins are shown in Figure 2.6. It is important to note that the plans are easily adaptable to smaller sizes. High school or college shop classes or a volunteer local carpenter may be good sources to tap for construction of shelving units.

4. *Open patron-access shelving with/without security devices.* Two companies, 3M and Checkpoint, offer magnetic and radio frequency security systems that can be adapted for use in library video collections. 3M's Tattle-tape system uses narrow ¼-inch-by-7-inch adhesive metal-coated strips that can be attached under the videocassette label. These strips remain sensitized in the library and, if they are not checked out by desensitizing the label, they will set off an alarm in a security gate. The Tattle-tape system was originally designed for books, and the sensitizing/desensitizing is actually a powerful electromagnet that can erase images (or cause distortion) on videotape. 3M has developed a weaker sensitizing unit that can be used with videocassettes, and the existing security gates can be maintained. Ronald J. Tworek of 3M's Safety and Security Systems Division indicates that (1988) prices for the videotape Tattle-tape system for libraries with preexisting Tattle-tape book systems are as follows: sensitizing/desensitizing equipment, $49–$195; magnetic strips, 1,000 per box, $.16 per strip.

3M also markets a similar system for retail video stores called the Whisper-tape system. The Tattle-tape equipment is not compatible with this system. Shorter magnetic strips are used and the strips have a weaker magnetic orientation than the Tattle-tape system. This system is costly and not recommended for libraries. Cost for equipment and installation is about $7,500. 3M's address is 3M

1-TOP
1-BOTTOM (SAME AS TOP)
14"
36 1/4"

72 1/2"
59 3/4"

10-Shelves
5"
35 3/8"

2 Base pieces 36 1/4" x 12" (illustration not shown)

All router cuts are 3/4" wide and 3/8" deep

Entire unit is 72 1/2" (H) x 37" (W) x 14" (D)

Sliding glass doors - 59" x 35 1/2"
2 locks
8 Adj. shelf brackets 60" long
40 shelf brackets
12 screen door molding 72" x 3/4"

59 3/4"
1-Center Divider
36 1/4"

(continued)

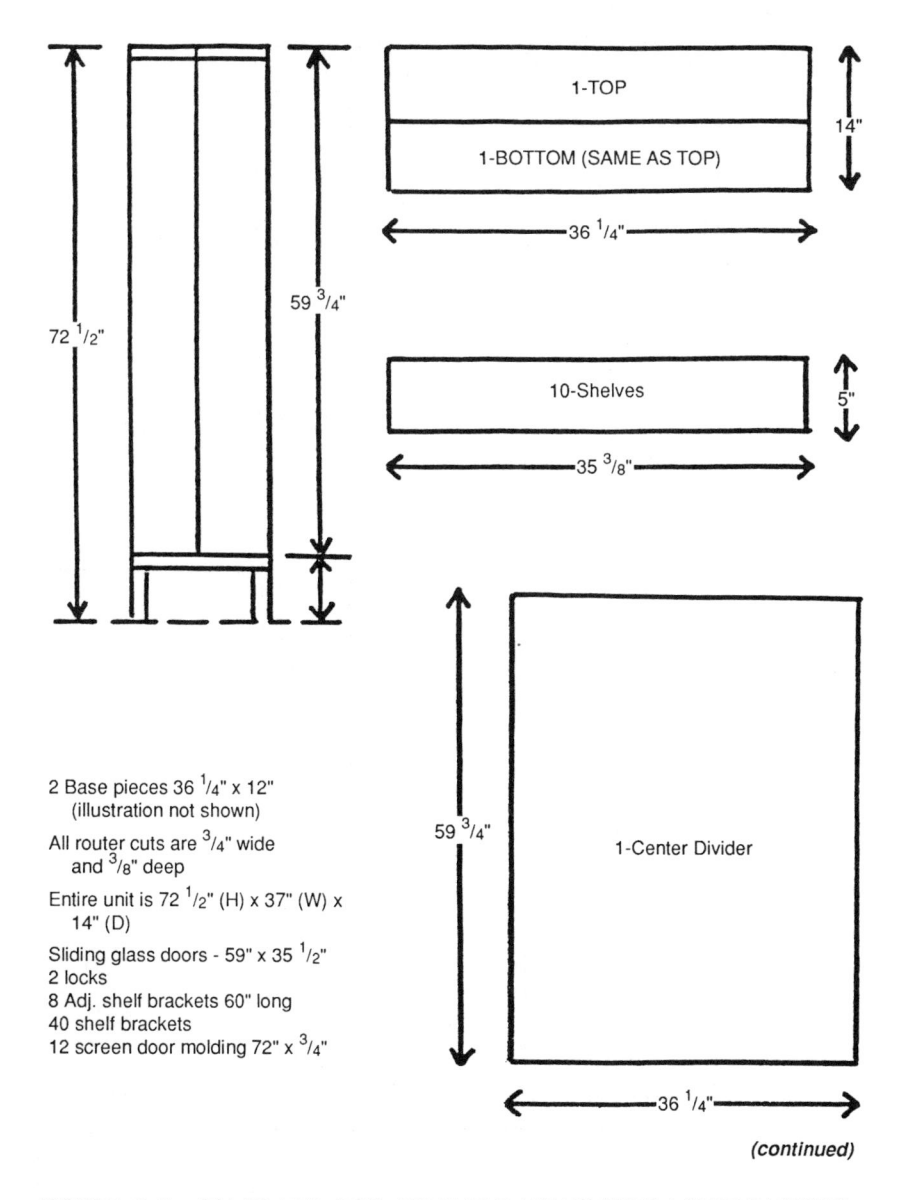

FIGURE 2.5 DIAGRAMS FOR SIX-SHELF HOME-BUILT VIDEOCASSETTE UNIT. These diagrams outline the dimensions and cuts for the videocassette units used in the Decatur Public Library (Photo 2.2). The plans can be modified for low, double-aisle shelving. It is suggested that, in the six-shelf unit, a weight be fastened to the underside (middle) of the unit to prevent it from being tipped over. Plans courtesy of Owen Richardson, head of maintenance, Decatur Public Library.

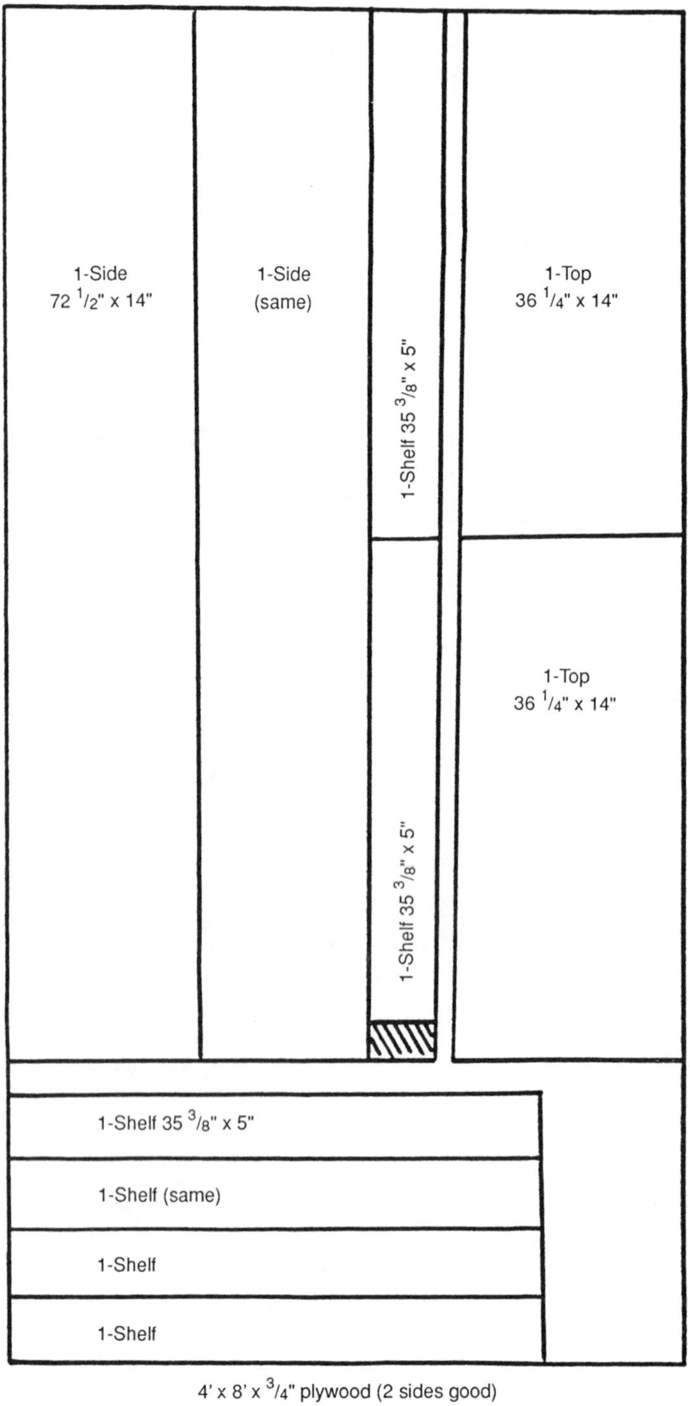

1-Side
72 $\frac{1}{2}$" x 14"

1-Side
(same)

1-Shelf 35 $\frac{3}{8}$" x 5"

1-Top
36 $\frac{1}{4}$" x 14"

1-Top
36 $\frac{1}{4}$" x 14"

1-Shelf 35 $\frac{3}{8}$" x 5"

1-Shelf 35 $\frac{3}{8}$" x 5"

1-Shelf (same)

1-Shelf

1-Shelf

Figure 2.5 (continued)

4' x 8' x $\frac{3}{4}$" plywood (2 sides good)

1 Center divider
36 $\frac{1}{4}$" x 59 $\frac{3}{4}$"

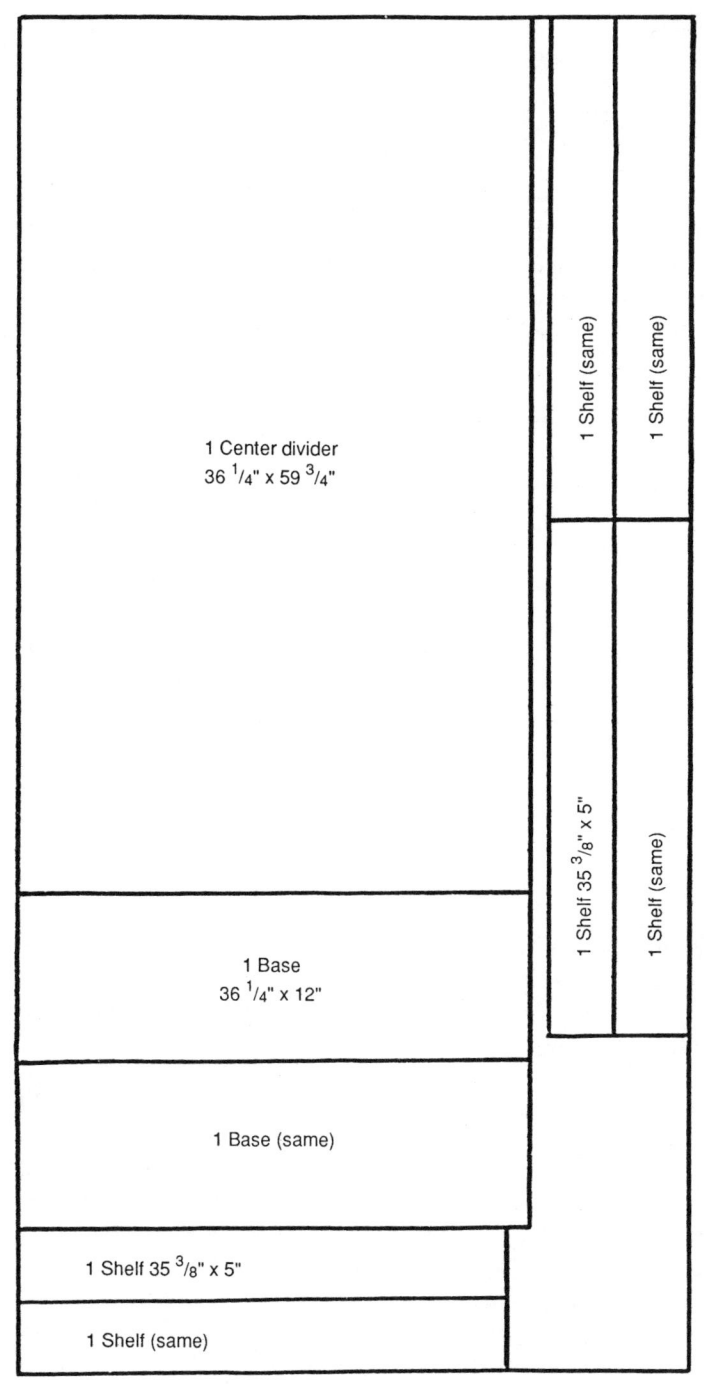

1 Shelf (same)

1 Shelf (same)

1 Shelf 35 $\frac{3}{8}$" x 5"

1 Shelf (same)

1 Base
36 $\frac{1}{4}$" x 12"

1 Base (same)

1 Shelf 35 $\frac{3}{8}$" x 5"

1 Shelf (same)

4' x 8' x $\frac{3}{4}$"

**Figure 2.5
(continued)**

Safety and Security Systems Division, 903 Commerce Drive, Oak Brook, IL 60521-1904; (800) 323-4087, (312) 920-4266.

The Checkpoint system uses a small foil adhesive square that reflects radio frequencies when passing through a security gate. The 1½-inch foil square is difficult to hide on the physical videocassette, and the orientation is weak when the cassette is passed through the gate at odd angles. Checkpoint Systems can be contacted for prices and more information at 550 Grove Road, Mid-Atlantic Park, Thorofare, NJ 08086; (800) 257-5540.

Security systems offer the advantage of open patron access and eliminate the need for an extra storage/shelving unit or extra staff to unlock the cases or serve patrons in a behind-the-counter situation. The display shelving serves as both display and video storage. However, the cost is prohibitive to most small and medium-sized libraries, which may find either open access or a version of closed access to be just as cost-effective and less cumbersome than using a security system. Large urban libraries with collections exceeding 5,000 items with an annual volume loss of 15 percent or more should consider costing out a security system versus additional staff time.

☐ PURCHASING EQUIPMENT

When purchasing video equipment, librarians should consider the function they want that equipment to perform. There is no sense in buying a Porsche when a Chevrolet will do, but the buyer must be careful not to get stuck with a Model T. Equipment obsolescence is inevitable, but it can be delayed by careful planning. The librarian will have to consider these important questions: Will the equipment be used only for individual in-house viewing or group viewing? Will the library also offer cable television viewing? Will the library loan videoplayers to patrons? Will the library want to produce some in-house programs?

Individual viewing carrels should each contain a television monitor and a VCR for private, in-house viewing. Playback-only units are slightly less expensive than recorders and should be considered if no other use will be made of the VCR. Since hi-fi stereo VCRs are becoming very popular, librarians may want to consider purchasing equipment to handle stereo broadcasts or radio/television simulcasts. Hi-fi VCRs do not reproduce sounds in stereo without hookup to a hi-fi television or stereo speakers and an amplifier. A cable-ready VCR or television is already set to receive the RF signal instead of UHF/VHF. Some type of inspection/

RECORD BIN PLANS

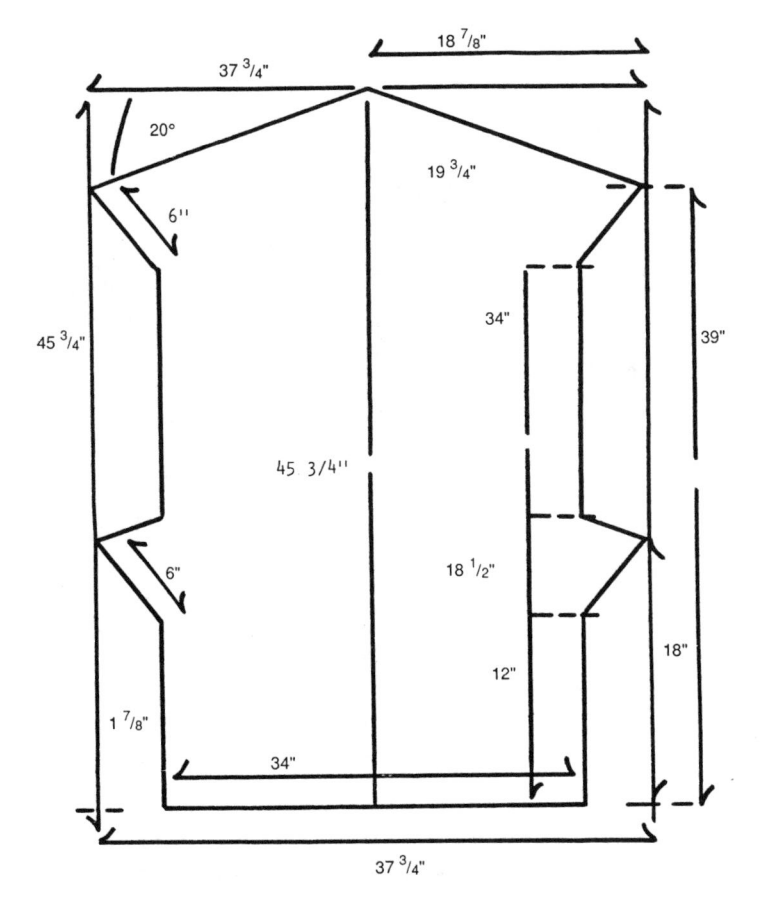

Plywood Needs (2 sides good)
  2 pieces 45 3/4" x 37 3/4" (ends)
  5 pieces 11 1/2" x 73 3/4"
  5 pieces 6" x 73 3/4"
  2 pieces 3" x 73 3/4"
  2 pieces 34" x 73 3/4" (floor)
  6 pieces 2" x 32 1/2" (braces)
  16 pieces for dividers (cut after assembly)

(continued)

FIGURE 2.6 DIAGRAMS FOR 20-BIN RECORD DISPLAY UNIT. These diagrams outline the dimensions and cuts for the record display units used in the Decatur Public Library (Photo 2.3). Plans courtesy of Owen Richardson, head of maintenance, Decatur Public Library.

**Figure 2.6
(continued)**

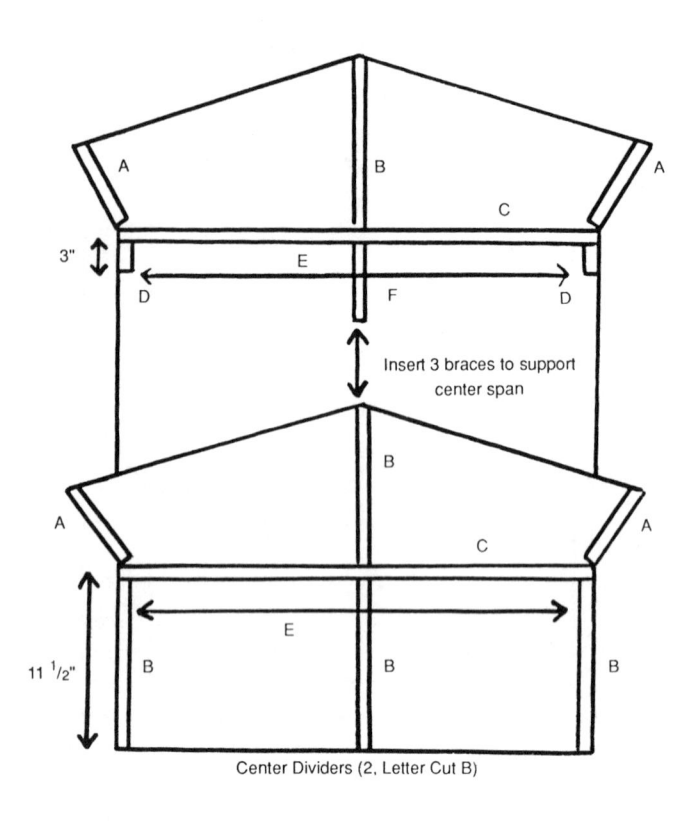

Insert 3 braces to support center span

Center Dividers (2, Letter Cut B)

PLYWOOD CUTS

Letter Cut	Dimension	Quantity
A	6" x 73 3/4"	4
B	11 1/2" x 73 3/4"	5
C	34" x 73 3/4"	2
D	3" x 73 3/4"	2
E*	2" x 32 1/2"	6
F	6" x 73 3/4"	1

* there are 3 of these spaced evenly to support top/bottom bin floor

STARTING THE COLLECTION 53

Figure 2.6
(continued)

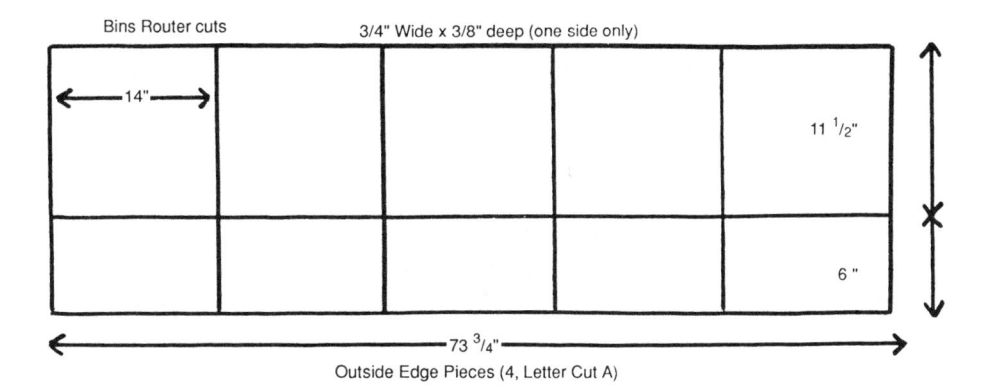

Bins Router cuts   3/4" Wide x 3/8" deep (one side only)

← 14" →

11 1/2"

6 "

← 73 3/4" →

Outside Edge Pieces (4, Letter Cut A)

cleaning machine should be purchased to assist in keeping videotapes clean and assessing damage. Also, a tape rewinder may prove beneficial. A portable recorder and/or tuner used with a television camera can provide a rudimentary program production and editing station, but for refined editing more advanced and expensive equipment is needed. It is important to plan for future equipment needs and to purchase equipment that lends itself to adapting add-on units. Either the television monitor or the VCR should have an earphone jack; also, a multiple ear jack adapter may be desired.

Three authoritative periodicals to consult when selecting equipment are *Video Review, Stereo Review,* and *Hi Fidelity. Consumer Reports* also has equipment tests and reviews, but they are not as up-to-date as the other three titles. Mail-order electronics centers and discount houses can be excellent places to save money on video equipment, but the buyer is buying sight unseen and must really know equipment; otherwise, an unsatisfactory purchase will result. It is advantageous to purchase known brand names such as JVC, Panasonic, Sony, Magnavox, Zenith, Curtis Mathes, and Hitachi. Industrial model VCRs usually have a metal case and sturdier components that can withstand continuous transportation. Prices are usually higher for industrial models. Equipment should be purchased with current and future service needs in mind; then those needs must be translated into equipment functions. Do not let the equipment, or a persistent salesperson, dictate those needs.

☐ STAFFING AND WORKFLOW

Providing adequate staffing is an important factor that can mean the difference between a successful or an unsuccessful service. Too often video collections are started by utilizing the existing library staff and not establishing a separate AV department. This practice places a substantial drain on staff and produces negative effects. In medium to large libraries, a separate AV department should be set up with a minimum of one full-time professional and one part-time viewer's advisor. Depending upon how the workload is distributed, additional drains will be felt in hidden ways in departments such as acquisitions, cataloging, circulation, and reshelving. One reshelving page should be designated to handle check-ins and shelving on a daily basis. Again, there are no magical formulas for determining adequate staff size. The circulation and shelving methods used and the extent to which the library wishes to provide carrel viewing and viewer assistance will dictate numbers. Retail stores are just now learning that staff attitudes are important ingredients in the success of video lending. In order to beat the competition, it is no longer sufficient simply to be pleasant and answer questions only when asked, while otherwise ignoring patrons. All staff should be outgoing, possess a positive attitude toward aiding patrons, be informed about the collection, and show enthusiasm while helping patrons. Generally, open-access shelving protected by a security system will reduce staffing requirements, but these systems are expensive in both initial capital outlay and continuation expenses. Providing visible reference sources, such as movie guides, annotated videographies, and the card catalog, will also help.

An interesting concept in organizing collection space and staff, based on perceived user habits, was developed by the Phoenix Public Library (Arizona). Results from a previous use survey indicated that most patrons used the library as browser/readers. The library staff was utilized at the lowest level of their effectiveness. Patrons experienced minimal contact with professional librarians. The library then developed a "popular library"—a highly visible branch within the central building that concentrates on providing reader advisory services along with a collection of general interest, popular fiction, new books, magazines, and paperbacks. This area is adjacent to the circulation desk and the main entrance. It is the first stop in the traffic flow and facilitates quick stops by patrons.[12] Because of the collection's high visibility, special merchandising (department store) techniques can be used effectively. This method of collection reorganization would be ideally suited for videocassette collections.

☐ SECURITY NEEDS AND EASE OF ACCESS

Security and patron/staff ease of access are ultimately tied to space allocation, organization, and staffing. Today, as Roy Smith observes, librarians "are in danger of treating video as timidly as they did picture and record lending."[13] Videocassettes are expensive and particularly susceptible to theft because of the high street resale value, especially in urban areas. However, videocassette prices are decreasing steadily and the newness of the video technology is wearing off; therefore theft may become less of a problem in the near future. Videos should not be perceived as expensive and fragile items to be put under lock and key nor to be circulated from behind the desk on a patron request basis. As video collections grow in size, library administration is experiencing large drains upon staff.[14] Security is a matter of opinion: one librarian may feel that the additional cost of a security system or closed-access shelving is prohibitive and be willing to tolerate negligible losses due to theft. A New York state public library director with a large video collection came to the conclusion that his open-stack approach and resultant "theft shrinkage" cost less than paying staff to open and close cases. He found that not only were his losses relatively low, but that circulation tripled as patrons were free to browse the collection.[15]

This author feels that no matter what the replacement materials cost, no loss is acceptable when left unchecked. If yearly theft losses commonly exceed 5 to 6 percent, possibly another method of circulation should be examined. Locked cases are not a good option because they inhibit browsing. Closed-access shelving with display dummies is a better method, although two sets of shelf space are required and the circulation staff workload is much greater. Both of these procedures will require more staff and, over the long run, will cost substantially more than a security system such as 3M's Tattle-tape or the Checkpoint system. Security is dependent upon a variety of factors that vary with each individual library's ultimate perception of its mission and goals within its community. Likewise workspace designs and space utilization must be tailored to each library's specific goals and objectives.

☐ ACQUISITIONS, PROCESSING, CATALOGING, AND COLLECTION ARRANGEMENT

Acquisitions, processing, cataloging, and video collection arrangement are grouped together in this discussion because they all require workload and staffing redefinition. The acquisitions procedure should be organized *before* selection begins, although, in practice, selection precedes materials acquisition. A differentiation should be made between acquisition policy and procedures. *Policies* state, in broad terms, what will be done and rationalize those ideals. *Procedures* indicate standard operational guidelines dictating how those policies will be implemented in day-to-day tasks. Acquisition is the process by which materials are obtained by the library, including identifying and selecting vendors, confirming title availability and price, organizing discounts, order verification, order transmission and fulfillment, and tracking back-orders and budgetary funds.[16]

One of the most formidable tasks for a video librarian today is in acquiring the product itself. The market is diffuse and often disconnected from large producers and commercial distribution sources. Also, there are relatively few review tools that pull together a large selection of quality titles.

Today, many librarians may want to purchase titles that include public performance rights so that they can legally use them for in-house showings such as story hours. Many titles are simultaneously being offered by the home-use market and the public performance market. Usually, the prices between the two vary widely, the latter being much more expensive. In the last two years, large quantities of public performance titles have been released at home video prices varying from $50 to $150. Large producers like AIMS Media, Pyramid Films, Encyclopaedia Britannica, MTI/Coronet, Films Inc., and Weston Woods have lowered their prices to compete with home video. Some producers have even entered the home video market with subsidiary companies like Weston Woods/C. C. Studios and Films, Inc./Homevision. The purchase of high-cost items should be governed primarily by each library's collection needs and expectations rather than price. But realistically, many libraries do not possess the budgets to buy high-priced videos; therefore a reasonable price ceiling (such as $10 per minute) should be set. When purchasing public performance titles, at the time of purchase, discounted damage replacement and duplication rights should be discussed.

The video industry has many jobbers and distributors who offer a wide range of price discounts; therefore the librarian must shop around for the best price, subsequently doing business with many producers, distributors, and jobbers. Most of these businesses produce catalogs that can be extremely useful in identifying titles and prices. Librarians should actively seek out and maintain up-to-date files of video producer, distributor, and jobber catalogs for title identification and price comparisons. In large libraries, most often different people handle materials selection and acquisitions procedures. Staff in charge of materials selection should also choose the vendor from which the title should be ordered.

Choosing Vendors
Videocassette vendors can be divided into three groups: producers, distributors (wholesale and retail), and jobbers. A producer is the entity who actually produced the program and, in most cases, possesses the copyright and public performance rights. Direct buying from producers can save money but often results in added paperwork because of many individual purchase orders rather than a bulk order from a distributor. In dealing with producers, librarians must be prepared to haggle over prices, and often can negotiate lower prices and special deals.

Distributors are usually organized to do business on a regional or national basis. Some distributors are producers as well; others just sell other producers' products. Distributor catalogs offer a wide variety of titles from many producers. Some distributors specialize in certain types of video titles such as specialty (nonfiction) titles or features, while others offer a mixture of both types. Most often, the video titles are for home use only because distributors do not negotiate public performance rights. Also, set discount prices are available, but usually not negotiable. Today, many distributors offer more intense customer service—distributor newsletters and product hotlines abound. Wholesale distributors usually have lower prices and sell to retailers and retail distributors, who in turn sell for a marked-up profit. Librarians would be wise to purchase materials from a wholesale distributor because the dollar savings can be substantial.

A jobber is a wholesale distributor who offers a large product line, usually at substantial discounts based on volume purchased. Jobbers usually stock backlogs of titles in-house; therefore many back-order problems can be eliminated by purchasing from them. A jobber possesses the buying power to offer a tremendous variety of producer and distributor titles. Jobbers usually do not negotiate public performance rights; therefore all titles are for home use only. Generally, a wholesale vendor can supply products at discounts above most retail vendors, but shopping around for the best deal makes good fiscal sense. Occasionally, a title may be exclusively available through only one source.

58 STARTING THE COLLECTION

Vendors should be chosen for five reasons:

1. Gives the best price or standard volume discount
2. Gives timely and pleasant service—knows the product, offers individual customer service, with billing/invoice procedures and forms understandable and adaptable to library methods
3. Has geographical proximity or easy access via an 800 number
4. Offers a full title line in terms of variety and possesses an attractive, easily usable catalog and/or special newsletter
5. Possesses methods of handling back-orders and returns in a timely, accurate, and acceptable manner

Many jobbers and distributors give two discounts, a net title discount plus another one based on volume orders. Librarians should check into this option and batch volume orders together. Many small libraries and library systems could band together for direct producer volume purchases or batched vendor orders and receive substantial discounts. Also, producers and distributors may offer two-tiered pricing, where a distinction between home use and institutional use is made on a price basis.[17]

A List of Vendors

WHOLESALE JOBBERS
These jobbers offer mostly features on video with a very limited selection of specialty video. Currently, the three major video jobbers are

Baker & Taylor Video, 7000 North Austin Avenue, Niles, IL 60648 (monthly updated catalog); (800) 227-2812

Commtron Corporation, 400 Airport Executive Park, Spring Valley, NY 10977 (catalog plus flyers); (914) 425-3191

Ingram Video, 347 Reedwood Drive, Nashville, TN 37217 (quarterly *Videopedia* title listings, biweekly microfiche title updates, newsletter, *Check It Out*); (800) 251-5900, (615) 361-5000

Other wholesale distributors:

Artec, Inc., Pine Haven Shore Road, Shelburne, VT 05482 (catalog); (800) 372-7007, (800) 541-1413, in New England (800) 451-5160

Coronet Feature Video, 108 Wilmot Road, Deerfield, IL 60015 (catalog, features only); (800) 621-2131, (312) 940-1260 in IL

East Texas Distributing, 7171 Grand Boulevard, Houston, TX

77054 (monthly catalog updates); (800) 235-3108, (713) 748-2520

Metro Video Distributors, 92 Railroad Avenue, Hasbrouck Heights, NJ 07604; (800) 876-3876

M. S. Distributing Company, 1050 Arthur Avenue, Elk Grove Village, IL 60007 (flyers, features only); (312) 364-2888

Professional Media Service Corp., 13620 South Crenshaw Boulevard, Gardena, CA 90249 (catalog and monthly annotated title update, *In the Groove*, catalog card sets and processing available); (800) 223-7672, (800) 826-2169 in CA

Publisher's Central Bureau, 1 Champion Avenue, Avenel, NJ 07001-9987 (flyer/catalog); (800) 772-9200, ext. 503

Star Video Entertainment, 550 Grand Street, Jersey City, NJ 07302; (800) 251-5432, (201) 333-4600

RETAIL DISTRIBUTORS

Apple Video, P.O. Box 345, Palatine, IL 60078; (312) 359-1115

Blackhawk Films and Video, One Old Eagle Building, P.O. Box 3990, Davenport, IA 52808 (catalog; classic, old-time features plus nonfiction titles unavailable elsewhere); (800) 826-2295; (319) 323-9735

C. A. I. Software Inc., 168 Express Drive South, Brentwood, NY 11717; (800) 247-7009, (516) 231-1220 in NY

Chip Taylor Communications, 15 Spollett Drive, Derry, NH 03038 (features only); (800) 342-0268, (603) 434-9262

Discount Video, Park Square Station, P.O. Box 15403, Stamford, CT 06901; (800) 962-9099, (203) 323-9099

Evergreen Video Society, 213 West 35th Street, Second Floor, New York, NY 10001 (flyer updates, features, specializes in out-of-print and hard-to-find titles); (800) 225-7783, (212) 714-9860 in NY

Facets Video, 1517 West Fullerton Avenue, Chicago, IL 60614 (features only; foreign, classic and independent films); (800) 331-6197, (312) 281-9075 in IL

Filmic Archives, P.O. Box C, Sandy Hook, CT 06482 (catalog, specializes in classic titles and Canadian Film Board titles); (203) 426-2574

Movies Unlimited, 6736 Castor Ave., Philadelphia, PA 19149 (catalog, mostly features)

Tamarelle's International Films, 110 Cohasset Stage Road, Chico, CA 95926 (catalog; foreign features, public performance); (916) 895-3429

Walden Video, P.O. Box 9497, Department 603, New Haven, CT 06534–0497; (800) 443-7359

Zenger Video, 10,000 Culver Boulevard, Room 932, P.O. Box 802, Culver City, CA 90232-0802; (catalog; mostly nonfiction, some features); (800) 421-4246, (213) 839-2436 in CA

SPECIALTY DISTRIBUTORS

Alternative Video, 604 Davis Street, Evanston, IL 60201 (catalog); (800) 777-2223, (312) 328-2221

Brodart Video, 500 Arch Street, Williamsport, PA 17705 (catalog); (800) 233-8467, (717) 326-2461

Classical Video, 162 B Cabot Street, West Babylon, NY 11704 (opera, ballet, and symphonic video); (516) 420-1059

Clearview Media Corp, Route 1, Box 25, Bowling Green, VA 22427 (catalog, same as Videotakes; monthly review source *Librarian's Video Review*); (800) 624-0894

Greenleaf Video, 3230 Nebraska Avenue, Santa Monica, CA 90404 (catalog, newsletter); (800) 255-4687, (213) 557-2043

Librarian's Video Service, 184 East Main Street, P.O. Box 468, Middletown, CT 06457 (catalog plus flyers, specialty video only); (800) 828-4450, (203) 346-2979

Library Video Company, Dept. M-8, P.O. Box 40351, Philadelphia, PA 19106 (catalog, specialty video only, catalog card set available); (800) 627-6667, (215) 627-6667 in Canada

Playing Hard to Get, 580 Old Mine Office, Madrid, MN 87011 (catalog; music video only, classics and new titles); (505) 471-7814

Polo Video Sales Company, Roosevelt Island, 688 Main Street, New York, NY 10044 (catalog); (800) 348-3425, (212) 759-7779

Quality Life Video Publishing, 2995 Wilderness Place, Suite 101, Boulder, CO 80301 (review newsletter plus computer printouts of title listings); (303) 440-9109

S.I. Video, P.O. Box 310, San Fernando, CA 91341 (catalog); (800) 228-5002, (818) 845-5599

University of Illinois Film/Video Center, 1325 South Oak Street, Champaign, IL 61820 (catalog plus an extended lease plan for nonfiction, public performance); (800) 252-1357, (800) 367-3456

V—The Mail-Order Magazine of Videocassettes, 1690 Oak Street, Lakewood, NJ 08701 (monthly review catalog, features and nonfiction); (800) 426-1859

The Video Schoolhouse (Sallyforth), 2611 Garden Road, Monterey, CA 93940 (catalog); (800) 367-0432, (800) 345-1441 in CA

Videotakes, 220 Shrewsbury Avenue, Red Bank, NJ 07701 (catalog); (800) 526-7002, (201) 747-2444

Video Trend, 5490 Milton Parkway, Rosemont, IL 60018 (catalog, features and nonfiction); (800) 451-7185, (800) 323-1257 in IL, (312) 678-3700

EDUCATIONAL PRODUCERS/.DISTRIBUTORS

Agency for Instructional Technology, Box A, Bloomington, IN 47402 (catalog, children's education); (800) 457-4509, (812) 339-2203

The Annenberg/CPB Project, Distributed by Intellimation, 2040 Alameda Padre Serra, P.O. Box 4069, Santa Barbara, CA 93140-4069; (catalog, educational materials); (800) LEARNER

GPN: Instructional Television Library, P.O. Box 80669, Lincoln, NE 68501 (catalog, children's education); (800) 228-4630, (402) 472-2007

Guidance Associates, Communications Park, Box 3000, Mount Kisco, NY 10549 (catalog, features and nonfiction); (800) 431-1242, (914) 666-4100

National Audiovisual Center, General Services Administration, Information Services Section/PN, Washington, DC 20409 (catalog); (301) 763-1896

PBS Video, 1320 Braddock Place, Alexandria, VA 22314-1698 (catalog, educational programming); (800) 344-3337, (800) 424-7963

Processing Acquisitions

Processing is the stage in which the item is made ready for circulation and collection addition. Usually it involves several steps, including title and defects checks, identification labeling, and adding a protective but attractive case. Classifying and cataloging the title along with adhering descriptive labels is also part of this stage. Security strips and circulation barcodes are adhered at this stage also. Various labels, cards, pockets, and generic protective cases are used depending upon a library's processing procedures.

After the materials have been acquired by the library, they must first be checked against the invoices for title match-up *before* the shrink-wrap is removed. This is a very important step, because most video jobbers and distributors will not allow returns of titles with the shrink-wrap removed. Each video should be checked for physical damage, then for sound/video damage (a portion should be viewed using a VCR). Many jobbers do not allow returns or give credit for titles that are physically damaged, feeling that the mail carrier is responsible. All jobbers will replace titles with defective sound/video. It is extremely important that the AV librarian be aware of the jobber's return policy *before* doing business.

The next step involves processing the video for protection, identification, marketing/display, and accessibility. Placing a label identifying the owning library is perhaps the most important step. Copyright warning/protection labels with the library's name and address can be purchased from many library supply companies like Demco and Highsmith, as well as video retailing stores like the Video Shopper.

Marketing is very important, and librarians should not avoid or neglect this element, because it will substantially increase circulation. The commercial cases in which videos are packaged are, for the most part, less than desirable as library circulating protective boxes. Some commercial packaging is no more than a cardboard sleeve open at one end. Plastic, generic videocassette cases are the best answer to the protection problem and offer the added advantage of uniform size, thus saving shelf space. Cases are available with a wraparound clear Mylar sleeve that accepts the commercial box frontispiece, thereby making the video more attractive to the browsing patron.

Cataloging and Shelving

Another problem arises in using the commercial boxes for product identification information. There are three areas of title location on a videocassette. The primary cataloging source is the title frame on the actual video. Secondary variant sources include the commercial packaging and the videocassette label. The *Anglo-American Cataloguing Rules*, 2d edition (*AACR II*) states that the primary source should be used to describe the item if possible.[18] Variant titles should be relabeled to match the primary source to avoid confusion. However, this presents a peculiar problem in that many videos are advertised and known by a variant title rather than by the primary one. One solution is to put an added title entry into the card catalog.

The term *cataloging* actually describes two library functions—

STARTING THE COLLECTION 63

descriptive cataloging and item classification. Descriptive cataloging is the process of actually describing the physical item using a standard bibliographic style. The *AACR II* describes the rules and standards for determining the necessary author/title information and its proper organization on the catalog cards. It is not the purpose of this text to discuss the elements of descriptive cataloging, because they are covered in detail in a variety of textbooks. For general purposes, however, a quick rules index to *AACR II* for videocassette cataloging is given in Table 2.2.

Cataloging videocassettes is somewhat more complex than cataloging books because, not only are different descriptive elements used more extensively, but they are not at all consistent from title to title. The librarian must utilize a VCR to actually view the front part of a program in order to ascertain important bibliographic information. Most often, books are described by their primary source, the title page; they usually possess an author or editor as the primary source of responsibility and are published by one company. In contrast, a video has three title sources, all of which may vary. Usually, a video is not the sole effort of one person; therefore the title is the main entry. There are also usually multiple "publishers"—a producer, distributor, and purchase source. The

TABLE 2.2 Index to AACR II cataloging rules for videos

AACR II CHAPTER NO.	RULE DESCRIPTION
1.0	General rules; where to find sources of information, punctuation, cataloging levels
1.1	Title and statement of responsibility, punctuation, General Material Designator
1.4	Imprint information (place, producer, date)
1.5	Collation (physical description area)
1.6	Series area (see Appendix D)
1.9 – 1.10	Items made up of several types of materials and supplementary items (see also Series)
2.1	Items without a collective title
2.7	Notes area
7.0	Motion pictures and videorecording general information
26.4	Uniform titles

video *Yellowstone in Winter* by Karl Lorimar will serve as an example of the complexity and difficulty in cataloging video. (Bracketed words refer to bibliographic elements or are added to clarify terms.)

1. Primary source states: Nature [series title]/ *Yellowstone in Winter* [title]/ WNET [producer]
2. Secondary source, videocassette label states: Nature [series title]/ *Yellowstone in Winter* [title]/ EBC [the letters stand for Encyclopaedia Britannica, the distributor]/ 60 min. [length]/ color
3. Secondary source; the commercial packaging states: Nature, Vol. III [PBS series]/ *Yellowstone in Winter* [title]/ EBC (Encyclopaedia Britannica) [distributor]/ Lorimar Home Video [distributor, home rights]/ New York: WNET [produced by]/ 1987 [year of distribution, shown EBC 1987]/ 60 min. [length]/ color/ not rated/ closed captioned/ photographed by Wolfgang Bayer [in description on box, notes]

In this particular case, the primary source has the least amount of information; therefore, it must be supplemented with secondary

FIGURE 2.7 MAIN ENTRY CATALOG CARD FOR YELLOWSTONE IN WINTER.

Yellowstone in Winter [videorecording]/New York: WNET; [distributed by] Lorimar Home Video; EBC, 1987.
60 min. col. VHS
(Nature series, Vol. III)
Portrays the winter beauty of Yellowstone National Park and the struggle of the wildlife to survive the frigid depths of winter.

                       I. Nature [series]
II. Bayer, Wolfgang [photographer]

O

source information. Figure 2.7 illustrates the descriptive cataloging of this title (Level 2, *AACR II*).

A further complication in terms of *Yellowstone in Winter* is that some important information is not discernible unless the cataloger is versed in video products. This program is an update of an earlier 27-minute version of the same title produced in 1983. Also, this title is simultaneously distributed by Wolfgang Bayer Productions (1986) and Lorimar Productions (1987).

After the video has been physically described, its contents (subject and genre) must be described by using a consistent set of headings that promotes accessibility. Two standard subject lists commonly used are *The Library of Congress List of Subject Headings* and *Sears List of Subject Headings*. These subject headings (and added entries) are shown in the tracings of a unit card. The subject headings for *Yellowstone in Winter* might be 1. Yellowstone National Park, or possibly a broader heading, 1. National Parks. Also, videos that are closed-captioned for the hearing-impaired should be noted on the spine label and as a subject heading on the catalog card. Nonfiction titles can be described relatively easily by using these sources. Feature films are more difficult to describe and, for simplicity's sake, should be modified in genre categories as illustrated below.

Action and adventure	Children's features
Comedy	Drama
Foreign films	Music videos
Musicals	Mystery and suspense
Romance films	Science fiction/fantasy
Horror films	Westerns
War films	

Another example of subject/genre categorization and arrangement is illustrated in Chapter 7.

The use of catalog cards for patron access is advocated by the author, but some librarians may prefer to develop a book catalog/title list instead. A personal computer is very useful for revising lists. Many librarians are currently using OCLC on-line cataloging for books and audiovisual materials. OCLC is not very useful for cataloging home video titles. Most of the titles are not in the data base, and when they are, there are multiple "incorrect" listings. It is much more efficient to purchase personal computer card catalog reproduction software and do it yourself.

Shelving arrangements should accomplish three functions: (1) facilitate ease of browsing and title locations; (2) be organized in a logical manner readily apparent to patrons; and (3) be kept as simple as possible but with subject/genre areas sufficiently delineated to avoid confusion.

This text also advocates the use of the Dewey decimal classification system for subject arrangement of nonfiction titles. Librarians possessing small collections may feel that Dewey is too complex and may choose to use a few broad subject categories such as feature films, music, documentary, instructional, and children's films. The Dewey system provides for an orderly shelf arrangement of subject videos and facilitates transitional continuity from print to nonprint. Arranging feature films alphabetically by title with genres denoted using colored labels seems to work the best. Genre labels are available from the video store sources previously listed, and also from United Ad Label Company, P.O. Box 2165, Whittier, CA 90610. These labels facilitate easy location and patron browsing.

☐ CIRCULATION AND USE POLICIES AND PROCEDURES

Now that the videocassettes have been purchased, acquired, processed, cataloged, and arranged for patron access, they are ready for circulation. The actual process of circulating videos is no more complicated than circulating other library items; however, there are some special problems to be addressed. Loan periods should be established to facilitate equitable use. They should not be arbitrarily set to inhibit patron use. The average loan period for public libraries is two to three days, but a week may be required for many nonfiction titles. A two-tier circulation period (three days for features; one week for nonfiction) may work fine. A written circulation policy addressing the following concerns should be established before any circulation occurs:

- Loan time limits and number of videos per patron per circulation period
- Age limitations (if any) for use of collection, or any part of the collection
- Registration/responsibility card for video users or for minors' parents to sign
- Overdue fines—cost per day or per hour

- Replacement/damage policy—sliding discount scale based upon use or current replacement cost and repair cost
- Overdue penalty—a suspension of service after so many overdues within a certain time period
- Circulation fees or handling charges.

Videocassettes should be physically examined upon their return. Damage inspection and evaluation is performed for three reasons: (1) to be assured that the case and the cassette match (mix-ups are extremely common) before the mix-up becomes untrackable; (2) to evaluate the condition of the item so that damage/replacement fees can be assessed; and (3) to make sure the video is in good working order. Some library inspection procedures actually involve viewing a portion of the tape upon return, but this is not cost-effective in terms of staff time or results. The physical cassette should be visually inspected for any breaks or cracks, excessive rattles, tape crinkles or tears, hanging out of flip-up lid, and excessive tape oxide shedding. A repair fee schedule should be determined that delineates labor and parts costs for all repairs. The circulation policy covers all the elements of daily circulation operations and is likely to be the one most questioned by patrons; therefore it is essential that the library be well prepared to field patrons' questions and protect the library's integrity.

CONCLUSION

The importance of strategic planning in starting any new collection cannot be stressed enough. Strategic planning lets the library administration act out various scenarios that give insight into the best plan of attack. In this manner, all available resources, including physical facilities, budget money, and staff, can be more efficiently utilized. Although no plan is without faults, and unexpected day-to-day emergencies arise, the administration that possesses a strategic plan (and the accompanying policies) can direct its staff energies toward solving those emergencies with the comfort of knowing they are headed toward a specific set of goals. However, it should also be stressed that a strategic plan is a dynamic set of documents that is continually reviewed and revised. A strategic plan enhances administrative vision and forecasting and enables the library to keep pace with the constantly changing and growing video/society environment.

NOTES

1. Barbara Tolliver, "Collection Development: Problems and Opportunities," *Catholic Library World* 58 (March/April 1987): 225.
2. Vernon E. Palmour, "Some Reflection on Strategic Planning in Public Libraries," *Drexel Library Quarterly* 21 (Fall 1985): 48.
3. Ibid., 51.
4. Ibid., 54.
5. Ray Serebrin, "Video in Public Libraries: A Guide for the Perplexed," *Library Journal* 119 (15 May 1987): 29.
6. David Spiller, *Book Selection*, 3d ed. (London: Clive Bingley, 1980), 61.
7. Ibid., 62.
8. Peter P. Schillaci, "Video Trends: Past, Present, & Future," *Sightlines* 20 (Winter 1986/1987): 8.
9. David L. Perkins, ed., *Guidelines for Collection Development*, (Chicago: American Library Association, 1979), 55.
10. William E. McGrath, "A Pragmatic Book Allocation Formula for Academic and Public Libraries with a Test for Its Effectiveness," *Library Resources and Technical Services* 19 (Fall 1975): 361.
11. John Rutledge and Luke Swindler, "The Selection Decision: Defining Criteria and Establishing Priorities," *College & Research Libraries* 48 (March 1987): 127.
12. T. D. Webb, "A Hierarchy of Public Library User Types," *Library Journal* 111 (15 September 1986): 47–50.
13. Roy Smith, "Lending Video," *New Library World* 84 (November 1983): 181.
14. Jack Short, "Video in the Collection," *Collection Management* 7 (Fall 1985/Winter 1986): 242.
15. Ibid.
16. Phyllis J. Van Orden, *The Collection Program in Elementary and Middle Schools* (Littleton, CO: Libraries Unlimited, 1982), 227.
17. Serebrin, "Video in Public Libraries," 29.
18. Michael Gorman and Paul W. Winkler, eds., *Anglo-American Cataloguing Rules*, 2d ed. (Chicago: American Library Association, 1978), 166.

3
COLLECTION DEVELOPMENT POLICY

Collection development is probably the single most important and difficult library theory to effectively put into practice because it requires so much preplanning and a broad scope of vision. However, it is the number one priority and the foundation of effective library service. For the most part, librarians have been inundated with patrons demanding video and, consequently, have been forced to perform within the narrow scope of satisfying those immediate needs. The larger picture of overall collection development policy has been neglected. Today, almost anything on video will circulate, but relatively soon the market will be overburdened by similar-subject/genre titles. Consumers are rapidly becoming more eclectic about what they choose to watch. These factors together will ultimately spell the downfall of the ephemeral collection because the library will have to keep purchasing more and more new hit titles to keep up with the demand while the old forgotten hits such as *Rambo* and *Rocky IV* gather dust on the shelves.

Planning is the buzzword for the 1980s. It must not be an end in itself but a foundation upon which to put goals into action and a framework on which to build selection standards. Collection development must relate to the library's purpose and mission and be directly linked to accomplishing goals. Statements of purpose describe the parameters of the library's clientele and community and define broad-based service and collection goals.

Careful management of any library's collection is crucial to meeting patron needs, resulting in more effective and efficient use of library space, funds, and staff. Not only must the *how* and *what* of a collection be managed, but the *why*, *when*, and *where* must also be controlled.[1] These concerns are addressed in the library's written collection development policy, which serves several functions:

1. It establishes a planning guideline and working tool for selectors
2. It operates as a communications medium between the library and external administrative bodies
3. It states the codified rationale for decisions in budgetary matters where materials are concerned
4. It helps achieve a unified view of what areas of the collection should be developed
5. It helps develop coordination between different individuals responsible for the collection
6. It helps achieve consistency in materials selection by clarifying specific objectives and reducing the number of ad hoc decisions related to the selection process
7. It provides for methods of performance evaluation for continuation of the collection-building cycle

Libraries with automated circulation systems can adapt to a program such as this very quickly. However, those with manual systems will find evaluation to be the hardest, most time-consuming step. Evaluation is the most important step because without it the entire cycle breaks down. Small collections such as video are particularly well suited to the collection development concept because genre/subject strengths and the resulting circulation can be monitored with relative degrees of accuracy.

A collection development policy provides librarians with the means to conduct systematic materials selection according to a set of predetermined guidelines founded upon community wants and needs and quality standards. The policy should never be set in stone but rather should be flexible and attuned to the changing community environment. However, rational thought coupled with consideration of long-term effects should always provide the impetus for those changes and not spur-of-the-moment decisions.

Two documents of value in providing goal delineation regarding materials are the materials selection policy and the overall collection development policy. The latter policy consists of very broad statements that define the scope and nature of the library's various collections and provide a guide for allocating the materials budget. Materials selection policies usually address specific material types (i.e., books, periodicals, videocassettes, phonorecords, etc.). These policies are then included in the broader collection development plan. Each selection policy literally spells out the various criteria and guidelines for selection. It is important that every material type have its own policy because this clarifies the unique nature of each format and integrates each format into the budget structure.

SPECIFIC COMPONENTS OF A COLLECTION DEVELOPMENT POLICY

The following collection development components will only consider elements specifically applicable to the video format, combining some of the larger concepts of the collection development policy with the video selection policy.

A collection development policy usually includes the following elements:

1. Introduction
2. Mission or general philosophy statement and institutional goals
3. Description of structure and community served
4. Selection process defined and delineated
5. Detailed analysis of specific collections, subject areas, and selection criteria
6. Weeding and gifts
7. An acquisitions policy
8. Collection evaluation guidelines/goals
9. Policies and procedures for reconsideration of challenged material[2]

Items 7, 8, and 9 do not have to be specifically defined within the smaller videocassette policy. They can be addressed along with the total collection development policy.

☐ DESCRIPTION OF POLICY FACTORS

1. The introduction establishes the uses of the document, states the governing body legally responsible for materials selection, and defines the scope and purpose for the policy.
2. The mission statement identifies the general function and philosophy of the institution and the various collections, creating a theoretical foundation on which the more practical

sections will be built. Many libraries include references to the "Library Bill of Rights" and "Freedom to View" (see Appendix) in this section. If the library has formal goal statements, they should also be included here.
3. The structure and community service section recognizes the principles that will guide the growth of the collection. Issues to be addressed include:
   a. Description of those responsible for selection.
   b. Description of the clientele to be served—demographics and general population parameters. Clientele with special needs such as children, disabled, etc., are described here.
4. The general selection process is outlined:
   a. General collection subject boundaries—defining the subject intent, coverage limits, special interest, curriculum-related or extracurricular interests.
   b. Programs or user needs supported—specifies the types of subject coverage to be included in the collection; for example, instructional, general informational, or recreational materials.
   c. General priorities and limitations governing selection, such as specific funds allocated to special interests, forms of materials to be excluded and included, and materials duplication.
5. A detailed analysis of specific collections identifies all collection types as well as specific genres such as children's, features, nonfiction. This section should consider current levels of collecting, offer guidelines for future growth, and include a clear statement identifying the person(s) responsible for selection. Selection criteria should be listed here, possibly broken down by genres and/or subject areas.
6. In the weeding and gift acceptance section, specific criteria are outlined.
7. The acquisition policy section describes the methods and rationale of obtaining materials.
8. Collection evaluation ensures that specific collection levels established in the policy are followed and makes provisions for continual evaluation and policy revision. Weeding is also discussed in this section.
9. The policies and procedures for reconsideration of challenged materials provide directions for handling complaints concerning collection inclusion, censorship, and labeling. Specific complaint forms may be appended.

A SAMPLE COLLECTION DEVELOPMENT POLICY

The following sample collection development policy was formulated by the author of this text by combining two existing policies from the Seattle (Washington) and Decatur (Illinois) public libraries. It should serve as a guide for libraries wishing to develop their own policies. As noted above, items 7 through 9 are not addressed in this policy because they should be included in the larger total collection development policy and need not be repeated. Many books on collection development address these three elements in depth.

SMITH COMMUNITY DISTRICT LIBRARY
Videocassette Collection Development Policy

The Smith Community District Library Board of Trustees hereby adopts the following collection development policy on this date, 1 December 1987. This document will be used as a guide to direct the library director and all department heads in the various aspects of collection development, including selection, acquisition, and discarding of materials.

Purpose
The Library acquires, makes available, and encourages the use of videocassettes to serve the general information, education, and recreation within the diverse needs of the community. The collection strives to complement, rather than to compete with, local video rental stores by offering a different collection focus. The collection strives to be general in nature, and does not contain specialized material for the exclusive use of one particular group. Materials selection is guided by a general design to maintain a 50/50 split between nonfiction and feature films representing a wide variety of general subjects and genres. The collection does not include materials purchased specifically for school or college curriculum use. The Library subscribes to the "Library Bill of Rights" and "Freedom to View" and does not label or censure materials.

Community Served
Videocassettes are selected to serve the broad, general interest ranges of the Smith District. Smith is a medium-sized district with a population of 60 percent white-collar workers, 30 percent blue-collar workers, and 10 percent persons under the age of 18. Library cardholders are 40 percent of the community.

Structure
Videocassettes are made available in the audiovisual (AV) department of the main library and through request at the two bookmobiles. Selection of materials is the responsibility of the AV department head.

Selection Process
The AV department employs the AV department head to coordinate the selection, acquisition, and discarding of materials within the video collection. Items are considered for collection inclusion based on favorable reviews from authoritative reference sources. Regularly scheduled, weekly selection meetings are held where all the department heads gather to discuss and review potential purchases.

General Selection
There is no single set of criteria that can be applied to all items because of the great diversity of materials. Some items are judged primarily in terms of artistic merit or documentation of the times, while others are selected to satisfy the recreational and informational needs of the community. The library encourages purchase suggestions from the public and will give them serious consideration. Selection decisions are based upon reviews in professional review magazines and books such as *Halliwell's Film Guide, Motion Picture Guide, Library Journal, Booklist, Video Review, Librarian's Video Review*, and others. Currently, only VHS videocassettes are included in the collection.

Selection Criteria by Subject of Material
In selection of material by subject, consideration should be given to such matters as popular (and timely) demand for the item, the relationship of the material to the existing collection and to other materials available on the

subject, the likely attention of critics, opinion makers, and the public to the item, its importance as a document of our times, the cost of the item as compared with comparable material on the same subject, and the cost-benefit ratio compared with an alternative expenditure. Acquisition of such material will include videotapes of an informational, cultural, recreational, and instructional nature with collections that contemplate and emphasize serious use while also recognizing the legitimacy of entertainment purposes. Acquisitions are limited to works for which an acceptable level of quality has been determined in one or more of the following ways:

1. By the opinion of qualified reviewers in recognized, authoritative review sources. At least one positive review is required.
2. Through recognition by prizes, awards, etc., given by critical organizations or institutes or associations of peers of producing artists, such as the New York Film Critics Circle, the Television Academy of Arts and Sciences, Cannes Film Festival, CINE awards, U.S. and international film festivals, etc.
3. Materials reissued in videoform from filmed material or reproduced 20 years or more after the original production shall be assumed on the basis of longevity of appeal to meet standards for acquisition.
4. Materials that have appeared on public television networks.
5. In-house review evaluation by the department head.
6. If an artist, in seeking realistic representation of the human condition, includes material that is sexually candid or dialogue with vulgar diction, such inclusion will not be considered reason for rejection if the video otherwise meets standards for acquisition.

General quality criteria include the following:

1. Is of present and potential relevance to community needs
2. Provides insight into human and social needs
3. Accurately presents factual information
4. Is useful for its intended audience
5. Satisfies public demand resulting from the attention of critics and reviews

6. Provides high-quality performances and accurate content
7. Is produced with technical skill
8. Provides a presentation most effectively or appropriately delivered by the video format
9. Provides information or presentation that is unique to or only available in the format

SPECIFIC CRITERIA: NONFICTION, CHILDREN'S AND YOUNG ADULT, AND FEATURE FILMS

Nonfiction. Nonfiction video is purchased when the format provides a useful and eclectic way of presenting information to a clientele. All general subjects will be acquired with particular emphasis upon cooking, travel, craft how-to, and sports videos. All video programs advocating exercise or special diets must receive certification, approval, or a favorable review from an authoritative subject source such as The Aerobic and Fitness Association of America or the American Dietetics Association.

Children's and young adult. These materials should be useful and relevant to their everyday needs, interests, and activities. Children's materials will be purchased for the age group ranging from preschool through eighth grade. Special emphasis will be placed on a child's developmental needs for stimulation of imagination and mental growth. Young adult material will emphasize current, popular, lively themes that contribute to the development and pleasure of this group. Concept films, folktales, and fairytales will be emphasized in children's video. Programs such as *ABC Afternoon Specials* will be included for young adults.

Feature films. Feature films will be purchased to satisfy the public's need for recreational materials and to serve differing tastes and interests. Owing to the relatively high cost of video materials and limited library budgets, it is impossible for any library agency to adequately satisfy public demand for high-interest feature films. Classics, long-term, popular features and musicals, award winners, as well as other broad-based genres will be included. Popular, ephemeral music videos will not be included.

Collection Maintenance

FORMAT SELECTION AND MULTIPLE COPIES

Information in diverse video formats will be acquired and made available if the format is judged to be useful in satisfying the immediate and long-range needs of the community. A substantial portion of the community must desire the format. Multiple copies will be provided based on demonstrated and anticipated user interest, availability of funds, and availability of similar items already in the collection.

REPLACEMENT OF MATERIALS

Programs will not automatically be replaced because of loss or damage. Replacement decisions will be based upon (1) demand for title, (2) number of copies already held, (3) existing coverage of a subject/genre in the collection, and (4) availability of newer or better materials on the subject.

WEEDING

In order to maintain active, up-to-date, useful collections, selectors, as assigned, will periodically examine all video materials in terms of relevance to user needs and selection criteria. Last copy, out-of-print titles will usually be retained if of local historical interest or significance, or if the information they contain is of use to the community and cannot be acquired elsewhere. Other factors to be considered include lack of use, physical and playing condition, and accuracy and datedness of information.

EVALUATION

The collection is continually evaluated in terms of circulation performance, currency, content inclusion, scope and depth of coverage, and popularity. Continuous weeding and responsible replacement of damaged or lost titles helps maintain a collection that reflects changing community needs and library goals.

GIFTS

Gift materials will be accepted by the AV department with the understanding that they become the property of the library. They will be evaluated against the same criteria as purchased materials. Donors may not place any special conditions upon the loan or handling of the items. Department heads will make the final decision on use and disposition of all donations and will determine the conditions of display, storage, and access to the materials. Materials *not* included—work that achieves its appeal strictly by sensational, erotic, scatological, or other cheap and exploitative means. Material that is strictly ephemeral in nature and is dependent upon speedy acceptance encouraged by massive publicity will not be acquired.

SUMMARY

A well-defined collection development policy, put into place before the collection is started, will enable the librarian to express the library's clearly defined service goals in terms of specific materials that will satisfy those goals. The collection development policy is not a static document to be written once then placed in the closet. It is a dynamic policy outlining a plan of action relative to specific collection needs. The community and the library are constantly changing; therefore the policy must reflect those changes. Care must be taken not to mistake ephemeral trends and local fads for change—the librarian must not be too reactive in nature. Libraries will have a much better chance to respond positively to change if they have prepared themselves with a thorough collection development policy.

NOTES

1. G. Edward Evans, *Developing Library Collections* (Littleton, CO: Libraries Unlimited, 1979), 22.
2. Ibid.

COLLECTION DEVELOPMENT GOALS AND EVALUATION AND SELECTION GUIDELINES

Proceeding from theory to practice, a video collection development program is the next logical step after library policy has been established. Four premises underlie sound collection development. (1) Collection development should be geared primarily to community needs rather than to an abstract standard of quality. (2) It must be responsive to the total community's needs inasmuch as that information is ascertainable. (3) It must be based on goals and objectives that are translated into material needs. Even though selection is a title-by-title process, the broader scope of the entire collection must constantly be viewed. (4) Finally, the process will always be subjective and biased; therefore more than one person should be involved in selection. It requires constant practice in order to develop proficiency.[1]

In other words, a comprehensive collection development program should be a dynamic, self-perpetuating activity whereby the library staff brings together a variety of materials to meet patron demands. If well defined, a collection development program can serve a secondary function of helping libraries justify themselves to local government by showing that libraries are receptive to community needs and do not house materials chosen indiscriminately.

A solid collection development program includes five functions: (1) assessment of community information needs, (2) expressing those needs in terms of goals and measurable but attainable objectives, (3) establishing policies for materials selection based on those goals and objectives, (4) systematic collection maintenance and weeding, and (5) monitoring and evaluation of collection performance including collection use studies. Given the sequential relationship of these elements, it is possible to diagram the cycle (see Figure 4.1). These elements are generally agreed upon; what is open to debate is how much emphasis should be placed upon individual steps in the process, and the interrelationship of all the elements. As Phyllis J. Van Orden says,

> Few librarians would question the need or value of patron input, but the question is, how much should there be? The best answer would seem to be, as much as the library can afford to handle and as much as the community is willing to provide.[2]

This chapter will focus on the process of translating community video needs into concrete collection goals and on the nuts and bolts of selecting and evaluating videocassettes for the collection. Later chapters will cover collection maintenance and performance.

IMPORTANT VARIABLES IN DETERMINING VIDEO COLLECTION GOALS

Translating the needs of the community and library patrons into concrete goals for a video collection and developing a workable set of selection/evaluation criteria from those goals are two of the AV librarian's most important challenges. A number of often competing needs must be weighed when charting the course for a video collection. The video medium is especially subject to short-lived, intense, changing pressure for popular titles, and AV librarians must develop concrete guidelines for integrating these short-term patron demands with long-term patron needs and library goals. *Patron demands* is broadly used to mean what the patrons presently need or want as well as what may be needed or wanted in the future, and not to simply refer to persistent user requests for the latest best-selling materials. The library must always keep in mind its duty to offer in-depth and wide-ranging services also to less vocal members of the community.

It is an oversimplification to reduce the philosophy of collection development to simple arguments of quantity versus quality. Librarians must consider many variables when setting up a development plan. For example, collection development should be partially driven by a library's perceived function, as well as by demand. Public libraries serve a broad-based, general public; therefore, they

COLLECTION DEVELOPMENT GOALS AND GUIDELINES 81

must be sensitive to popular cultural phenomena. School and college libraries perform a curriculum support function for specific clienteles and thus have different functions and require different sorts of video collections.

FIGURE 4.1 COLLECTION DEVELOPMENT PROCESS MODEL. This is a conceptualization of the interrelationship between the library's patron community and the library staff in the materials selection process. The selection process is really a continuous cycle. Reprinted with permission from Libraries Unlimited from G. Edward Evans, *Developing Library Collections* (Littleton, CO: Libraries Unlimited, 1979), 19.

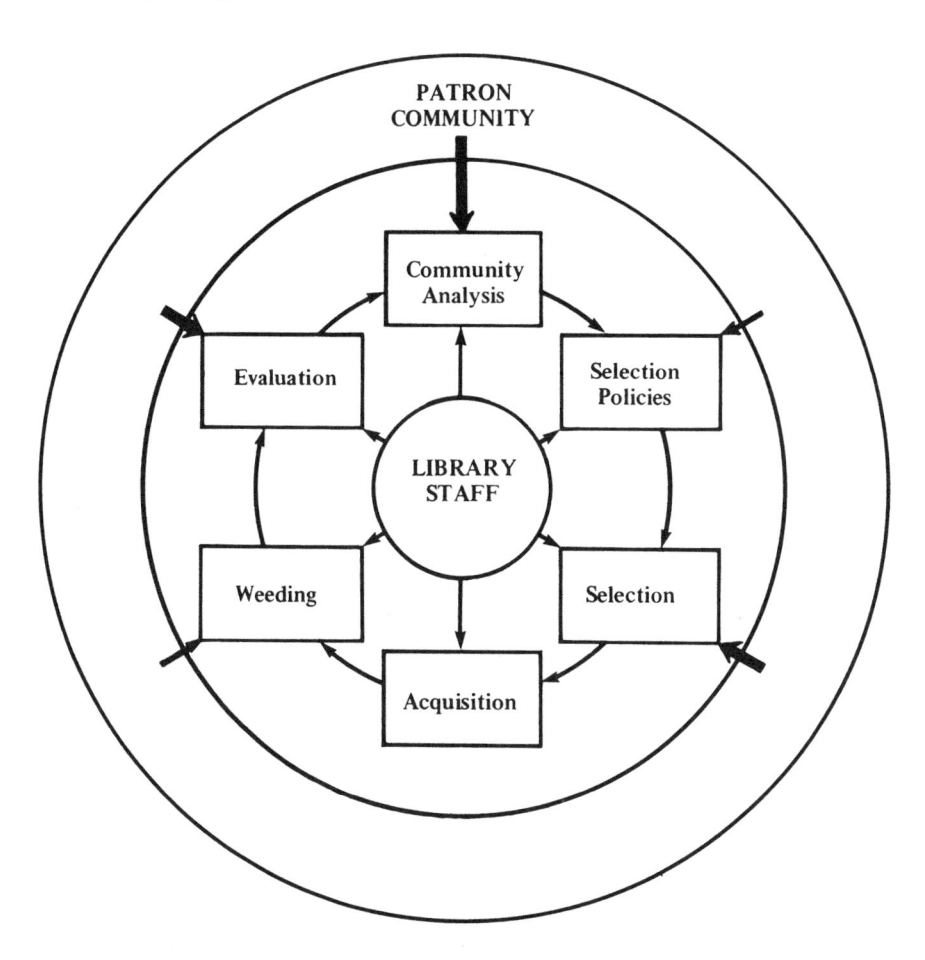

Librarians must also question what makes a good library video collection. Is there any way to know if a collection is good or not? Something that is good or useful is valuable—but to whom? Most librarians equate *good* with *highly used*, but are these terms equivalent? This is a superficial conclusion at best. How many times does an item have to be used in order to make it useful? Should various subject areas of the video collection have different use criteria? Does the definition of a good collection change with the goals and priorities of the library? Should the collection be looked upon as a collection of individual items or as a collective whole? What constitutes a developed video collection? Is a plateau ever reached at which a collection has too many volumes/titles? Can collections become overcrowded with items that should not be there? Do patrons know what they need when they see it? And finally, can the value of an item be accurately determined instead of merely tallying circulations as "use"?

☐ QUALITY VERSUS DEMAND

Regarding the issue of demand selection (give them what they want) versus quality selection (give them what they should have), this text advocates a compromise where quality standards are set, but special exceptions for items in constant demand are made.[3] This middle-of-the-road approach does not necessarily imply a 50/50 split. Quality selection standards should be applied to videos as well as all other library materials: items that receive poor reviews because of information inaccuracy, deletions, or poor production quality should not be purchased. However, if a poor review occurs because of the reviewer's subjective tastes or misunderstanding of the item's purpose, another review (or in-house preview) should be sought and the title considered for purchase. Video titles such as *The Care Bears*, *My Little Pony*, and *The Transformers* are examples of titles that are questionable library purchases. Although these titles were produced primarily to sell a product and have been criticized as such, they are well animated, have good production qualities, are not overly violent, and possess fairly stable plots. Yet, despite their popularity today, they will probably not stand the test of time in the same sense as the Disney classics. Acquiring high circulation should not be the sole purpose of any library collection; equally important is the acquisition of titles that will be used by the entire community.

As noted, it is a mistake to base quality solely upon circulation. The librarian who is content with buying only what is currently popular, besides abdicating the professional role as an information expert, is doing a serious disservice to the community by eliminating the educational mission of the public library. Quality materials selection provides the library with works of permanent value. What must be avoided is selection of materials for a single set of patrons whose tastes thus dictate the shape of the whole collection, although it must be kept in mind that the library simply cannot supply enough material to satisfy every special interest group to the full extent that they desire.

Librarians advocating fee-based library video collections often rationalize the acquisition of ephemeral, best-selling titles based on two reasons: (1) patrons pay for the service, so the library should acquire what the public wants; and (2) since a fee is charged, the item pays for itself (i.e., a $40 videocassette circulating 40 times for a $1 fee has paid for itself); therefore, title deaccession after that circulation limit has been reached results in virtually no loss. These are logical reasons for purchasing only popular titles. However, the library should theoretically strive to serve everyone equally. Fees are discriminatory to those unable to pay. To date, the attorney generals in at least two states have advised librarians not to charge fees for videocassette loans based on the premise of the tax-supported public library.

Guidelines for a Compromise Course

In truth, it is impossible and unrealistic to come down squarely on either side of the demand/quality issue; therefore an equitable compromise must be reached. Following are some guidelines that will aid in establishing this balance:

1. Establish purchasing objectives in terms of both number of features and nonfiction titles purchases and number and duplication rate of popular and standard titles. A good starting point is 60 percent features and 40 percent nonfiction, with popular titles representing not more than 20 percent of the total features.
2. Establish evaluation standards for judging all titles based on measurable, fairly objective quality criteria.
3. Strive to purchase only on the basis of favorable reviews from reliable sources, and acquire the best of any subject/genre. *Quality* should generally be interpreted to mean "appropriateness and expected use and value to the collection through the long term."

4. Duplicate known quantities first, rather than acquiring unknown titles, but duplicate sparingly based on previous performance.

It is relatively easy to determine what to duplicate, but extremely difficult to determine the duplication rate. Retrospective item circulation and the number of times that an item has been requested, but not available, must also be examined. For example, a library has a circulation period of three days. Theoretically, saturation would occur at 104 annual circulations; 52 circulations indicate that the title is on the shelf just as much as it is checked out. Any number exceeding 52 indicates that the title is out more than it is in. Library staff should keep daily lists of titles that are not currently owned by the library. Patrons may also express a desire to check out or reserve a title that is currently out. These titles should also be listed, as they will aid the librarian in deciding which titles to duplicate and how many duplicates to purchase. Also, backed-up item reserves could indicate that duplication is necessary. The demand versus quality and duplication decisions must be delicately balanced between intuition and collection development rationale. There are no hard and fast rules to be followed.

Following is a summary of some of the basic precepts of video collection development:

1. Buy multiple copies sparingly. It is not wise to purchase ten copies of *First Blood* and find that they sit on the shelf. A better use of funds might be to acquire one or two copies of a wide variety of titles.
2. Know the community's general and specific character and interests; be familiar with subjects of current interest; keep abreast of new releases to satisfy those interests; and provide materials for a broad range of interests.
3. Solicit and accept recommendations from patrons and provide feedback; actively search for published reviews in all types of sources.
4. Keep a want list of titles/subjects based on need; supply these as reviews and video software become available.
5. Provide for both the actual and potential viewer. Satisfy existing demand and anticipate those suggested by coming events, community conditions, and existing circulation trends.
6. Utilize collection evaluation instruments to accurately measure individual title and subject/genre performance.
7. Examine selection aids on a regular, systematic basis.

8. Practice impartiality in selection; possibly institute a selection committee of several coworkers with different backgrounds to aid in selection.
9. Maintain, so far as possible, promptness and regularity in supplying new titles, thus taking advantage of outside media promotions.
10. Utilize standard purchasing lists judiciously because they can become outdated quickly and do not take into consideration specific community needs.
11. Keep the budget streamlined so that all monies can be spent wisely without waste. Generally, libraries with larger budgets will purchase more titles and are likely to acquire more of the better, as well as more of the less good titles. However, there is a greater chance of acquiring lesser quality, nondemand items with a larger budget, especially when careful development plans have not been followed.

☐ CIRCULATION AS A FACTOR IN COLLECTION DEVELOPMENT

As noted above, the terms *good* and *highly used* are not necessarily synonymous, nor should they be. For instance, specific categories within any collection do not circulate equally; however, this circulation, or lack of it, does not necessarily predicate the relative usefulness of any one title. Circulation is not necessarily an accurate determinant of the degree of usefulness or value of an item, but it can be used as a guideline. For example, if a library serving a blue-collar community purchased some well-known foreign films such as *Knife in the Water* or *La Cage Aux Folles*, and they did not circulate, purchasing more foreign titles would not be wise.

☐ CIRCULATION STATISTICS

The collection should be divided into a number of small, manageable but related subjects and genres. In this manner, a collection map showing strengths and weaknesses can be developed when comparing volumes/titles held, circulations, and number of items in/out. Figure 4.2 illustrates a highly segmented Dewey arrangement. An accurate, continuous count of the number of titles/volumes held should be kept. Libraries possessing automated circulation systems such as CLSI can code each category so the computer can accurately count the circulations within those categories. The total circulations for any given category can then be divided by the

	No. of Titles	No. of Vol.	No. Months Held in Collection	Circulation	Avg. Circ.
000					
130-39					
150-59					
100's					
200-89					
270-99					
300-09					
330-39					
360-69					
370-79					
300's					
400's					
500-49					
550-99					
610-19					
620-29					
635-36					
640-49					
650-59					
690-99					
600's					
737-39 & 745-49					
700-69					
770-79					
780-792					
793-99					
811 & 821					
812 & 822					
817 & 827					
818 & 828					
800's					
900 & 909					
910 & 919					
920 & B					
930-39					
940-49					
950 & 69					
970-79					

FIGURE 4.2 SAMPLE VIDEO CIRCULATION STATISTICS SHEET.

number of titles (or volumes) held, resulting in an average circulation per category. Averages can be used as comparisons to individual titles to judge performance or popularity.

Manual systems might employ several systematic visual counts of titles/volumes in or out at any given time. These figures can then be compared with the total titles/volumes held, thus revealing use percentages of the collection. This type of data is very important for selection purposes. In this manner, similar titles can be purchased and increase the likelihood of responding to unexpressed or unactivated patron needs. Circulation statistics are valuable, but they should not be overrated in determining what to purchase.

THE SIZE AND SHAPE OF THE INITIAL COLLECTION

A small, well-selected collection will produce the maximum use per dollar expended. Librarians should start with a collection of 100 to 200 titles representing a wide and general range of genres and subjects with, as mentioned earlier, a division of 60 percent features and 40 percent nonfiction. Growth can occur based on planned expansion in response to collection goals designed to meet patron needs. The results from the patron survey (Chapter 2) along with planned buying, based on collection goals, will result in a well-used, long-term circulating collection.

The important thing to remember in collection development is that there is no universal right or wrong. There are basic tenets that can be adapted to situations, but no two library collections will be the same. A developed collection is reached when patrons stop asking the librarian for new materials; therefore, a limit is never reached. However, any collection can become overcrowded. In public libraries, the primary method patrons use to choose videos is browsing. Browsing becomes less attractive and less effective as the size of the collection increases. A video collection utilizing colorful packaging with descriptive content notes will enhance browsing and increase circulation.

☐ POPULAR FEATURES VERSUS SPECIALTY PROGRAMS

Although producers agree that the wave of the future in video is nonfiction or specialty programming, many libraries do not yet consider nonfiction video a viable collection item. Librarians cite a variety of reasons for this omission, for example: (1) longer circulation periods are needed for nonfiction titles; (2) prices for nonfiction videos are too high and resultant circulation is too low compared with features; and (3) purchasing nonfiction requires more patron advisory assistance. However, most of these objections are no longer valid. Libraries should not encourage short loan periods just to artificially inflate circulation and thus discourage the use of nonfiction video. Also, prices of nonfiction programming have dropped dramatically since 1984, and are currently averaging about $59 compared to features averaging $37. Finally, the already wide variety of titles and subjects is constantly growing, and distributor availability is also increasing. The library has the responsibility to provide for the informational and recreational needs of its community and should include a wide variety of subjects/genres within the collection.

Book fiction and video features are not that dissimilar in patron appeal; therefore we might look at the fiction circulation trends in public libraries for guidance. Historically, fiction has had higher circulation than nonfiction in public libraries. During 1985, Illinois public libraries loaned 51 percent fiction and 49 percent nonfiction (including AV materials). Based upon an average loan period of three weeks, fiction generally averaged 7.7 circulations annually per title compared with nonfiction's 2.2 circulations per title.[4] The data seem to indicate that smaller libraries stock more fiction because of budgetary and shelf space limitations. However, the data give no indication of the interest longevity of fiction as time goes on. Libraries that purchase more nonfiction than fiction seem to have more consistent, less volatile circulation, but their materials budgets are somewhat larger, and they must buy more titles to equal the circulation of a library concentrating on fiction. It might be wise for smaller libraries to concentrate purchasing efforts toward a feature video collection, but they should not neglect the nonfiction titles. Also, multiple-copy purchasing of the blockbuster movies will increase circulation for a short while, but eventually the library will be stuck with these copies of short-term popularity movies.

SELECTION AND EVALUATION STRATEGIES

The librarian must select videos that appeal to a heterogeneous population from a wide range of possible choices and a limited amount of reliable guidance for those choices. Selection should not proceed by chance or be directed by the personal interests of staff; it should be based upon written objectives and policies. It is a creative process—new materials selected will relate not only to user needs but to the developing collection as well. It is not enough to say that the library will purchase all titles that are well received or those that are in great demand. The role of the AV librarian rests heavily upon selection/evaluation decisions; therefore it is important to define and separate functions for a clearer understanding of the total process.

The terms *selection, evaluation,* and *collection development* are often used interchangeably, but are not synonymous. This text will use the term *selection* to refer to the process whereby materials are chosen for inclusion in the library collection from various review sources. Although it involves critical choice, the process depends entirely upon the review sources used, the reviewer's objectivity, and the subject variety/title inclusion presented.

Evaluation is the assessment or appraisal of any title against a predetermined set of standards. Primary evaluation occurs when material itself is reviewed in-house against a set of criteria. Secondary evaluation is a librarian's appraisal of reviews gauged against the criteria set. Evaluation provides more consistency, especially when two or more people are responsible for evaluating items. By using a collection development policy and selection aids, librarians are performing secondary evaluation within a framework of measurable collection objectives, rather than just performing arbitrary, title-by-title selection.

☐ EVALUATION CRITERIA

Evaluation usually takes the form of questions such as Will this title fill a void in the collection? Will it be popular? Is there anything similar in the collection that would argue against its purchase? Does it meet all the local primary evaluation criteria? Below are three sets of evaluation criteria.

Content

Is the subject suitable for the video format?

Does the program satisfy its intended purpose, audience, and subject matter?

Is the content accurate, current, and presented in an organized, easily followed, and pleasant manner?

Does the content seem honest, authentic, and objective, or slanted and biased?

Do plot, character development, and subject comprehensiveness appear adequate?

Do the performance, dramatic interpretation, use of medium, overall effectiveness, and any use of special effects seem cinematically valid?

How is the overall pacing of the program and edit sequencing?

Do the style, point of view, overall approach, and creativity seem original, fresh, and inventive?

Are elements of sound (articulation, intonation, wordiness, faddishness, jargon use, and level of sophistication) of professional quality?

Technical Aspects

Consider these aspects of camera work: expressiveness, mobility, multiple camera work, viewpoint, resolution and clarity, and color and contrast.

Sound elements should be evaluated for appropriateness in approach, music and narration/dialog balance, synchronization, general speech clarity and pacing.

Do these elements of editing seem smooth: pacing and rhythm, length of sequences, use of dissolves, fades, and other special effects?

Are the script, narration, and visuals technically correct?

Packaging

Is the original case protective? Is it oversized, or does it contain another cassette/s or additional material, and will this cause shelving and circulation difficulties?

Does the outside information accurately, attractively, and effectively advertise the contents? Is the title the same on the case, cassette, and title frame?

In addition to the above criteria, Ingram's Dick Fontaine has several ingredients for a successful video program:

Repeatability in viewing.

Interaction—If the video is not repeatable, and its subject matter can be assimilated in one viewing, then the tape must promote interaction between the viewer and itself. Titles such as *Strong Kids, Safe Kids,* and *Gary Coleman's Safety in the Neighborhood* are prime examples of interactive videos because they involve the viewer in role-playing situations that keep interest high.

Product identification—Whether it is a matter of using a best-selling author like Robert Haas in the *Eat to Win* tape or starring Ed Asner in the *Less Stress* tape, many publishers feel that a star name is important in making a successful tape.

Price—A lower retail price from $30 to $9.[5]

These are all valid criteria that the experienced evaluator is aware of, consciously or unconsciously, while screening a video. Good and bad qualities in a program should be considered as appropriate or inappropriate for its intended audience and use. The librarian must make selections based not just on cost or convenience alone, but on a thorough understanding of the strengths and weaknesses of each available format. The role of the AV librarian relies heavily on a knowledge of community wants and needs and the translating of those needs into evaluation criteria that allow purchase of necessary materials. The entire process builds upon the previous information acquired and is a continuous cycle.

☐ EVALUATING REVIEW SOURCES

The biggest problem within the video field today is the lack of available reviews proportional to the number of titles available. Feature film reviews do not present as much of a problem because reviews are usually available when the film is released to movie houses. Finding reviews of nonfiction video is a serious problem because a large percentage of titles remains an unknown quantity. After locating the reviews and deciding whether to purchase the item, librarians must make decisions on where to purchase based on price evaluation and other factors.

At this point, it must be noted that the selection process is not a passive one; it is extremely active. Librarians should not just sit at their desks and select from whatever sources happen to come across them. Each source should be carefully sought and chosen for need, genre/subject, objectivity, quality of reviews/titles, and its usefulness in fulfilling collection goals and objectives.

Selection aids usually come in two formats, monographs and periodicals. Generally speaking, monographs are most useful for retrospective purchasing. Most often, they contain more titles and have a greater subject/genre variety, but they tend to become out-of-date more quickly. Periodicals usually contain a more limited title selection but, because issued more frequently, are more up-to-date. Locating retrospective reviews presents the additional problem of finding an index that gathers those periodical reviews in an organized manner. Librarians should exercise care in choosing selection aids because the intended audience and purpose of the aids vary widely. Selection sources directed toward the general population, rather than professional librarians, are sometimes thought to be of questionable quality. Most often, prices of periodicals, for instance, are considerably lower with these general, consumer-oriented sources.

It is one thing to have the tools and know how to use them, but quite another to assess their value related to specific collection needs. Evaluating the reference aids before including them as part of the selection arsenal is just as important as evaluating and selecting individual titles themselves from those sources. Performing a systematic evaluation of selection aid material is essential.

The first step, obviously, is to acquire this material for review. Many publishers will send copies on a preview basis; also, interlibrary loan as well as a larger area library, regional library system, or state library are excellent sources for obtaining examination copies of periodicals and reference sources. A visit to a neighboring library already possessing a video collection may also prove helpful. Local video stores may give or lend copies of selection sources to the library upon request. The local magazine outlet always has a variety of titles available. Each of the following elements should be examined when looking over review sources:

Authorship—author's and publisher's credentials, often stated in the preface.

Preface—should state the author/publisher authority, discuss the inclusive scope and coverage depth of the work.

Publication data—Is the work new and kept up-to-date by supplements, new editions, or serial issue? How long has it been in circulation, and has it been published under the auspices of the same title/publisher during that time? Is the work cumulative, or are back issues/editions necessary? If so, are they available?

Information—Is the information given in a complete enough form so as to facilitate content evaluation and purchase? Is it current and accurate? The reviews should be consistent and should contain contrasts and comparisons with other titles. Is it objective or biased in presentation, and does it make judgments? Also, reviews should be as objective as possible, based on overt concepts of technical quality, content accuracy, and cinematic quality. All statements and opinions should be reinforced with specific examples when possible.

Scope and coverage—What is the apparent purpose of the work? What subjects or genres does it cover? Is it international or regional/national in scope, covering what time periods? How specific or general is the coverage?

Arrangement—The information should be easily accessible and conveniently arranged for use. Are there cross-references by performer, genre, subject, or keyword? The format should be pleasant to the eye, easy to use and to read. Arrangement may be subject-oriented, then alphabetically organized within each subject, or one large alphabetical arrangement with a detailed subject index. Different types of users will find different arrangements appealing.

Physical characteristics—Generally, with reference books it is advantageous to purchase hardback copies that have heavy-duty bindings, especially if the source will double as a selection/patron reference guide. Are the print and page large enough to read and handle? Is the layout consistent? What is the quality and durability of the paper?

Uses—How can it be used? Does it have multiple uses? Does it complement other selection aids already in use?

Special features—Does it contain articles of interest? Does it utilize photographs or special directional aids to facilitate the location of information (e.g., indexes, table of contents, etc.)?

Cost—Is the cost reasonable when compared to prices of similar selection aids? Are replacement copies of microforms available? At what cost?

Periodicals usually do not include all of these parts, but often, once a year, the publisher runs a "Statement of Inclusion" that addresses some of the same concerns. Usually, signed reviews are an assurance of quality. Fastidious choices in selection aids should give the librarian an excellent range of materials from which to choose, as well as ensuring that they get the most for their money.

☐ OVERVIEW OF THE FUNCTION OF SELECTION AIDS

Buying guides—These can be used for ascertaining availability, comparative prices, and subject/genre variety and depth. Producer and distributor catalogs fall into this category. Since there is no price fixing in the video market, prices can vary widely and are in a continual state of flux.

Reference tools—Most selection tools are not primarily intended for reference purposes, but some reference tools can double as selection aids, such as *Halliwell's Film and Video Guide*, *The Motion Picture Guide*, the *Encyclopedia of Film*, and *Shoot 'Em Ups* (a guide to westerns). Reference tools do not usually specify prices or availability; therefore a current, primary source such as a buying guide should also be used.

Checklists—The professional librarian is always concerned with how the collection measures up to some standard of an acceptable collection in terms of size, title inclusion, and material type. Currently there is no comprehensive select list of videocassettes; however, several lists can be put together to approximate a comprehensive list. Feature films have a variety of checklists/award winners including Academy awards, Golden Globes, and various film festivals such as the American and the Cannes Film Festival. Books such as *Halliwell's 100* offer select listings of quality films. There are also many awards given to nonfiction titles. Each year an Academy award is given for the best documentary film and for the best animated short. *Video Review* magazine publishes an annual list of VIRA awards, which include nonfiction titles as well as features. The CINE Golden Eagle awards are perhaps the most prestigious of all documentary/nonfiction annual awards. *Media Review* provides an annual list of CINE winners, and citation references to award winners can be found in the *Reader's Guide to Periodical Literature* and *Library Literature*.

Indexes—Currently there are only two indexes that are helpful in locating videos: the *Reader's Guide to Periodical Literature* and *Media Review*. In *Reader's Guide*, under the subject heading "Motion pictures—reviews," features can be found, and, starting with the 1985 bound edition, videocassette reviews can be found under the heading "Videocassettes—reviews." *Media Review* covers film and video as features and nonfiction. However, considerable time is needed before a title is listed in the index. *Library Literature* does not list specific reviews by title but does make reference to special articles and/or columns occurring in professional periodicals.

Evaluative tools—If there is a concern for quality, selection aid tools that evaluate materials can be of considerable assistance, especially when they help eliminate the often tedious and time-consuming task of in-house evaluation. Unfortunately, a great percentage of the home video market does not receive reviews; however, this situation is improving. Professional periodicals such as *Booklist, Choice, Science Books and Film,* and *Library Journal* fall into this category, as do *Video Review* and *Home Viewer* on the consumer end.

In-print directories—Currently, there are three comprehensive directories that list in-print video titles: NICEM's *Film and Video Finder* (1987), *The Video Source Book* (9th ed.), and *Variety's Complete Home Video Directory* (1988). These directories are analogous to the directory *Books in Print* for monographs. These three sources provide short, one-sentence content notes for each title as well as producer, production year, running time, and genre/subject information. The *Film and Video Finder* contains fiction, nonfiction, and some features in 16mm film and videotape format. *The Video Source Book* contains features and nonfiction appearing in videodisc and in three-quarter and half-inch video formats. Librarians and educators are the primary audience because of the inclusion of public performance videos in both titles. A relative newcomer to the scene, *Variety's Complete Home Video Directory* is designed for video stores and libraries. It lists only home-use features and nonfiction video titles in VHS, Beta, and laserdisc formats. These sources are useful for locating a title, but they should not be used as selection tools because they are not evaluative lists.

☐ A SELECT LIST OF VIDEO REFERENCE GUIDES

The following pages include a basic, annotated bibliography of selection aids. New sources are always being published; therefore this list is not all-inclusive. *The Video Librarian,* an excellent source of reviews in its own right, lists *Billboard, Variety, Rolling Stone, People, Stereo Review,* and *High Fidelity* as possible periodical review sources. In short, the subject should guide the search; automotive repair videos may be found in *Road and Track* or *Car and Driver*, while furniture repair/refinishing and woodworking titles may be found in *Fine Woodworking*.[6] Today, special-interest video advertisements and reviews can be in just about any magazine. However, general periodicals such as *Time* and *Newsweek* should not be overlooked.

Books

The Black Video Guide. St. Louis, MO: Video Publications, 1987. $70.

This 400-page reference work identifies approximately 2,500 videocassettes that feature or concern black people. Produced in conjunction with NICEM, the guide alphabetically lists features as well as nonfiction. Extensive indexing incorporating African and U.S. history, art, biography, civil rights, and feature films is its strength. Actors, directors, producers, composers, and choreographers are also indexed. Recommended for special collections emphasizing black culture.

Connoisseur's Guide to the Movies. James Monaco. New York: Facts on File, 1985.

A checklist of 1,450 feature films alphabetically arranged using symbols to designate quality. It is international, includes all genres, and is historical (and up-to-date) in scope. The symbol system is very hard to follow and complicated, however.

500 Best American Films To Buy, Rent, or Videotape. New York: Pocket Books, 1985.

An annotated, alphabetical guide to feature films selected by the National Board of Review of Motion Pictures and Editors of *Films in Review*. Each descriptive annotation is one page in length and has some critical notes. No indication is given as to current availability on video.

Halliwell's Film and Video Guide, 5th ed. New York: Charles Scribner's Sons, 1985.

An annotated, A-to-Z listing of feature films including review excerpts. Many plots are not thoroughly described, the main annotation being mostly evaluative in nature. Titles are rated by a star index of one (poor) to four (excellent). The fact that this

COLLECTION DEVELOPMENT GOALS AND GUIDELINES   97

volume uses review excerpts that do not completely describe title plots makes it rather undesirable as a viewer's advisory reference. The strength of this source is its wide coverage of historical and international films. This may be the only source where Russian, Japanese, Chinese, and Slavic films are annotated. Its two-column, small-print format includes approximately 10,000 titles. Complete cast, length, release date, MPAA rating, and award information are given. No indication as to current availability on video.

Kidvid: A Parent's Guide to Children's Videos. Harold Schechter, Ph.D. New York: Pocket Books, 1986. $4.95.

An alphabetical, annotated listing of some 300 titles, features and nonfiction, for preschool to age ten. One page per title, these reviews are suspect because many titles are ephemeral in nature. Complete producer information, plot, and criticism are given.

Leonard Maltin's TV Movies and Video Guide. New York: Signet, 1988. $4.95 (paper).

This new edition of Maltin's book contains over 17,500 annotated titles in 1,154 pages. The reviews are consistently crisp and insightful, although each entry averages only four sentences. However, the alphabetization is based on the logical but awkward letter by letter premise; for example, *I, the Jury* follows *It Happened One Night*. Also, there are some slip-ups pertaining to video availability. Recommended as a viewer's advisory source.

The Motion Picture Guide. New York: Cinebooks, 1985. 12 vols. $850. Distributed by R. R. Bowker.

This multivolume work promises to be the most authoritative source on film titles from 1927 to 1983 ever produced. It is very thorough and an ambitious project. The two-column, small-print format with boldface titles is easy to read. Complete cast, plot, length, release date, MPAA rating, awards, genre, and video availability are given. Annotations are mostly descriptive. This is an excellent information source for patrons to use. Index volumes (11 and 12) not seen.

Music Video Guide. John Chu and Elliot Cafritz. New York: McGraw-Hill, 1986.

An annotated, categorized genre listing of music videos alphabetically arranged within each genre, e.g., rock, jazz, musicals, operas, etc. Short descriptions with some critical evaluations. Black-and-white photographs included in text. This source promises to be a good retrospective guide for music videos; however, the genre is so volatile that titles may be ephemeral.

Roger Ebert's Movie Home Companion. Kansas City, KS: Andrew, McNeel & Parker, 1988. $10.95 (paper).

An alphabetical, annotated listing of 700 films from 1980 to 1987 complete with star ratings, from bomb to four-star. The reviews are rather lengthy. The list is very subjective in its inclusion of titles, emphasizing current movies rather than classics. However, it is already out of date—midsummer 1987 releases such as *La Bamba, Summer School,* or *Superman IV* are not found. A good companion to Maltin.

Variety's Complete Home Video Directory. New York: R. R. Bowker, 1988.

This new work is primarily a listing of 25,000 home videos, with only titles and short descriptive annotations. There are 40 genre and subject categories with indexing by genre and performer/director. Lists of titles that have won major awards are closed-captioned, and a list of over 400 distributors and producers with names, addresses, and phone numbers is included. There are four completely updated directories per year for approximately $100. This source is a good buy for the money, particularly for public libraries.

The Video Movie Guide 1988. New York: Ballantine, 1987. $5.95 (paper).

Written by Mick Martin and Marsha Porter, this concise volume rates over 5,000 feature films from *The Great Train Robbery* to *Top Gun.* All are available on video. The rating system is a series of stars from one (poor) to five (excellent). There are eight genres; titles are listed alphabetically within each genre, and each annotation gives cast, director, year, and running time. Annotations are mostly descriptive, but there is a one-sentence qualitative review in every entry. The one claim to fame this book possesses is its extensive cross-index. It is the only guide that lets the reader look up a star or director to find a film title; otherwise, the entries are bafflingly categorized, wildly incomplete, and inaccurate.[7]

The Video Source Book, 9th ed. Syosset, NY: National Video Clearinghouse, Inc., 1987.

The *Books in Print* of the video world, this publication is an annotated, alphabetical title list of every videocassette currently produced. About 50,000 titles are listed in 1,900 pages. The annotations are one to two sentences in length and are purely descriptive. Through the use of a broad subject index, subject/genre access of titles is possible. Each annotation contains descriptions, audience level, subject/genre, format, length, cast, awards, release dates, and ratings. A distributor name index is also included. It is updated every six months with a free supplement. Libraries still possessing a 16mm film collection or with educational emphasis should consider purchasing NICEM's *Film and Video Finder,* which gives short, descriptive annotations to features and nonfiction titles. It is recommended as a companion to *The Video Source Book.*

The Video Tape & Disc Guide to Home Entertainment. Syosset, NY: National Video Clearinghouse, Inc., 1987.

This is a smaller, consumer-oriented version of *The Video Source Book,* listing some 10,000 features and nonfiction titles with partial descriptive annotations and pertinent plot information.

Periodicals

Booklist. Chicago: American Library Association. Semimonthly, 22 issues per year.

Nonfiction only. Reviews 10 to 20 titles per year except for quarterly feature "Home Video for Libraries," where about 60 to 90 titles (each issue) are reviewed.

Home Viewer. Philadelphia, PA: Home Viewer Publishers, 1986. Monthly.

"The chief advantage of this magazine," according to *The Video Librarian,* is its extensive listing of new releases; however, it only reviews about 35 feature films per issue."[8] The reviews seem to be more descriptive than critical.

Library Journal. New York: Bowker. Semimonthly, 22 issues per year.

Nonfiction only. Mostly higher-priced public performance videos. There are about 10 to 15 signed video reviews in each issue.

Librarian's Video Review. Bowling Green, VA: Clearwood Media, 1986. Quarterly.

About 220 to 250 nonfiction titles are thoroughly reviewed in each issue. The reviews are medium-length and highly evaluative in nature. A star system and an index provide a cumulative quick-reference system. One to two articles on trends, equipment, and other items pertaining to video are included. Although the publisher is also a video wholesale distributor, the publication does not endorse for sale any title appearing in the publication. This is a very authoritative source containing many reviews per issue. Recommended for all public libraries.

VCR. Prospect, KY: Falsoft Building, 1986. Monthly.

The Video Librarian gives this publication a mixed review, saying, "Started in 1986, this source does not make a good first impression because of some inaccuracies. However, the premier issue had 38 reviews, and it may improve. The first issue (February 1986) seemed to be hastily constructed, listing reviews of tapes that had not been released yet (*Cocoon*, for instance)."[9]

Video. New York: Reese Communications, 1978. Monthly.

Video has been called the granddaddy of popular video magazines. The emphasis is on hardware and test reports. An average of 35 titles (features) are reviewed per month.[10]

The Video Librarian. Bremerton, WA: Pitman. Monthly.

Published by Randy Pitman, AV librarian at the Kitsap Regional Library, this is an excellent source for reviews and keeping up with market trends and industry news. All libraries should consider this as a first purchase. It contains concise, informative articles on trends, equipment, sharing common concerns, and a wide range of other video-related topics. Features and nonfiction titles are reviewed; average number of titles reviewed is about 35 per issue, with the total newsletter running 16 pages.

COLLECTION DEVELOPMENT GOALS AND GUIDELINES 101

Video Review. New York: Viare Publishing. Monthly.

This is probably the most popular of all the video magazines around today and is comparable in quality to *Stereo Review.* It is directed toward the consumer but has applications for the library as well. Both features and nonfiction are reviewed, with the number varying from 10 to 20 reviews. The bulk of the magazine is advertisements and equipment articles. Highly recommended as a circulating item as well as a selection aid.

Video Software Dealer. Los Angeles: Video Software Dealer. Monthly.

This 80-page magazine is free to qualifying libraries and the trade only; a letter requesting a subscription on library letterhead stationery must be submitted. This magazine is an excellent source for keeping up to date with current trends and new releases. It lists new releases for the month, giving cost, plot, release date, length, MPAA ratings, and distributor information. The strength of this periodical lies in its industry trend reporting (from the retail standpoint) and current new titles with point-of-purchase information.

V: The Mail-Order Magazine of Videocassettes. New York: Fairfield Publishing, 1987. Monthly.

This unique magazine is both a retail catalog and a review magazine. It is a glossy publication with a lot of meat; over 200 feature films and nonfiction titles are reviewed per issue with signed reviews. Some of the reviews are inserted into specialty articles. Full-color photographs with full-length articles on video genres/subjects are included. The reviews are slightly critical, but most are descriptive. This is a good source to purchase because of the variety and number of reviews presented, but the lack of critical reviews limits its use as an objective review source.

Other sources include *School Library Journal, Choice, Science Books & Films,* and *Video Insider.* Also, some traditional 16mm film review sources include *Film File 1984–1985, Lander's Film Review,* and *Media Review Digest.*

Distributor Catalogs
AV librarians should make a concerted effort to acquire as many up-to-date video product catalogs as they can. Although *The Video*

Source Book lists some 40,000 titles, it quickly becomes out-of-date. Also, the annotations are often too short for ascertaining content. Below are listed some major distributors/jobbers who have well-developed, descriptive video catalogs.

> Brodart Video. 500 Arch Street, Williamsport, PA 17705. Nonfiction and features.
>
> Clearview Media Corporation. Route #1, P.O. Box 25, Bowling Green, VA 22427. Nonfiction and features.
>
> Greenleaf Video. 3230 Nebraska Avenue, Santa Monica, CA 90404. Nonfiction.
>
> Librarian's Video Service. P.O. Box 468, Middletown, CT 06457-0468. Nonfiction and features.
>
> Library Video Company. Department M-B, P.O. Box 40351, Philadelphia, PA 19106. Nonfiction and features.
>
> Movies Unlimited. 6736 Castor Avenue, Philadelphia, PA 19149. Nonfiction and features.
>
> Professional Media Service Corporation. 13620 South Crenshaw Boulevard, Gardena, CA 90249. Nonfiction and features.
>
> S. I. Video. P.O. Box 310, San Fernando, CA 91341. Nonfiction.
>
> The Video Schoolhouse. 2611 Garden Road, Monterey, CA 93940. Nonfiction and features.
>
> Video Shack. 1608 Broadway, New York, NY 10019. Nonfiction and features.
>
> Zenger Video. 10,000 Culver Boulevard, Room 932, P.O. Box 802, Culver City, CA 90232-0802. Nonfiction and features.

Television and Newspaper Film Critics

Today there are several regional and national television shows that review new movie features, such as *Entertainment Tonight*, PBS's *Sneak Previews*, and *At the Movies*. These programs can be used to supplement printed reviews, but unless they are videotaped and indexed they should never be used as the single review source for purchases. Retrospective access to reviews is essential if title inclusion is ever questioned. Local newspaper film critic columns are also good indicators of community movie tastes. The reviewer's credentials, objectivity, and standardized set of review criteria should be ascertained before including any source in the selection aid repertoire.

The video industry is just now realizing that video and film are two distinctly different entities; many box office flops are successful in the video arena. Although box office success is a good measure of community interest, a title should never be acquired just because it is an award winner. Titles should be acquired based on popularity and longevity. Extremely popular but ephemeral titles should be reserved for the video stores. The emphasis should be on developing a long-term, consistently circulating collection rather than an occasionally used film archive.

THE BILLBOARD CHARTS: A TEST OF POPULARITY

Within the library field, the use of *Billboard*'s "Top Videocassettes" sales and rental charts as selection aids has been hotly contested. Generally it is best not to regard these charts as indicators of quality since there is a considerable amount of dross included. However, when questions of subject/genre composition, longevity, and popularity are addressed, this is the first place to look. Although consumers prefer to rent rather than purchase videocassettes, rental popularity is based only on those extremely popular titles video stores carry. Also, the sales charts seem to be slightly less volatile than rentals—weekly rankings do not distort to the same degree as in the rentals. There also seems to be a wider title and subject variety within the sales charts. For these reasons, the sales charts are the best determinant of *popularity* for libraries to follow.

Figures 4.3–4.6 give *Billboard*'s "Top Videocassettes" sales and rental charts for the year ending 16 August 1986 and for one-week periods in 1987. Many older titles such as *The Sound of Music, Casablanca, The African Queen, The King and I, The Maltese Falcon, Patton, Gone with the Wind, West Side Story,* and *South Pacific* were all in the top 40 titles. At the same time, 7 nonfiction titles were in the top 40 as well. Almost 25 percent of the sales chart was composed of original, made-for-video programming. Children's programming was also strongly represented. Music video showed signs of increased popularity, but only 5 titles were listed in the top 40. Only 2 titles, *The Sound of Music* and *Alien*, have remained on the charts since 1980. *Jane Fonda's Workout* is closing in on 300 weeks as a top-40 member, with future sales looking to keep it there.[11] From an analysis of the sales charts from 1980 to the present, the following popularity/longevity guidelines have been determined: (1) classics and older films that have been on the chart for

TOP VIDEOCASSETTES RENTAL HIT CHART

A Billboard Spotlight

Following is a recap chart of the top videocassette rentals during the eligibility period of Aug. 17, 1985 to Aug. 16, 1986.

1. **BEVERLY HILLS COP** (Paramount Home Video)
2. **PRIZZI'S HONOR** (Vestron)
3. **THE BREAKFAST CLUB** (MCA Dist. Corp.)
4. **GHOSTBUSTERS** (RCA/Columbia Pictures Home Video)
5. **THE KARATE KID** (RCA/Columbia Pictures Home Video)
6. **RAMBO: FIRST BLOOD PART II** (Thorn/EMI/HBO Video)
7. **AMADEUS** (Thorn/EMI/HBO Video)
8. **RETURN OF THE JEDI** (CBS-Fox Video)
9. **WITNESS** (Paramount Home Video)
10. **MASK** (MCA Dist. Corp)
11. **DESPERATELY SEEKING SUSAN** (Thorn/EMI/HBO Video)
12. **GREMLINS** (Warner Home Video)
13. **THE KILLING FIELDS** (Warner Home Video)
14. **A SOLDIER'S STORY** (RCA/Columbia Pictures Home Video)
15. **A NIGHTMARE ON ELM STREET** (Media Home Entertainment)
16. **BACK TO THE FUTURE** (MCA Dist. Corp)
17. **COMMANDO** (CBS-Fox Video)
18. **COCOON** (CBS-Fox Video)
19. **FALCON AND THE SNOWMAN** (Vestron)
20. **STARMAN** (RCA/Columbia Pictures Home Video)
21. **SILVERADO** (RCA/Columbia Pictures Home Video)
50. **THE MEAN SEASON** (Thorn/EMI/HBO Video)
51. **JAGGED EDGE** (RCA/Columbia Pictures Home Video)
52. **A PASSAGE TO INDIA** (RCA/Columbia Pictures Home Video)
53. **GOTCHA!** (MCA Dist. Corp)
54. **STICK** (MCA Dist. Corp)
55. **DEATH WISH 3** (MGM/UA Home Video)
56. **PLACES IN THE HEART** (CBS-Fox Video)
57. **INTO THE NIGHT** (MCA Dist. Corp)
58. **SWEET DREAMS** (Thorn/EMI/HBO Video)
59. **MISSING IN ACTION** (MGM/UA Home Video)
60. **SUMMER RENTAL** (Paramount Home Video)
61. **YEAR OF THE DRAGON** (MGM/UA Home Video)
62. **SILVER BULLET** (Paramount Home Video)
63. **MRS. SOFFEL** (MGM/UA Home Video)
64. **REMO WILLIAMS: THE ADVENTURE BEGINS** (Thorn/EMI/HBO Video)
65. **PERFECT** (RCA/Columbia Pictures Home Video)
66. **BLOOD SIMPLE** (MCA Dist. Corp)
67. **LOST IN AMERICA** (Warner Home Video)
68. **2010—THE YEAR WE MAKE CONTACT** (MGM/UA Home Video)
69. **A CHORUS LINE** (Embassy Home Entertainment)
70. **MICKI & MAUDE** (RCA/Columbia Pictures Home Video)
71. **BABY ... SECRET OF THE LOST LEGEND** (Touchstone Home Video)

FIGURE 4.3 *Billboard*'s "Top Videocassettes Rental Hit Chart" for 17 August 1985 to 16 August 1986. (Copyright 1987 by Billboard Publications, Inc. Reprinted with permission.)

15 weeks or more will continue to be popular; (2) current hit titles that have been on the chart for 30 weeks or more will be popular, unless the range of movement from week to week is extremely erratic; (3) nonfiction titles that have been on the chart for 26 weeks or more will be popular; and (4) children's titles that have been on the chart for 20 weeks or more will be popular.

Librarians can use these guidelines of popularity to acquire a collection that will deliver long-term, consistently high circulation. However, libraries seeking to preempt and predict video popularity will have to rely on intuition, a thorough knowledge of their community's movie tastes, and their local newspaper's movie critic's columns.

TOP VIDEOCASSETTES SALES HIT CHART

Following is a recap chart of the top-selling videocassettes during the eligibility period of Aug. 17, 1985 to Aug. 16, 1986.

1. JANE FONDA'S WORKOUT (Karl-Lorimar Home Video)
2. JANE FONDA'S NEW WORKOUT (Karl-Lorimar Home Video)
3. PINOCCHIO (Walt Disney Home Video)
4. BEVERLY HILLS COP (Paramount)
5. PRIME TIME (Karl-Lorimar Home Video)
6. GONE WITH THE WIND (MGM/UA)
7. THE WIZARD OF OZ (MGM/UA)
8. THE BEST OF JOHN BELUSHI (Warner Home Video)
9. RETURN OF THE JEDI (CBS-Fox Video)
10. WRESTLEMANIA (Coliseum Video)
11. MOTOWN 25: YESTERDAY, TODAY, FOREVER (MGM/UA Home Video)
12. GHOSTBUSTERS (RCA/Columbia Pictures Home Video)
13. THE SOUND OF MUSIC (CBS-Fox Video)
14. PRINCE AND THE REVOLUTION LIVE (Warner Music Video)
15. WE ARE THE WORLD—THE VIDEO EVENT (MusicVision)
16. MARY POPPINS (Walt Disney Home Video)
17. RAMBO: FIRST BLOOD PART II (Thorn/EMI/HBO Video)
18. CASABLANCA (CBS-Fox Video)
...
55. BUGS BUNNY'S WACKY ADVENTURES (Warner Home Video)
56. SEVEN BRIDES FOR SEVEN BROTHERS (MGM/UA Home Video)
57. THE KILLING FIELDS (Warner)
58. SOUTH PACIFIC (CBS-Fox Video)
59. PEE—WEE'S BIG ADVENTURE (Warner)
60. THE TERMINATOR (Thorn/EMI/HBO)
61. THE BLUES BROTHERS (MCA Dist. Corp.)
62. ST. ELMO'S FIRE (RCA/Columbia Pictures Home Video)
63. JOHN LENNON LIVE IN NEW YORK (Sony Video Software)
64. THE GOONIES (Warner Home Video)
65. JAGGED EDGE (RCA/Columbia Pictures Home Video)
66. PURPLE RAIN (Warner Home Video)
67. WHITE NIGHTS (RCA/Columbia Pictures Home Video)
68. FRANK SINATRA—PORTRAIT OF AN ALBUM (MGM/UA Home Video)
69. STARMAN (RCA/Columbia Pictures)
70. PALE RIDER (Warner Home Video)
71. AUTOMATIC GOLF (Video Associates)
72. TINA TURNER—PRIVATE DANCER (Sony Video Software)
73. THE BEATLES LIVE—READY STEADY GO! (Sony Video Software)
74. ...

A Billboard Spotlight

FIGURE 4.4 *Billboard*'s "Top Videocassettes Sales Hit Chart" for 17 August 1985 to 16 August 1986. (Copyright 1987 by Billboard Publications, Inc. Reprinted with permission.)

SUMMARY

Establishing a total collection development program involves many factors, all of which are dependent upon one another. If any part of the cycle breaks down, the entire process fails. Collection development is based upon interpreting patron demands, translating them into library goals and objectives, and satisfying those needs inasmuch as possible within budget constraints. These goals are formulated into working policies providing a framework for selection. Whether conducting a patron survey, evaluating a selection tool, or considering a single item for collection inclusion, evaluation is the single most important factor that keeps the cycle moving.

A video collection is particularly suited to the collection development concept because of its relatively small size and current

FOR WEEK ENDING MARCH 28, 1987

Billboard ©Copyright 1987, Billboard Publications, Inc. No part of this publication may be reproduced, stored in any retrieval system, or transmitted, in any form or by any means, electronic, mechanical, photocopying, recording, or otherwise, without the prior written permission of the publisher.

TOP VIDEOCASSETTES™ SALES

Compiled from a national sample of retail store sales reports.

THIS WEEK	LAST WEEK	WKS. ON CHART	TITLE	Copyright Owner, Manufacturer, Catalog Number	Principal Performers	Year of Release	Rating	Suggested List Price
			★★ No. 1 ★★					
1	NEW▶		TOP GUN	Paramount Pictures Paramount Home Video 1629	Tom Cruise Kelly McGillis	1986	R	26.95
2	1	23	JANE FONDA'S LOW IMPACT AEROBIC WORKOUT ▲	KVC-RCA Video Prod. Karl Lorimar Home Video 070	Jane Fonda	1986	NR	39.95
3	2	73	JANE FONDA'S NEW WORKOUT ▲	KVC-RCA Video Prod. Karl Lorimar Home Video 069	Jane Fonda	1985	NR	39.95
4	4	2	ALIENS	CBS-Fox Video 1504	Sigourney Weaver	1986	R	89.98
5	5	10	CALLANETICS	Callan Productions Corp. MCA Dist. Corp. 80429	Callan Pinckney	1986	NR	24.95
6	3	21	SLEEPING BEAUTY	Walt Disney Home Video 476	Animated	1959	G	29.95
7	16	50	ALIEN ▲ ◆	CBS-Fox Video 1090	Sigourney Weaver Tom Skerritt	1979	R	29.98
8	7	66	STAR WARS	CBS-Fox Video 1130	Mark Hamill Harrison Ford	1977	PG	29.98
9	6	11	SECRETS OF THE TITANIC	National Geographic Video Vestron 1063	Martin Sheen	1986	NR	29.95
10	17	87	THE SOUND OF MUSIC ▲ ◆	CBS-Fox Video 1051	Julie Andrews Christopher Plummer	1965	G	29.98
11	10	3	RUTHLESS PEOPLE	Touchstone Films Touchstone Home Video 485	Danny DeVito Bette Midler	1986	R	79.95
12	9	86	PINOCCHIO ◆	Walt Disney Home Video 239	Animated	1940	G	29.95
13	12	40	KATHY SMITH'S BODY BASICS ▲	JCI Video Inc. JCI Video 8111	Kathy Smith	1985	NR	29.95
14	15	140	STAR TREK II-THE WRATH OF KHAN ▲ ◆	Paramount Pictures Paramount Home Video 1180	William Shatner Leonard Nimoy	1982	PG	19.95

FIGURE 4.5 *Billboard*'s "Top Videocassette Sales" chart for 28 March 1987. (Copyright 1987 by Billboard Publications, Inc. Reprinted with permission.)

popularity. However, the AV librarian must be constantly in tune with video industry events and new video software in order to be an active respondent to community needs. Today's video industry is a chameleon—title popularity is always changing. Selection decisions must be made under the guidance of a predetermined plan of action and a standard set of evaluation criteria, thereby maximizing patron use per budget dollar spent. Community needs, quality, objectivity, consistency, longevity, authority, and comparative evaluation are the seven key words to keep in mind during the selection process. The AV librarian must be totally responsible for the selection process and establish a coordinated collection development policy.

FOR WEEK ENDING MARCH 21, 1987

Billboard

©Copyright 1987, Billboard Publications, Inc. No part of this publication may be reproduced, stored in any retrieval system, or transmitted, in any form or by any means, electronic, mechanical, photocopying, recording, or otherwise, without the prior written permission of the publisher.

TOP SPECIAL INTEREST VIDEOCASSETTES™ SALES (A)

Compiled from a national sample of retail store sales reports.

HEALTH AND FITNESS™

★ ★ NO. 1 ★ ★

THIS WEEK	2 WKS. AGO	WKS. ON CHART	TITLE	Copyright Owner, Manufacturer, Catalog Number	Remarks	Suggested List Price
1	2	11	JANE FONDA'S NEW WORKOUT	KVC-RCA Video Prod. Karl Lorimar Home Video 069	Beginner and advanced routines designed to strengthen and tone.	39.95
2	1	11	JANE FONDA'S LOW IMPACT AEROBIC WORKOUT	KVC-RCA Video Prod. Karl Lorimar Home Video 070	Jane Fonda's newest workout focuses on stretching and toning.	39.95
3	4	11	CALLANETICS	Callan Productions Corp. MCA Dist. Corp. 80429	Callan Pinckney presents deep muscle exercise techniques.	24.95
4	3	11	RICHARD SIMMONS AND THE SILVER FOXES	Karl Lorimar Home Video 158	Fitness program for people over 50 includes warm-ups and aerobics.	24.95
5	6	11	KATHY SMITH'S BODY BASICS	JCI Video Inc. JCI Video 8111	Fitness video gets down to basics and is designed for the beginner.	29.95
6	8	11	KATHY SMITH'S ULTIMATE VIDEO WORKOUT	JCI Video Inc. JCI Video 8100	Strenuous program designed for intermediate and advanced exercisers.	29.95
7	5	11	JANE FONDA'S PRIME TIME WORKOUT	KVC-RCA Video Prod. Karl Lorimar Home Video 058	Calisthenics and aerobics for any age at a slow and easy pace.	39.95
8	9	11	DONNA MILLS: THE EYES HAVE IT	Donna Mills Inc. MCA Dist. Corp. 80384	Donna Mills shares her make-up, beauty and skin-care secrets.	19.95
9	13	11	RAQUEL, TOTAL BEAUTY AND FITNESS	HBO/Cannon Video 2651	Raquel Welch combines exercise and yoga with tips on staying youthful.	19.95
10	10	11	KATHY SMITH'S TONEUP	JCI Video Inc. JCI Video 8112	Comprehensive workout for all fitness levels designed to shape and tone.	29.95
				Video 202	Judi Sheppard Missett's newest video all-new aerobic dance routines.	29.95
19	NEW▶		JANE POWELL'S FIGHT BACK WITH FITNESS	Karl Lorimar Home Video 170	Program aids arthritis sufferers on how to minimize pain & stiffness.	24.95
20	18	5	BODY BY JAKE: DON'T QUIT!	MCA Dist. Corp. 80114	Workout combines speed and continuity to build endurance and tone muscles.	19.95

BUSINESS AND EDUCATION™

★ ★ NO. 1 ★ ★

1	4	11	LIVING LANGUAGE SPANISH LESSONS	Karl Lorimar Home Video 060	Learn to speak Spanish at your own pace in six easy weeks.	29.95
2	5	7	LIVING LANGUAGE FRENCH LESSONS	Karl Lorimar Home Video 059	Learn basic French in just 6 weeks-look, listen, and repeat the phrases!	29.95
3	1	9	CONSUMER REPORTS: HOW TO BUY A HOUSE, CONDO, OR CO-OP	Karl Lorimar Home Video 079	How to evaluate, purchase, and finance a home.	19.95
4	13	9	TOO SMART FOR STRANGERS	Walt Disney Home Video 736	Winnie The Pooh teaches kids to deal with strangers and protect themselves.	29.95
5	6	11	SAY IT BY SIGNING	Crown Publishing Corp. Crown Video	Basics of sign language with emphasis on useful words & phrases.	29.95
6	3	11	STRONG KIDS, SAFE KIDS	Paramount Pictures Paramount Home Video 85037	Henry Winkler educates parents and children about child abuse.	24.95
	7	5	THE VIDEO SAT REVIEW	Random House Home Video	Improve test-taking skills for those entry SAT tests.	69.95

(continued)

FIGURE 4.6   Billboard's "Top Special Interest Videocassettes Sales" charts for 21 March 1987 (A) and for 28 March 1987 (B). The appearance of special-interest charts in Billboard emphasizes the growing market for these types of videocassettes. (Copyright 1987 by Billboard Publications, Inc. Reprinted with permission.)

FOR WEEK ENDING MARCH 28, 1987

Billboard
©Copyright 1987, Billboard Publications, Inc. No part of this publication may be reproduced, stored in any retrieval system, or transmitted, in any form or by any means, electronic, mechanical, photocopying, recording, or otherwise, without the prior written permission of the publisher.

TOP SPECIAL INTEREST VIDEOCASSETTES™ SALES (B)

Compiled from a national sample of retail store sales reports.

RECREATIONAL SPORTS™

THIS WEEK	2 WKS. AGO	WKS. ON CHART	TITLE	Copyright Owner, Manufacturer, Catalog Number	Remarks	Suggested List Price
** NO. 1 **
1	2	13	GOLF MY WAY WITH JACK NICKLAUS	Worldvision Enterprises Inc. 2001	Easy-to-follow guide for the beginning golfer.	84.95
2	1	13	AUTOMATIC GOLF	Video Reel VA 39	Bob Mann's methods increase players' drive by 30 to 80 yards.	14.95
3	4	13	JAN STEPHENSON'S HOW TO GOLF	Karl Lorimar Home Video 147	Program addressing aspects of golf such as putting and tee shots.	29.95
4	5	13	HOW TO PLAY POOL STARRING MINNESOTA FATS	Karl Lorimar Home Video 018	The pool master reveals his secrets for shooting to win--every time.	19.95
5	3	13	WARREN MILLER'S LEARN TO SKI BETTER	Karl Lorimar Home Video 098	A definitive guide to the art of skiing.	24.95
6	NEW▶		1986 MASTERS TOURNAMENT	LCA Video New World Video C20170	Highlights of last years annual golf classic.	39.95
7	16	11	NFL CRUNCH COURSE	NFL Films Video	Profiles of football greats plus the NFL's greatest hits.	19.95
8	6	7	JOHN MCENROE AND IVAN LENDL: THE WINNING EDGE	Vestron	Learn the secrets and tips from the	
20	19	5	FISHING WITH JIMMY HOUSTON #1	Video City	Tips include information on casting, the PH breakline, and worm fishing.	29.95

HOBBIES AND CRAFTS™

** NO. 1 **

1	2	13	CHEF PAUL PRUDHOMME'S LOUISIANA KITCHEN, VOL. 1	J2 Communications	Unique techniques are revealed in this video on Cajun cooking.	19.95
2	1	13	CHEF PAUL PRUDHOMME'S LOUISIANA KITCHEN, VOL. 2	J2 Communications	How to prepare Cajun and Creole classics from scratch.	19.95
3	4	7	JULIA CHILD: MEAT	Random House Home Video	The preparation and carving of roasts, steaks, hamburger, and chops.	29.95
4	10	7	JULIA CHILD: FIRST COURSES AND DESSERTS	Random House Home Video	From mousses and pates to crepes and tarts, as well as chocolate cakes.	29.95
5	11	3	CHEERS! ENTERTAINING WITH ESQUIRE	Esquire Video ESQCH01	Esquire magazine presents this foolproof guide to giving great parties.	14.95
6	15	13	JULIA CHILD: SOUPS, SALADS, AND BREAD	Random House Home Video	Making French bread, tossed salads, and light and hearty soups.	29.95
7	8	5	THIS OLD HOUSE	Crown Video	Numerous home repair and restoration ideas presented in an easy-to-do style.	24.95
8	RE-ENTRY		LAURA MCKENZIE'S TRAVEL TIPS- HAWAII	Republic Pictures Corp. H-7352-1	Visits to Oahu, Maui, Diamond Head, and Waikiki.	24.95
9	7	13	CRAIG CLAIBORNE'S NEW YORK TIMES VIDEO COOKBOOK	Warner Home Video 34025	Preparation and presentation of over 20 of his favorite recipes.	29.95
10	3	5	PLAY BRIDGE WITH OMAR SHARIF	Best Film & Video Corp.	Step-by-step bridge techniques and strategies.	34.95
11	13	5	BENIHANA'S CHINESE COOKING	Best Film & Video Corp. B100	The use of Chinese utensils, the wok, and perfect slicing are shown.	39.95
12	9	5	MR. BOSTON'S OFFICIAL VIDEO BARTENDER'S GUIDE	Karl Lorimar Home Video 064	Learn to mix your favorite drinks with easy instructions.	19.95
13	14	9	JULIA CHILD: POULTRY	Random House Home Video	How to prepare the perfect chicken, holiday turkey, and special roast duck.	29.95
14	6	5	D.I.Y. BASIC CARPENTRY	Do It Yourself Inc.	Includes use and choice of tools, paneling, shelving, etc.	19.95
15	5	9	VIDEO AQUARIUM	The Video Naturals Co.	For the fish lover whose time or bad luck makes owning live fish impossible.	19.95

◆ International Tape Disc Assn. certification for a minimum sale of 75,000 units or a dollar volume of $3 million at retail for theatrically released programs, or of at least 25,000 units or $1 million at suggested retail for nontheatrical titles. SF short-form. LF long-form. C concert. D documentary.
Next week: Health And Fitness; Business And Education.

Figure 4.6 (continued)

BILLBOARD   MARCH 28, 1987

NOTES

1. Janet French, "The Evaluation Gap: The State of the Art in A/V Reviewing with Special Emphasis on Filmstrips," in *Expanding Media*, ed. Deidre Boyle (New York: Oryx Press, 1977), 87.
2. Phyllis J. Van Orden, *The Collection Program in Elementary and Middle Schools* (Littleton, CO: Libraries Unlimited, 1982), 92.
3. S. L. Baker, "Does the Use of a Demand-Oriented Selection Policy Reduce Overall Collection Quality? A Review of the Evidence," *Public Library Quarterly* 5 (Fall 1984): 30.
4. Illinois State Library, *Illinois Library Statistical Report 21*, (Springfield, IL: Illinois Secretary of State's Office, October 1986), 1–5.
5. Linda Sunshine, "The Videocassette Business: Is There a VCR in Your Future?" *Publisher's Weekly* 227 (15 February 1985): 39.
6. Randy Pitman, "Video Sources: Reference and Review," *The Video Librarian* 1 (1 March 1986): 5.
7. Ibid., p. 5.
8. Ibid., p. 5.
9. Ibid., p. 5.
10. Ibid., p. 4.
11. Jim McCullaugh, "Videobeat '86: Reading the Clear Signposts to the Sell-Through Market," *Billboard*, 30 August 1986, V38.

5. A GUIDE TO SELECTING AND MAINTAINING VIDEO EQUIPMENT

Strategic planning includes planning for equipment needs as well as for the physical collection area, circulation methods, and other policies and procedures. Today, video technology is changing rapidly, and uneducated choices can mean costly mistakes, nonworking or obsolete equipment, and expensive service bills.

This chapter is designed to familiarize librarians with the history/development, vocabulary, basic principles, and simple maintenance and repair of videocassette recorders (VCRs). Today, because the VCR is increasingly being considered a household necessity rather than a luxury, a greater number of patrons are becoming video-wise. They speak the video language and are up to date on technological advances and new hardware and software. Librarians should feel obligated to develop a fairly thorough working knowledge of the videocassette world so they can converse intelligently with salespeople, repairmen, and patrons.

The discussion is divided into three segments: (1) technological development and fundamental principles, (2) equipment needs in varying situations, and (3) repair and maintenance of that equipment. In discussing equipment, particular brand names and models will only be mentioned as reference points. Some equipment, such as cleaning machines, will be recommended, but with this technology's rapid advancement, a literature search should precede purchase. Librarians wishing to survey the scene for the most appropriate equipment should consult issues of the following magazines: *Stereo Review* (particularly the yearly *Video Buyer's Guide*), *High Fidelity,* and *Video Review.*

BRIEF REVIEW OF VIDEO RECORDER TECHNOLOGY

It is helpful to compare definitions of film and video before delving into the technological aspects of video. Film is a physical/chemical medium, relying upon light to initiate a chemical change on film resulting in a photographic image. When these images are shot in rapid sequence and projected back in a continuous manner, they give the illusion of movement. Film sprockets facilitate the controlled movement of film through the projector, while sound is reproduced through electrovoltaic light fluctuations within a physical soundtrack. In contrast, video is an electronic/magnetic medium relying upon the distribution of magnetic fields on a tape that are interpreted by rotating magnetic heads to form sound and moving images. Magnetic audiotape is very similar to videotape, although the play head is stationary rather than rotating. Hereafter, the terms *reading* and *writing* will be used to describe the play and record functions, respectively.

True video recording began with the Ampex invention of the Quadruplex (Quad) recorder in 1956. This system used a 2-inch tape that traveled at 15 inches per second (ips), across which four recording heads spun at very high speeds. An audio track was laid longitudinally along the top of the tape, using a stationary record/replay head. Quad is still in use, but is widely being replaced by helical scan machines. All home VCRs are helical scan machines. Instead of spinning the heads at right angles to the direction of tape travel, they spin on the same axis as the tape motion.[1]

At first, all recorders were open reel-to-reel, black-and-white reproduction only. The tape was either 1-inch or ½-inch. Sony introduced the ¾-inch U-Matic cassette system in 1970. Today, this cassette format is used extensively within the broadcasting industry and in academic institutions. Sony also introduced the first home video format in 1975; called Betamax, it utilized a small cassette containing ½-inch-wide tape. Philips/Grundig beat Sony to the punch with its own ½-inch VCR system, but these are now obsolete.[2] The Japan Victor Corporation (JVC), a subsidiary of the giant electronics manufacturing company Matsushita, developed the VHS format in 1976, incorporating features lacking in Beta.

It might be well to stop here and discuss the recording method that made the Beta and JVC ½-inch formats possible, that of aximuth or diagonal recording (Figure 5.1). Audio recording uses a magnetic tape that moves across a stationary head. This head is actually a miniature electromagnet that either reads or writes in-

SELECTING AND MAINTAINING VIDEO EQUIPMENT

formation upon the tape. A video signal is much more complex than its audio counterpart. If stationary heads were used, it would take an astronomical amount of tape passing by the head to record even a single minute. In order to solve this tape-consumption problem, both the tape and the heads were made to move within the same plane.

Videotape moves around an angled, rotating drum (see Photo 5.1). Small magnetic video heads are placed 180 degrees apart from one another within a single large, rotating drum. The heads protrude out of the drum slightly and, as the drum rotates, trace an angled pattern across the tape. Each single head pass is called one video field; two fields constitute one video frame. Each 525-line television frame consists of two 262 ½-line fields, the lines of which are interleaved on the screen.[3] Opposite heads scan separate diagonal tracks for the two interleaved fields. One picture is made up of 30 frames of 525 video lines (resolution) per second. Each head makes 60 passes per second, which, in the United States, is analogous to the 60 cycles per second (cps) in alternating current. This is called the

FIGURE 5.1 AZIMUTH RECORDING AND TRACKS ON VIDEOTAPE. This diagram illustrates the path of the rotating video head as the tape flows around it. The diagonal lines illustrate the concept of azimuth recording. The video track is laid down in the center of the tape, while the control and sound (mono) tracks are laid longitudinally on the bottom and top of the tape, respectively. In stereo recording the video track and separate audio tracks are laid in alternating azimuth paths in the center track.

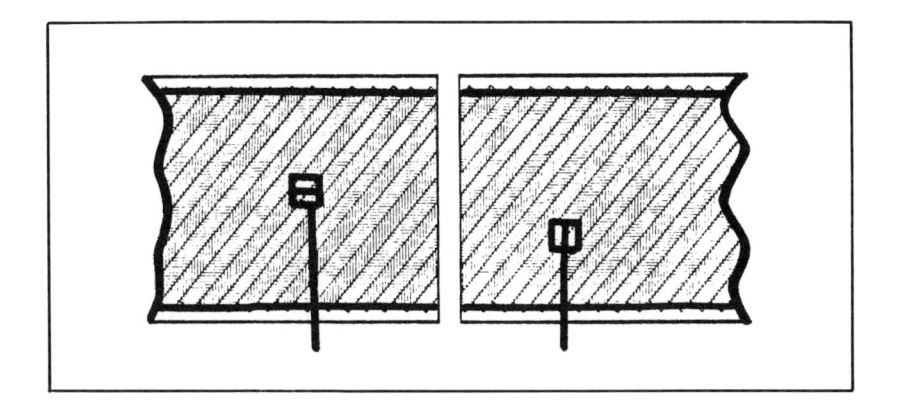

PHOTO 5.1 CLOSE-UP OF A VCR VIDEO DRUM. Some of the various guides and capstans that direct the tape around the video drum containing the video heads can be seen here. Unlike an audiotape recorder, which moves magnetic tape across stationary heads, a VCR moves tape across a rotating drum at extremely high speeds.

NTSC standard of recording. Most European countries use one of two systems, **PAL** or **SECAM**, which are not compatible with the U.S. system because of the alternating current variance. Each head is placed in the drum at a slight angle (6 degrees in Beta and 7 degrees in VHS), which results in paired diagonal bars (Figure 5.1). This technique permits each bar or track to abut without interference from its neighbor.[4]

☐ BETA VERSUS VHS

Beta and VHS represent the bulk of today's video market. They are incompatible with one another—a VHS tape will not play in a Beta machine. Ever since the two systems have coexisted there has been an ongoing war as to which system is better in terms of quality. The Beta camp, spearheaded by the leader Sony, said that their system was easier on the tape and mechanical parts because the tape was always wrapped around the drum, unlike VHS, which continually engaged/disengaged. This aspect also made freeze frame and rapid, shuttle forward/reverse visual search available first on Beta. VHS offered more tape within its slightly larger cassette, which resulted in extended play/record time. Today, the reproduction quality in both systems is virtually equal. Beta has developed Super Beta; VHS has S VHS (although Sony is now marketing a high quality EQ Beta, the company has recently positioned itself to manufacture the S VHS system and has thus answered retailer questions concerning Beta's future). Both result in enhanced picture reproduction.[5] True stereo high-fidelity recorders are also available. At present VHS constitutes almost 90 percent of the international market. However, the advent of newer, incompatible formats such as C, 8mm, and 4mm, and CD-LV have made the process of choosing a VCR more complex than ever before. Format inclusion decisions should be based upon community popularity. However, it should be noted that, by choosing one format over another, the library will be able to supply more titles per dollar than if both VHS and Beta were purchased.

Beta

Today, almost all prerecorded videocassettes are available in both VHS and Beta, but increasingly many distributors are not stocking Beta because of a dwindling market. Software availability may be a problem in the future. However, with a worldwide installed base of more than ten million machines, Sony will not abandon the Beta format altogether.

Beta I was introduced into the United States in 1975. It has the shortest play/record speed but results in the highest picture quality. The ½-inch tape travels at 1.57 ips and has 1 hour of recording time. Lack of room in the cassette prevented more tape from being added, so to extend the recording time, the tape speed was decreased to 0.787 ips (Beta II), and to 0.523 ips (Beta III), resulting in 3.25 and 5 hours recording/playback time, respectively.[6]

When a Beta cassette is inserted into the VCR, the tape guides pull about a foot of tape out and wrap it over the audio, erase, and control heads and around the drum. The tape is threaded in a B shape (Figure 5.2).

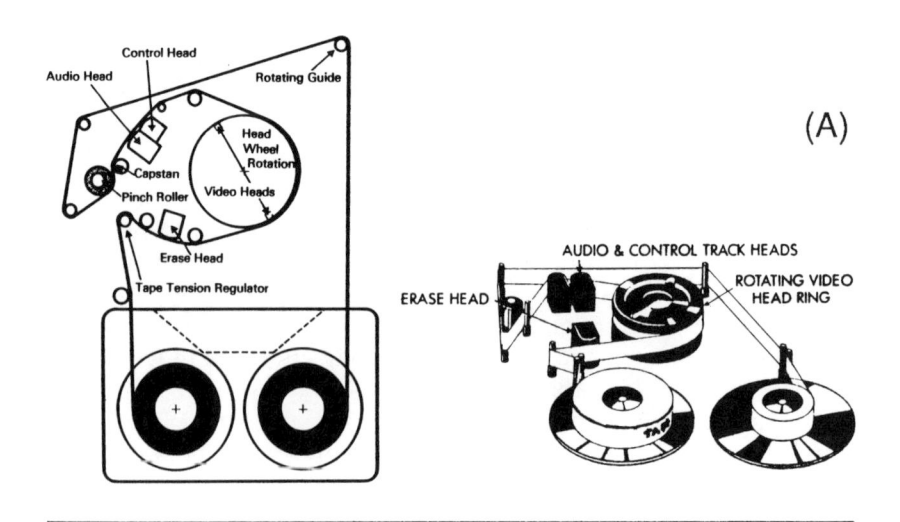

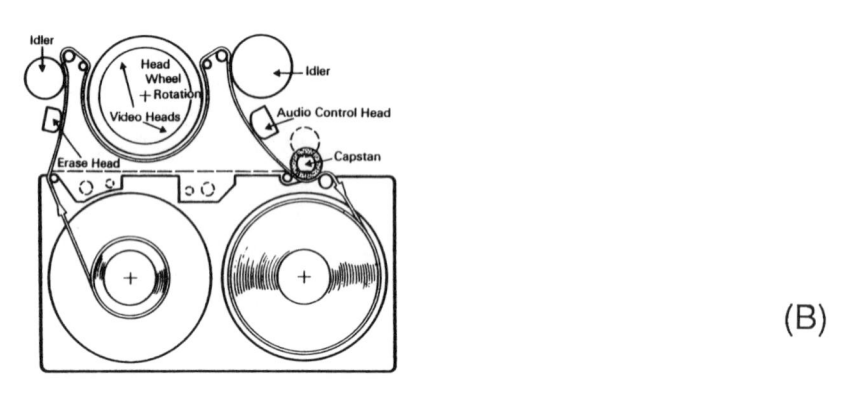

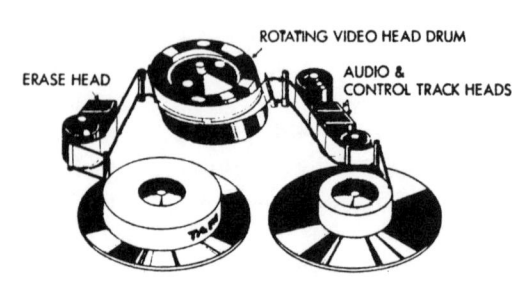

FIGURE 5.2 ILLUSTRATIONS OF VIDEOTAPE PATHS. (A) Beta B wrap of the tape from two different angles; (B) VHS M wrap around the video drum and various capstans and guides.

VHS

The Video Home System (VHS) was introduced in 1976. The physical cassette is larger than the Beta format and contains more tape, providing increased recording/playback time. Like Beta, there are three recording speeds: SP (Standard Play, 2 hours), LP (Long Play, 4 hours); and EP (Extended Play, sometimes called SLP, 6 hours). The SP tape speed is 1.32 ips. The heads rotate across the tape at about 1,800 rpm, so that almost 16½ feet of tape is effectively flowing under the heads every second.[7] The tape is threaded into the machine in an M wrap pattern (Figure 5.2).

MAGNETIC VIDEOTAPE

The magnetic medium of videotape is what makes all this technology possible. Videotape consists of four very thin layers (Figure 5.3). A layer of polyester forms the base to which a layer of oxide, capable of magnetization by the writing heads, is bonded. The oxide is commonly iron, though some newer types include chromium dioxide, cobalt-doped, metal, and metal-evaporated tapes. The newer types produce improved frequency response, greater signal-to-noise ratio, and consistent color and picture resolution because of the increased magnetic density. The third coat is a highly polished topcoat overlaid on the oxide to protect the heads and improve head contact. The fourth layer, located on the back side of the polyester base, consists of antistatic carbon to aid in reducing static as the tape passes across the head guides.

The tape itself must be extremely strong and flexible as well as flake- and stretch-resistant because video drums spin at rates exceeding 1,800 rpm. It must stand up to repeated plays and the constant wear and tear of special functions such as pause and slow motion.[8]

The tape itself is magnetically divided into three separate segments (see Figure 5.1). The video portion is laid down in the center track via diagonal, azimuth recording. The audio track is located on the top and is read by a separate stationary head. The control track acts as the speed and synchronization timer, analogous to film sprocket holes.

Several terms are often used to refer to the audio/video quality of videotape. These are *dropout, frequency response, noise, snow, video S/N ratio,* and *tracking. Dropout* is a loss of a portion of the audio/video signal caused by dirt or missing oxide particles. It appears as small white holes in the picture. *Frequency response* is a

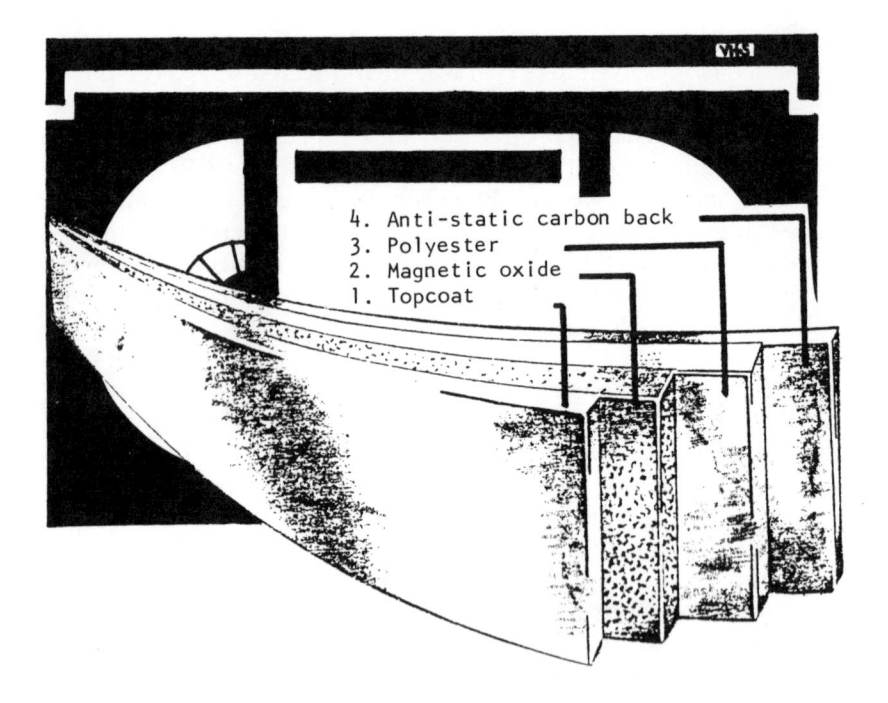

FIGURE 5.3 VIDEOTAPE LAYERED COMPOSITION. Videotape is composed of four different layers: (1) topcoat, (2) magnetic oxide, (3) polyester base, and (4) the antistatic carbon backing.

measurement of the range of frequencies a tape is capable of reproducing. Unwanted or crossed signals sometimes appear in the picture and cause *noise*. *Snow* can actually be noise or dropout. The *video S/N* is the ratio of pure video signal to noise. The higher the ratio between the signal and unwanted noise, the better. The *tracking* control feature on a VCR controls the angle at which the tape passes the heads. Some picture distortion and horizontal roll can be corrected by using this control.

SELECTING THE EQUIPMENT

The task of choosing a VCR is made formidable by the virtually unlimited number of manufacturer brands and models available on the market today. Selection is relatively simple when carried out methodically, however. The decision should rest solely upon the expected use of the equipment and the expansive, as opposed to potentially obsolete, capabilities of that equipment, viewed within the future needs of the library.

VCR manufacturers tend to add features to their models in groupings, going from entry-level to step-up to midline to high-end models. Overall quality and versatility improve as the price increases. Today, many manufacturers are discontinuing their midline models in favor of the two-step hierarchy—low-end and high-end models only. The high-end models offer maximum versatility, but these models possess various functions that some libraries will never need. The bottom line is that consumers may pay more for the functions they want because other, possibly unnecessary, functions are included. In today's market many brands are actually manufactured by the same company and are identical or nearly identical to one another. The quality may vary, but many times the internal workings are the same, only the external packaging is different. Matsushita is the original equipment manufacturer (OEM) for Magnavox, Panasonic, JVC, Technics, Quasar, and General Electric. Pioneer's Beta-format VCRs are made by Sony, while its VHS model is made by Hitachi. NEC manufactures for Marantz, and Hitachi for RCA. Mitsubishi supplies VCRs to Emerson and others.[9] Librarians need not be concerned about who makes what for whom; they should concentrate on purchasing a machine that will fulfill the expected library functions and have reliable local service available. Because of the latter constraint, mail-order and discount houses should be eyed with care. Many times a good purchase deal becomes an expensive service item.

Most libraries will probably utilize a VCR in the most rudimentary way—that of playback only for in-house patron use. Some libraries will want to loan out the VCRs to patrons. Others, especially school libraries, will want a machine to record programs off-air. Many libraries are producing their own cable shows or at least videotaping local historical events. In the future, the library may wish to access high-fidelity/stereo simulcast programs or access visual text. All these various needs require different choices for the overall and long-term use of equipment. As noted, when the purchase of equipment is planned in relation to current and future needs, optimum use per dollar amount expended is possible, thereby minimizing the possibilities of obsolescence.

The various functions that VCRs may play within a library are outlined below with reference to specific equipment for particular uses.

Equipment loan. A play-only portable unit for heavy-duty use is appropriate. The power source should be 110-volt, household current, not battery powered. Tabletop models and home-use portables usually cannot stand the transportation stress. One RF 4-foot-long cable and a 75/300 ohm converter should also be loaned with the equipment.

Patron in-house use. If the major function for in-house use will be for playback only, portable units should be considered. Playback carrels should be private but secure, and can be of two types—patron activated/controlled or staff activated/controlled.

Private viewing carrels should consist of a VCR and a receiver/monitor with headphone attachment. Many VCRs and receivers now come with headphone jacks, but a jack can be installed in a regular television as well. Extremely comfortable seating should be avoided as this will lull patrons to sleep. Electrical outlets and RF cables are also needed.

Patron abuse of playback time and equipment/software security problems may enhance the rationale of having a closed-access VCR bank with the monitor only in the private patron carrel. Library staff may then control the use time more effectively. VCR-to-TV ratios are still one to one; however, the VCR is not in the control of the patron. Long runs of RF cable, sometimes utilizing amplifiers, are needed for this closed-access scenario.

In-house production. These needs vary widely with the function desired: off-air programmable taping, local history or training tapes (nonbroadcast quality), or local station/cable broadcasting. Off-air programmable taping requires a VCR with a built-in tuner. Also, it should be cable-ready. A satellite dish may also be desired to enhance channel availability. Purchasing a camera for local production is a major step. Most VHS cameras now come with a variety of special effects and character-generator capabilities. These functions can save much time and money by making it unnecessary to purchase individual component parts. Portable VCRs, individual tuners, and battery and self-contained lighting packs should be considered. Utilizing equipment for editing and broadcasting requires a substantial equipment upgrade and dollar investment. When proper planning is utilized, much of the equipment can be used for dual purposes. VCRs with flying erase heads can be connected with editing equipment to produce smooth edits. Reel-to-reel, four-track tape recorders and sound-mixing units are a must for inserting narration and dubbing. Only individual special-effects generators will provide broadcast quality results. High-quality resolution cameras must also be used.

FEATURES AND FUNCTIONS OF VCRs AND EQUIPMENT

☐ **VCRs: PORTABLE AND TABLETOP**

VCRs vary greatly in their special feature/function offerings. Basically, there are two types of VCRs, the tabletop model and the portable unit. The tabletop model has the video player and the tuner combined. The portable unit provides increased mobility and flexibility regarding camera hookup, but needs a few other pieces of equipment, often sold separately, to be utilized as a tabletop model. The tuner allows the VCR to receive and record off-air/cable programs through its radio frequency (RF) input. Depending upon the model, a variety of self-programming options are available. The number of programs that a VCR can be programmed to record can vary from one event over seven days to eight over a full year. The norm is four to eight programs over seven to fourteen days. Some users find the programming procedure highly complex; however, some models offer simple on-screen prompts and instructions.

Tabletop models can be adapted for use with a camera by buying a camera adapter that hooks up through the video and audio (RCA plug) inputs, but this is very cumbersome. Its use is also limited to facilities with 110-volt household current. Portable units offer the dual flexibility of being used as tabletop models and portable studios. Most often the VCR player/recorder and the tuner are sold separately. Off-air television or cable reception and off-air taping cannot be accomplished without the tuner. Many times the AC/DC adapter is only included in the timer. Portable units operate on 12-volt battery power supplied by a built-in or external battery pack. An adapter for hookup through a car cigarette lighter can even be purchased. Today, there are several portable play-only VCRs on the market. These would be excellent choices for libraries wanting to loan equipment or for in-house patron use.

Basic recorders provide only the essential tape transport functions: stop, pause, play, fast-forward, and rewind. Some have a shuttle visual-scan feature (forward/reverse) for fast program searching. Others have slow motion, freeze frame, and double-speed play. The freeze-frame function is enhanced by an add-on single-frame advance control. This is useful for achieving clean edits between scenes when commercials are being deleted from a tape.[10]

Most basic, low-cost VCRs are two-head machines. They will do an adequate job if used to record and play back in the EP speed or to play back prerecorded tapes in SP if no special effects are needed. VCRs with three to seven heads are recommended; today, most midline models have four. Additional heads are needed to provide the special-effect functions and improve video quality. Some machines limit the scan and freeze-frame functions to the slowest recording speeds. Generally, the shortest recording time (Beta I and SP) give the best audio/visual quality. VHS hi-fi units utilize two heads on the drum for audio recording. These audio heads may be included in the VCR specification sheet. Test reports and specification sheets are fine, but when it comes right down to the final purchase, the unit should be seen in operation. A recording from a live broadcast should be made, then played back, comparing it with the broadcast original. Picture detail (clarity and sharpness), picture noise (snow and colored interference), and color reproduction accuracy should be examined. Also, all recording speeds should be tested.

On most VCRs only the standard VHF and UHF channels can be received. An external converter is required to access some channels. Advertised as "cable-ready," this option is a must for in-house use if television programs will be viewed. Most cable-ready VCRs are able to receive 107 or more channels. High-end units can receive up to 181 channels. However large the tuner's capacity is, most VCRs can only tune in 12 to 16 preprogrammed channels at one time. Midline units have dial tuners, while high-end units have electronic, lockable random-access ones that enable channel entering from a numeric keypad.

Sony introduced Beta hi-fi in 1983. VHS had offered Dolby-assisted stereo earlier, but it was not true high fidelity. Both the Beta and new VHS hi-fi systems utilize two drum heads to deposit the audio track in a side-by-side azimuth recording method with the video track. Hi-fi units can also play and record mono programs as well. Stereo recording needs stereo reception. Currently there are three sources of high-fidelity video programming. Simulcasts are programs that are simultaneously broadcast over television and FM radio. The VCR must be hooked up to the FM receiver. There is also a growing number of stereo-encoded prerecorded videocassettes. The third source is stereo television. To receive stereo television, a special multichannel television sound (MTS) decoder must be hooked into the system. The MTS unit is now a standard feature on most high-end units.

☐ TELEVISION AND RECEIVER/MONITOR

Next in importance to the VCR is the television or receiver/monitor. A television has VHF and UHF antenna connections, a speaker, and a channel selector (tuner). The VCR outputs video and audio signals to the television, using radio frequency (RF) transmitted through coaxial cable. Most televisions manufactured after 1982 are cable-ready, meaning they possess an internal RF modulator to which the VCR can be directly attached. Older televisions must be adapted for VCR use by adding a 75/300 ohm converter to the VHF terminals, then attaching the VCR using coaxial cable. Some older televisions must have a horizontal/vertical stabilizer added to prevent picture roll. Usually it is advisable to invest in new televisions rather than upgrade pre-1982 equipment.

A tuner performs the all-important channel selection function and has advanced significantly from the standard rotary knob. Cable-ready televisions are usually advertised as being able to receive X number of channels. Equipment possessing an electronic tuner capable of receiving up to 144 channels is very sensitive. Usually, both televisions and VCRs have a programmable limit of 14 to 20 channels, but when used in tandem they can give the viewer access of up to 40 channels without reprogramming.

Standard televisions usually deliver 250 to 300 lines of resolution. The television picture is actually made up of hundreds of small horizontal and vertical lines forming a grid pattern, similar to the way in which the colored dots in comic books give the illusion of a solid color. The proximity of these lines to each other determines the lines of resolution, resulting in improved picture clarity, sharpness, and focus. Presently, the Federal Communications Commission and NTSC broadcast standard is 525 lines of resolution. However, manufacturers are already starting to produce a third generation of receiver/monitor capable of reproducing a phenomenal 750 to 1,170 lines of resolution, delivering exceptional clarity. The receiver/monitor will only reproduce what is on the screen up to its maximum capabilities; therefore, the computer term "garbage in, garbage out" also applies here.

The receiver/monitors are slightly more complicated than a television set, offering a variety of functions that are not available on the standard television. Today's receiver/monitor combination is a complex piece of electronic wizardry made up of a large square screen in a relatively compact box. The popular screen size is 25 inches, measured diagonally. Digital components allow special effects such as a picture within a picture, enabling the viewer to watch two or more programs simultaneously. A broadcast monitor only receives pure audio and video signals through RCA video inputs. Usually speakers are not included and must be connected using the RCA audio outputs. Stereo television is complicated because it involves many factors: (1) A program must either be broadcast in stereo or be reproduced in stereo on cassette. (2) If it is a broadcast program, the local station must have the necessary bandwidth to transmit a stereo signal. An early innovation of stereo television was the simulcast method, having the audio portion transmitted over an FM radio band to be picked up by a stereo receiver. (3) If it is a cassette, it must be played on a stereo VCR. (4) The receiver must be capable of reproducing stereo sound and have two speakers. Digital stereo receiver/monitors are not cheap; a 25-inch diagonal can run from about $425 to $800. Librarians contemplating purchasing new components should purchase them in relationship to their present and future needs. However, one should purchase components possessing the most options and expansion capabilities per dollar, because this will forestall premature obsolescence.

Projection or large-screen television is very useful for small group presentations. Today's equipment is vastly superior in picture reproduction (lines of resolution and brightness) to that of a few years ago. Screen sizes range from 40 to 80 inches with prices ranging from $1,900 to $4,000.[11] Most offer direct inputs similar to the standard receiver/monitor. There are two classes: front projection and rear projection. In the former, the picture is projected onto the front of a screen; in the latter, the picture is "pushed" through the screen from the rear. Generally speaking, all projection televisions have either one or three picture tubes. One-tube sets are considerably less expensive. They use a small, portable television set inside a cabinet to project an image. Three-tube sets actually consist of three cathode ray tubes (red, green, and blue) and are superior in quality to one-tube units.

Basically, there are three types of projection televisions on the market. The first type is the two-piece system consisting of a projector and a separate screen. Screen sizes can range from 5 to 15 feet in diameter. Screen types vary; some are curved (high-gain), yielding a brighter picture. Others are flatter, sacrificing brightness for a better viewing angle. Prices for this type range from $2,500 to $5,000. The second type was originally the most popular, although now only one manufacturer (Mitsubishi) still produces it. Essentially, it is a front projection machine utilizing a mirror with the image, produced by three cathode tubes, reflected back up onto the screen. The screen is curved, and the viewing angle is not the best. The third type is the most popular—rear projection. It utilizes a Fresnel screen, which is actually a lens with one flat side and one curved side. The curved side contains concentric circles in the same shape as the lens curvature and focuses light in a concentrated manner. This type takes up the least amount of room because there are no mirrors to fold out. The screen is usually 37 to 45 diagonal inches. Prices run between $3,000 and $3,700. The VCR can be hooked up directly to a large-screen television. Projection televisions should be examined for color reproduction, clarity, graininess in picture enlargement, and keying. Many units do not fill the entire screen at the corners or exhibit substantial loss of clarity (focus) in those areas.

☐ ROUTING CONNECTORS AND SWITCHES

A routing connector is a special device useful for connecting one video input source or two or more video output devices. Whenever the RF signal is split, picture degradation will result. Over a short cable run to one extra VCR or monitor (such as for real-time duplicating) this loss is negligible, but for combinations exceeding this setup a signal amplifier is necessary. A simple amplifier can cost as little as $25; more complex amplifiers allowing multiple-output signal boost cost about $70 to $200. Multiple-output devices require coaxial cable connections. There is a new type of multiple-output device that transmits the signal from one VCR to another without using any cable connections. Known as the Rabbit, this device retails for about $80.

Another useful device for routing and switching various video input sources to one central output device is called a routing switch. By using this device, a computer, videodisc player, and several VCRs can be connected to one receiver/monitor and be interchanged with the flick of a toggle switch. While beneficial, whenever these devices are introduced into a system, the signal is weakened. Some devices, such as the Viditek SSV440, are designed to overcome this problem by amplifying the signal. External amplifiers can also be introduced into the system; most operate on alternating current and should be included in systems having long cable runs of 25 feet or more. Librarians wishing to utilize a central program distribution center for patron viewing will find the multiple-output devices and routing switches to be a necessity. In this type of setup, a patron chooses a video to watch, gives it to a staff member, and goes to a carrel containing a monitor. The staff member plays the cassette from a closed-access unit (behind the counter) that is connected to the monitor through a multiple-output or routing switcher. Staff time is not effectively utilized with this setup because of the constant monitoring of carrels, but this setup does provide a controlled viewing, theft-proof environment.

☐ THE VIDEO PROCESSOR

Another component is the "black box" or video processor, intended to improve sharpness and color in the television signal, and particularly useful in video editing, where two VCRs are used to duplicate or perform assemble/insert editing. There are three major types of processors: enhancers, processing amplifiers, and stabilizers. Enhancers boost the video signal and sharpen the picture detail. Processing amplifiers improve color and brightness by allowing manual control of chrominance (color) and luminance (brightness) individually. Stabilizers are used when duplicating prerecorded videocassettes encoded with the copy protector Copyguard. Often, these components introduce some problems of their own. Poorly designed equipment may actually produce too strong a signal, resulting in unwanted noise bars or distortion of the picture. A thoughtfully designed system can enhance viewing and component flexibility. An overloaded system will degrade quality.

☐ BROADCASTING AND EDITING EQUIPMENT

Although it is not the intent of this book to address broadcasting and editing in depth, it would be negligent not to briefly mention some considerations. If a library will be producing its own programs for broadcast, in-house training, or patron use, editing equipment should be considered. However, this equipment is very expensive, and technology is always improving and changing. The library should first investigate the local retail production facilities and production costs. Often, local television studios have ½-inch editing equipment.

A simple studio consists of a video camera and a portable VCR. Today, both VHS and Beta offer portable camera units that have the VCR unit inside the camera. Some versions use a smaller C format or 8mm (4mm is coming), which can be put inside a larger cassette for adaptation in standard units. These smaller cameras do not possess character generators and other special effects; therefore their usefulness in library situations is limited. A good-quality camera should be lightweight (3 to 5 pounds), have convenient handholds and controls, possess a character/special effects generator, have separate audio/stereo inputs with a stereo microphone, have autofocus and at least a 1.4F low lens range with possible interchangeable lenses, and possess insert editing capabilities with smooth assemble edits.

Basically, editing consists of two types, insert and assemble. Shooting scenes in sequence with a portable video camera is a type of assemble editing. Most cameras possess an automatic backspacing feature that occurs milliseconds after the camera record button is depressed. This feature provides smooth, no-noise bar-edit transitions from scene to scene, during which times the camera is turned off. Many cameras now have an insert editing feature whereby a sequence can be dropped in place of another sequence of the same duration.

Actual editing is a little more complicated than described. Most often it involves taking many sequences from more than one videocassette and assembling them onto one edited program. Panasonic makes a relatively inexpensive, high-quality home/studio (VHS) ½-inch editing unit with a computer sequencing controller. Sony manufactures a similar unit for Beta. These units utilize a computer-controlled flying erase head with backspace, which facilitates precise, smooth edits. Another essential component for the editing room is a reel-to-reel audiotape recorder with at least four separately controllable tracks. This recorder should be connected to an audio mixer. Many tabletop VCRs and cameras have audio dub capabilities. During this function, the audio portion of a cassette is erased and overlaid by input from a real-time microphone or audio recording. Only the linear soundtrack can be replaced. Since hi-fi sound is recorded alongside the video track by the spinning head drum, it cannot be replaced without erasing the picture. Audio dubbing is mainly used for adding narration or musical background to home-made videotapes. Some cameras have the video dub feature, which allows the video (and hi-fi sound) to be replaced without altering the linear soundtrack.

Another special component often required in the production/editing process is the title/special effects generator. This component enables titles to be added at any point. It also produces special effects such as fade to black, fade to white, windowing, and multiple images. In their simplest forms, most VHS cameras now possess some of these special effects. Beta format cameras do not possess this technology—individual components must be purchased for Beta units. However, a Beta/VHS camera pin adapter has been developed so that VHS cameras can be used with Beta equipment. Some functions will not work with specific adapters, so experimentation is a must. Home computers can also be hooked into video systems to provide text inserting.

Single-camera productions have certain visual limitations. Camera switchers enable two or more camera units to be utilized separately with one VCR. If a special-effects generator is also in the system, one camera can be simultaneously providing a window or split-screen effect. By utilizing the special features available on high-end VCRs and cameras, or by purchasing editing equipment, the entire realm of video production is opened up, yielding an endless variety of options.

VIDEOTAPE REPAIR AND MAINTENANCE

☐ HOW TO TEST, CLEAN, AND STORE VIDEOTAPE

Videocassette recorders and videocassettes need to be kept in top condition if they are to survive continuous circulation use within a public library. Today, there exist several types of videotape cleaning machines. Research Technology International (RTI), 4700 Chase, Lincolnwood, IL 60648, has developed the Tapechek 2100 and 320 cleaner/evaluator. Videotape passes by a dry cleaning tape that burnishes off dirt and excess oxide. It can clean a T-120 VHS tape in approximately 2 minutes and electronically inspects tapes for wrinkles, creases, and edge damage. These machines are of excellent quality and do extend videotape life, but the inspection function of the machines is of limited use. The Tapecheck 2100 has a printout that lists coded damage. However, the machine only detects physical edge damage; therefore magnetic tape imperfections or interior physical damage may go undetected. In the 320, damage is quantified by a counter from 0 to 99. The tape goes through the machine so fast that a difference in one number constitutes approximately 10 to 15 feet. The number does not indicate the extent of damage—a 1 might represent more damage than a 50. Even after all the analysis, not much can be done for a cassette that is extensively damaged, except replacement, anyway. The Tapechek 320 costs about $1,500, while the 2100 costs about $3,500. Models are available for ¾-inch U-Matic, VHS, and Beta.

Ambico manufactures a videotape cleaning system for Beta/VHS machines that utilizes a wet process, cleaning fluid. It cleans a T-120 tape in about 15 minutes and sells for $149.95. It is available from two sources: Tomorrow Today, 70 New Hyde Park Road, New Hyde Park, NY 11040; and Alpha Video, 48 Burd Street, Nyack, NY 10960.

The Nebraska Video Company, 206 North Brown Street, Pierce, NE 68767, sells the Video-Spec wet-process videotape cleaner. It sells for approximately $200 and cleans a T-120 tape in about 7 minutes. Kinma's Delux Video Cassette Rewinder ($49 to $100) will clean a standard T-120 tape in approximately 3 minutes. Some experts feel that wet-process cleaners leave a residue on the tape, but manufacturers say that this is not the case. In any event, it is advantageous for any library to develop a regular inspection/cleaning program. Videotapes should be visually inspected for physical tape/case damage after every circulation. They should also be cleaned on a regular basis at least four times per year.

☐ HOW LONG WILL VIDEOTAPE LAST?

The issue of tape life is particularly important now at a time when consumers and libraries are rapidly acquiring large collections of titles. Consumer ½-inch tape has only been around for about 13 years, not really long enough to be thoroughly tested regarding decomposition, stretching, and aging. Videotape engineers know that the chemical composition of the tape, the way it is used (or abused), and the environment in which it is stored are all factors of tape life. A tape that is played constantly may wear out long before it shows the effects of time. On the other hand, a poorly maintained tape that has never been used at all could decompose and become unplayable. The worst scenario is a poorly maintained tape that when played results in the malfunction of the VCR.

Video engineer John Godfrey estimates that today's professional videotapes, if used and stored properly, ought to last at least 20 years.[12] Usually, how tapes are used, rather than how they are stored, is the most important element in maintaining them. One pass through a dirty, maladjusted VCR may be sufficient to destroy a tape that has been stored properly. Even when tapes are used with well-maintained VCRs, tape life has to be measured by number of plays as well as in years. With a very clean VCR, 500 or more plays are possible, but under normal library use conditions 200 to 250 are average.[13]

Essentially, videotape is composed of tiny magnetic particles attached to a polyester base with a binding agent that glues them to the base. When the tape passes through the VCR, the particles are magnetized. In order to produce the image, the particles must remain magnetized and attached to the base. The tape must be free of any contaminants that would impede smooth running. The tape must also be free of any stretching or shrinking, as this will affect the recording tracks. Gradually, over time the magnetic particles will lose some of their magnetic charge. BASF's technical service manager, George Cribbins, explains, "[this magnetostrictive loss] is the equivalent of beating a metal bar with a hammer; it loses its magnetism because magnetism is dependent on molecular structure. Losses are small however; after 100 plays a tape's RF output may only be reduced by between 1 and 3 Decibels (dB)."[14] Wear on VCR parts can also damage the tape. High-speed rewinding in maladjusted machines is a major offender. Misaligned guides and capstans can cause the tape to fold over, crease, or tear.

Dust, humidity, and excessive heat and cold can also affect the life of tapes. The tape itself is fairly stable, but the plastic parts inside the cassette can break or fracture and cause damage to the tape itself.

Some guidelines to maximize the life of tapes are listed below.

1. Keep the VCR clean and away from dust. Use a dust cover. Develop a regular maintenance routine.
2. Programs should be recorded on high-grade tapes.
3. Never leave a tape in a VCR; always remove it before shutting off the machine.
4. Store videocassettes in plastic, dust-free cases. A constant temperature of about 68 to 70 degrees F is recommended. A 40 to 55 percent relative humidity storage level is recommended.
5. Videocassettes should be stored upright with the loaded hub below the empty hub. They should not be stored lying flat; this puts undue stress on the tape edges.
6. Tapes should not be exposed to excessive heat or cold, direct sunlight, or strong magnetic fields (such as on the top of a television). Tape manufacturers insist that tapes will withstand

SELECTING AND MAINTAINING VIDEO EQUIPMENT 131

temperatures of −40 to 176 degrees F, but it has been demonstrated that the binding agents begin to decompose at temperatures of 131 to 140 degrees F. The inside of a car can easily reach these temperatures in a few minutes on a hot summer day, even in indirect sunlight.

7. If the storage area is excessively cooler or warmer than the viewing area, allow the tape to acclimatize to room temperature before playing.
8. Before playing a tape that has been in storage more than three months (and not used) fast-forward and rewind the tape once.
9. Never store tapes half-played; always rewind.
10. All new tapes should be passed through a cleaning machine once before playing. This will clean off excess oxide and any cardboard/paper container sleeve particles that may have settled on the tape.

☐ VIDEO REPAIR

While the VCR itself is a complex piece of equipment that should not be repaired by amateurs, the videocassette is relatively simple to repair. Many librarians assume that videocassettes are not repairable and that it is not cost-effective to repair them anyway. *The Video Librarian* advocates repairing videos when repair is possible, because in the long run it is extremely cost-effective. Consider, for example, a $29.95 video whose leader has broken loose from the rewind spool after only 50 circulations. A simple repair such as this would take approximately ten minutes and cost about $10 in staff time, resulting in a $20 savings and avoiding the time-consuming hassles of acquiring a new title.[15]

In order to perform specific videotape repairs, some special but relatively inexpensive equipment is needed:

1. A small Phillips screwdriver. Do not use any magnetized tools. Most cassettes are made of two formed pieces of plastic held together by five Phillips-head screws. Increasingly, manufacturers are using four types of tamper-resistant screw heads, which make specialized screwdrivers a necessity for repairs (see Figure 5.4). These screwdrivers are available from the following sources ($14 each or $60 for a set that includes some extras): Multi-Video, Inc., P.O. Box 35444, Charlotte, NC 28235; Mr. Video, 5550 Fulton Avenue, Van Nuys, CA 91401; or The Video Store Shopper, 15759 Strathern Street, Van Nuys, CA 91406.

2. Tape splicer and a supply of splicing tape. Although there are many tape splicers available, this author prefers two: Total Video Supply's Tape Mender (available from Commtron), and the splicer from Bib Audio/Video Products, P.O. Box 27682, Denver, CO 80227. Either unit costs about $15 to $20 and both perform equally well.
3. Specific parts from salvaged videocassettes such as both pieces of the case, inner spools, and springs should be saved for use in repairs. The Video Store Shopper and Mr. Video offer empty shells for about $2 each.
4. In addition to these basic tools, a video rewinder and a tape cleaner/inspector should be purchased. Many machines perform the dual functions or rewind/forwardwind and cleaning.

The Video Librarian provides the following checklist for repairing videocassettes:[16]

1. Depending upon the size of the collection and the number of cassettes that are in need of repair, it is advisable to set aside a certain amount of time each day or week for uninterrupted repair.
2. Skin moisture and oils attract dirt; therefore hands should be washed and thoroughly dried before splicing.

FIGURE 5.4 VIDEOTAPE MANUFACTURERS' TAMPER-PROOF SCREW HEADS. Manufacturers are now inserting tamper-proof screws into videocassette cases, which make repair impossible unless the right screwdriver is available. Essentially, there are four different types of screws (left to right): (1) Mercedes-symbol screw, (2) rivet router, (3) nipple Phillips, and (4) de-clover. Multi-Video, Inc., makes a complete set of these screwdrivers, facilitating repair.

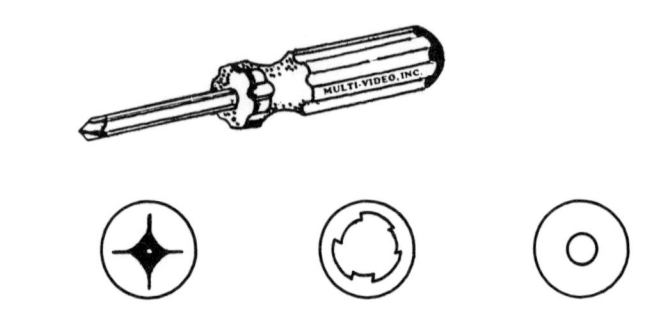

SELECTING AND MAINTAINING VIDEO EQUIPMENT

3. Splicing should be confined to the beginning and end of the tape. It should never be done within the program area, as this may cause damage to the sensitive video heads.

4. A broken shell means that the spools must be transferred into a new shell. Make sure that all pertinent labeling is also reaffixed.

5. A damage log file should be kept to record the repair date, type of trouble, and repair made. A card file could be kept, with each title having its own card. In this manner, it is easy to track the number of times a tape has been observed to have a certain type of damage and thus to decide if the tape is defective or possibly repairable.

To this list, this author adds the following points:

1. Before any attempts at repairing tape are made, the librarian should locate an expendable tape and take it apart to examine the "guts." Then it should be disassembled and reassembled several times. As mentioned before, splices should never be made in the middle of the program. The adhesive may smear across the surface of the tape and consequently become lodged in the play heads, ultimately damaging them. Splices should be made only on the antistatic base side, away from the video heads. Splicing can be performed without disassembling the cassette. It is advisable to wear smooth cotton film-inspection gloves when splicing videotape. Below are typical instructions for splicing:

    a. Position the cassette flat on a table with the flip-up lid facing the repair person.

    b. Locate a small button on the left side of the VHS cassette, just behind the flip-up lid. Depressing this button will enable the lid to be lifted, exposing the tape. Beta cassettes have the button located on the right side. A pen must be used to depress the button. Once the lid is lifted, a pen cap can be inserted between the shell housing and the lid, preventing it from closing.

    c. On VHS cassettes, the spools-ratchet mechanism must be released, enabling enough tape to be extracted from the cassette for repair. A pen inserted into a small hole on the underside (center) of the cassette will release the mechanism, allowing the tape to be pulled free. Beta cassettes do not have this mechanism; just pull out the tape.

    d. Now the tape can be inserted into the splicing unit and finger-rolled back in place when finished.

    e. Tape from the splicing kit is applied only to the side of the recording tape that does not make contact with the recording head. With the videocassette positioned as in step a, the side that does not contact the head is the one on the inside when the flip-up lid is lifted. On older videotape, this side is the dull side; the contact side is the glossy side.

  f. The tape should be inserted under the locking clamps with ends overlapping about ½ inch. A diagonal cut should be made and splicing tape applied over the cut. The surplus tape is removed, and the splice is complete.

2. When the shell is broken, both spools must be taken out and placed inside a new shell. In VHS cassettes there are essentially two different types of shells. The flip-up lid is slightly thicker and beveled a little differently to make them incompatible. The spools are slightly wider on some cassettes also. All cassette components must fit together exactly, without being forced, in order to work properly.

Any cassette labels (spine and front) should be removed first. Many simply peel off and can be reaffixed to the old cassette (or new one) after repair is complete. The cassette must be turned upside down and all the screws taken out. Then it is turned right side up, and the top lifts off. The flip-up back lid will come with the top. There is a small spring that controls the spring-action closing. If this comes off, it must be replaced. When this lid is closed, it must be flush with the top of the shell. If it is not, it will cause improper loading into the VCR.

3. Responsibility for damage is difficult to determine because a large percentage of damage is cumulative. Many of the problems patrons have with videos occur because they are unfamiliar with the correct functioning and operation of their VCRs. Generally, if two or more patrons have the same problem with the same cassette, the problem is with the cassette. The librarian should consult with the patron and try to duplicate the problem and the results in-house.

4. Water inside a cassette generally indicates a nonrepairable item. If a cassette is gotten to soon enough, however, it can be dried thoroughly (inside and out) and run through a videotape cleaning machine.

VCR MAINTENANCE

No VCR is immune to the problems of extended use and eventual wear of parts. Every machine will need repair and adjustment at some time within its life. By following a regularly scheduled maintenance program, potential problems can be eliminated, resulting in trouble-free operation. Besides inserting a VCR cleaning cassette into the machine every 30 to 40 hours of use, the librarian should not attempt to service any electronic parts or video heads. A first step in extending VCR life is learning how to recognize problems and symptoms as described by patrons.

The record/playback heads of a video recorder must be kept free of dirt and tape-shed oxide contaminants. Videotape passes around at least five different heads (erase head, at least two record/play heads, audio head, and control track head). The record/play heads are most susceptible to fouling because of the small gap cut into the face that contacts the tape. This gap must be kept clean. There are also various rollers, guides, idlers, and capstans that must be kept clean. All machines should be professionally serviced every 1,000 to 2,000 hours of use, but videocassette cleaners can do a good job between those times.

☐ VIDEO HEAD CLEANERS

There are many brands of video head cleaners on the market today. Basically, there are two types: wet and dry. All cleaning cassettes are made of a specially formulated cleaning material. Dry systems utilize material that is similar to videotape and actually scrapes dirt and contaminants from the tape path and heads. Wet systems employ a soft, interwoven fabric lubricated with a liquid/gas substance that attracts dirt to its surface. Dry systems offer better cleaning capabilities, but they are also extremely abrasive and could be harmful to the sensitive video heads if used often. Wet systems are slightly less effective, but are less abrasive. Some experts feel that wet systems leave a residue on internal parts, which only serves to attract more dirt. The manufacturers say that the drying capabilities of the liquid are almost instantaneous and feel that this need not be a concern. There is a wide variety of wet system types: internal, self-regulated flow of cleaning liquid; push-button control; and operator-applied control. Two companies offering both wet and dry high-quality systems, as well as a variety of wet systems, are Discwasher and Bib Audio/Video Products.

☐ TYPICAL PROBLEMS

VCRs often crunch or wrinkle tape in a machine. Inserting a tape in a front-load or top-load machine should be a simple, trouble-free operation. When the cassette is pulled out of the VCR and there is a tape loop hanging outside, there could be several causes. In Beta machines, the extraneous loop may indicate a fault in the motor that drives the threading mechanism. This mechanism is usually driven by a rubber belt that can slip with age. The VCR may be releasing the cassette lid before the tape is completely wound inside the shell. On VHS machines the VCR's reel brakes must operate correctly to keep the tape taut at the end of the rewind cycle.

A VCR that stops for no apparent reason may be suffering from too much back tension.[17] Tape is guided around the drum by various guides and capstans, and it must be held taut. However, too much tension activates a built-in VCR sensor that will automatically shut the machine off. A broken tape will make the machine shut down also. In this case, machines that have electronic eject will need to have the cover taken off in order to get the cassette out. Excessive back tension can also exhibit itself as picture bending or "skew" at the top of the screen. Sticky or jammed digital counters can also lead to machine shutdown. Sometimes wrinkled tapes may develop small "pinholes," where the oxide has flaked off the polyester base. VHS machines utilize light-sensitive sensors, which signal the machine to stop at the end of a tape or the beginning. Each end of the tape has a transparent leader that signals this shutdown. The pinhole will then act just like the transparent leader and shut down the machine. Careful application of a felt-tip marker on the tape may alleviate this problem; otherwise splicing is the only alternative.

The photolamp is essential to the operation of all VHS machines. If it is damaged or burnt out, the recorder will shut down. Some newer VCRs use invisible infrared light, others use a visible light source.

There are a variety of guides, capstans, drive belts, idlers, and rubber mountings that eventually will become glazed and brittle with age. These must be replaced. A VCR should operate with relatively little noise, except for the initial loading and unloading functions. Loud or strange noises emanating from the VCR are good cause for alarm, indicating worn belts, motors that need lubricating, or tape-threading problems. Front-load models often have initial threading problems because of a cassette that is improperly loaded. Some authorities advocate self-servicing of VCRs as a method of saving money. However, the video heads and other parts are so sensitive that improper use of swabs, cleaning agents, and even compressed air (canned air) can lead to serious problems that are expensive to correct. Therefore, it is best to let a professional service department handle problems and routine cleaning. Librarians possessing a basic working knowledge of a VCR can shorten service time by giving valuable symptom information to service people, thus expediting the repair process.

CONCLUSION

Librarians who develop a strategic plan for the purchase and use of in-house video equipment will have a variety of options available to them and be able to make informed decisions, thereby maximizing use of available funds. Obsolescence will inevitably occur, but, by planning ahead, equipment can be utilized more efficiently and be integrated with other components. Purchasing equipment without a plan is asking for trouble.

NOTES

1. David Cheshire, *The Video Manual* (Florence, KY: Van Nostrand Reinhold, 1982), 39.
2. Peter Lanzendorf, *The Video Taping Handbook* (New York: Harmony Books, 1983), 18–19.
3. Ibid.
4. Peter W. Mitchell, "The Hi-Fi VCR," *Stereo Review*, October 1985, 25.
5. Ibid.
6. Cheshire, *Video Manual*, 53.
7. Ibid., 51.
8. Ibid., 39.
9. "Hidden Secrets of Videotape," *Video Review*, September 1986, special advertisement section.
10. Gordon Brockhouse, "A Perfect Fit: Finding a VCR That's Just Right for You," *High Fidelity*, August 1986, 49.
11. Dawn Gordon, "How To Buy a Projection TV," in *Stereo Review's Equipment Directory: Video Buyer's Guide 1985* (New York: Ziff-Davis Publishing, 1985), 27.
12. James B. Meigs, "How Long Will Videotape Really Last?" *Video Review*, July 1984, 24.
13. Ibid., 25.
14. Ibid.

15. Randy Pitman, "Videocassette Repair Tips," *The Video Librarian* 1 (July 1986): 2–3.
16. Ibid., pp. 2–3.
17. Roderick Woodcock, "Home RX's for Sick VCR's," *Video*, 1983, 83.

6 SPECIAL PROBLEMS CONCERNING VIDEO

This chapter will discuss some potential problems facing librarians regarding circulating videocassette collections, including copyright, off-air program recording, fee-based videocassette loans, access by minors, and weeding.

COPYRIGHT

The use (and abuse) of copyrighted videocassettes by libraries and schools is probably one of the most hotly debated issues in the library field today. Librarians must be knowledgeable enough about the copyright law to interpret it to protect themselves, keeping the best interests of the library in mind. This section will address the following questions and concerns:

What is the copyright law in layperson's terms?

Can libraries loan videocassettes for home use?

What is the meaning of terms such as *private home use, public performance, nontheatrical exhibition,* and *semipublic and educational institutions* as regards the "fair use" section of the law?

Can libraries charge fees for videocassette loans?

Can libraries show videocassettes in-house to individuals and small groups?

Can libraries tape programs off the air, and how long may they keep them?

☐ THE LAW

The revised Copyright Act of 1976, Title 17 of the U.S. Code, Sections 101–810, which took effect on 1 January 1978, regulates the use of all copyrighted materials including videocassettes. The formidable job of comprehending the revised copyright law is made somewhat easier through a general knowledge of how the law is organized. A brief outline of some of the law's basic concepts, with sections enumerated, is given below.

Sections	Outline
101	Basic definitions of terms used throughout
102–104	Works protected by copyright
105	U.S. government works excluded
106	Right of fair use
108	Reproduction by library or archives
109	Effect of transfer of a particular copy
110	Performances and displays for nonprofit organizations
111	Secondary transmissions
118	Noncommercial broadcasting
401–406	Notice of copyright
501–506	Copyright infringement
504	Innocent infringement by libraries

As the video industry grows, so undoubtedly will the concerns over the copyright issue. The current Copyright Act is, at best, vague and unclear concerning library video operations. Librarians must protect themselves by complying with the exact letter of the law as much as possible. Much of the copyright law concerning library operations has not been challenged in the courts as yet; however, the day will come when it will be, and librarians must be knowledgeable and prepared.

A rule known as the first-sale doctrine regulates the copyright ownership of most materials. Generally, copyright controls over the ownership of the physical medium terminate after the first sale of each copy. The first-sale doctrine does not apply to videocassettes, thus copyright control remains with the originator. The motion picture industry failed to recognize the video rental business as a viable market until rentals far exceeded the outright sales of videocassettes. The problem is that copyright owners of motion pictures do not receive one penny directly from rentals. The film companies want royalties that are more directly related to actual consumer rental viewing. However, those companies are finding it difficult to show the kind of losses or damage to their commercial activities, as sustained by copyright, that would prod Congress to substantially revise the law.[1]

☐ THE ISSUE OF PUBLIC PERFORMANCE

One of the major questions librarians ask is, What is a public performance video, and how does it differ from the rental store (home-use) type? A public performance video is, generally speaking, any title for which licensing fees have been paid so that it may be shown in semipublic places, such as libraries and schools, and at semipublic programs, such as library story hours and club meetings. Most often this refers to group showings, but it may also apply to individuals in specific situations. The copyright law gives the author or originator of certain works the exclusive rights concerning production, distribution, and public performance. The 1976 law substantially revised the right to regulate performances and displays. It removed the for-profit performance-in-public limitation in the 1909 law and replaced it with two new sections, 106 and 110. The new law enhances proprietor's rights of control over performances and displays, but it also authorizes certain performances without permission or fees.[2]

Section 101 of the law defines *publicly* as a performance taking place anywhere "open to the public or at any place where a substantial number of persons outside of a normal circle of a family and its social acquaintances is gathered."[3] The term *family* in this context would include an individual living alone, so that a gathering confined to the individual's social acquaintances would normally be regarded as being private. Videotapes obtained at rental stores (or "for home use only" videos) are, by law, intended to be used only in a home setting. Customers may rent or buy "for home use only" videos, but ownership of the tape does not constitute ownership of the copyright.

Figure 6.1 contains the MPAA (Motion Picture Association of America) Warning Notice regarding home use. Some form of this notice should appear on the videocassette either as a label or before the title frame. Although the notice does prohibit performances in semipublic places including schools, the prohibition was not intended to exclude performances in face-to-face teaching situations within the context of school curricula.

WARNING!

"For Home Use Only" Means Just That!

By law, as well as by intent, the pre-recorded video cassettes and videodiscs available in stores throughout the United States are **for home use only**.

Sales of pre-recorded video cassettes and videodiscs **do not** confer any public performance rights upon the purchaser.

The U.S. Copyright Act grants to the copyright owner the **exclusive** right, among others, "to perform the copyrighted work publicly." (United States Code, Title 17, Sections 101 and 106.) Even "performances in 'semipublic' places such as clubs, lodges, factories, summer camps, and schools are 'public performances' subject to copyright control." (Senate Report No. 94-473, page 60; House Report No. 94-1476, page 64.)

Accordingly, without a separate license from the copyright owner, **it is a violation of Federal law** to exhibit pre-recorded video cassettes and videodiscs beyond the scope of the family and its social acquaintances—**regardless** of whether or not admission is charged. Ownership of a pre-recorded video cassette or videodisc **does not** constitute ownership of a copyright. (United States Code, Title 17, Section 202.)

Companies, organizations and individuals who wish to publicly exhibit copyrighted motion pictures and audiovisual works **must** secure licenses to do so. This requirement applies **equally** to profit-making organizations and nonprofit institutions such as hospitals, prisons and the like. Purchases of pre-recorded video cassettes and videodiscs **do not** change their legal obligations.

The copyright owner's right to publicly perform his work, or to license others to do so, is exclusive.

Any willful infringement of this right "for purposes of commercial advantage or private financial gain" is a Federal crime. The first offense is punishable by up to one year in jail or a $25,000 fine, or both; the second and each subsequent offense are punishable by up to two years in jail or a $50,000 fine, or both. In addition, even innocent or inadvertent infringers are subject to substantial civil penalties.

The companies listed below support the:

Film Security Office
Motion Picture Association of America, Inc.
8464 Sunset Boulevard, Suite 520
Hollywood, California 90028
(213) 464-3117

If **your** legal rights were violated **you** would insist upon seeking appropriate redress. So will the undersigned companies.

- Avco Embassy Pictures Corp.
- Columbia Pictures Industries, Inc.
- Columbia Pictures Home Entertainment
- Walt Disney Productions
- Walt Disney Home Video
- Filmways Pictures, Inc.
- Metro-Goldwyn-Mayer Film Co.
- Orion Pictures Company
- Paramount Pictures Corporation
- Paramount Home Video
- Twentieth Century-Fox Film Corporation
- Magnetic Video Corporation
- United Artists Corporation
- Universal Pictures, a division of Universal City Studios, Inc.
- MCA Videocassette Inc.
- MCA DiscoVision Inc.
- Warner Bros. Inc.
- Warner Home Video Inc.

FIGURE 6.1 MPAA COPYRIGHT WARNING NOTICE. This warning label describes the lawful limits of "for home use only" videocassettes and the infringement penalties.

☐ HOME USE, FAIR USE, AND EDUCATIONAL USE

Two important questions are, Does the home-use exemption apply to libraries? and Can libraries legally allow private individuals to view videocassettes labeled "for home use only" in viewing rooms or open carrels within the library? In attempting to answer these questions the following terms must be defined: (1) *home use* restricts viewing to the family unit, with admission charges strictly forbidden; (2) *nonprofit, nontheatrical exhibition* allows institutions such as libraries to use videos displaying these rights for in-house, group programming where no admission is charged; and (3) *theatrical exhibition* indicates a video may be shown for profit, such as in a movie studio setting.

Although, under the fair-use doctrine, the copyright law seems to allow the use of copyrighted materials in specific situations, noted copyright expert Dr. Jerome K. Miller holds that the doctrine applies solely to photocopying, not at all to video performance. He states that the Film Security Office of the MPAA has been sending out agents who go to public libraries, watch videocassettes on the premises, and file reports for possible future court action.[4] There are four key areas to be considered when deciding whether fair use is applicable: (1) the purpose and character of the use, including whether it is used for commercial or nonprofit educational purposes; (2) the nature of the copyrighted work; (3) the amount of the work used or copied and the number of copies reproduced; and (4) the effect of the use upon the potential market for or value of the copyrighted work.[5]

Copyright expert Debra Stanek feels that fair use does apply to in-house viewing of videos and argues that in-library (individual carrel) viewing would have little if any effect upon the particular market for any given title. She feels that copyright owners should be aware of the "ordinary use" libraries make of purchased materials, including in-library use.[6]

On the other hand, the MPAA sides with Dr. Miller, declaring, "Companies, organizations, and individuals who wish to publicly exhibit copyrighted motion pictures and audiovisual works must secure licenses to do so."[7] A letter from Warner Bros. Distributing, reproduced in Figure 6.2, states, "While lending tapes to patrons is permissible, exhibition anywhere except in the patron's home, without permission, is not."[8] Warner encourages librarians wishing to obtain public performance licenses for Warner private, home-use-only videos to contact certain licensing groups such as Swank Motion Pictures and the Motion Picture Licensing Corporation (see

Chapter 8 for address and full explanation of licensing). The MPAA's viewpoint cannot be ignored. In September 1986 a circuit court of appeals decision upheld a lower court's decision that it was not legal for a video store (Nickelodeon Video Showcase) to rent tapes to customers and allow them to use private booths within the store for viewing. Dr. Miller emphasized that that decision of the court was not based on the fact that money was involved; rather, "The Copyright Act speaks of performance at a place open to the public. It does not require that the public place actually be crowded with people."[9] The American Library Association (ALA) has taken the stand that "Even if a videotape is labelled 'For Home-Use only,' private viewing in the library should be considered to be authorized by the vendor's sale to the library with imputed knowledge of the library's intended use of the video."[10]

Fair use and *educational use* are often used synonymously, yet they are covered in two different sections of the law. Section 107 gives six examples of fair use: (1) criticism, (2) comment, (3) news reporting, (4) teaching, (5) scholarship, and (6) research. Educational use may be considered fair use, depending upon the specific circumstances surrounding it. Fair use should not be interpreted to mean "fair game."[11]

Section 110(1), "Limitations on Exclusive Rights," outlines an exemption for certain performances and displays of videocassettes for educational use, limiting the exemption to

> performance or display of a work by instructors or pupils in the course of [curriculum related] face-to-face teaching activities of a nonprofit educational institution.[12]

This face-to-face clause strictly prohibits the showing, without permission, of videocassette programs for recreation or entertainment, whatever their cultural value or intellectual appeal. To meet the educational exemption, the programs must be curriculum-oriented, must be an integral part of the teaching lesson, and must be shown in a "classroom or similar place devoted to instruction." Seven provisions should be met in order for Section 110(1) to be applicable to nonprofit schools, colleges, and universities:

1. Performances and displays must be shown using legitimate copies, not pirated ones
2. Showings must take place in a classroom or similar place devoted to instruction

WARNER BROS. DISTRIBUTING

Warner Bros. Distributing Corporation
4000 Warner Boulevard
Burbank, California 91522
818 954-6066
Cable Address: Warbros

D. Barry Reardon
President

July 25, 1986

Attention: Head Librarian

With the rising awareness of the importance of copyright laws affecting public libraries and especially concerning the use of videotapes, we would like you to know of Warner Brothers' position on the use of video tapes.

To give you some guidance in the matter, let us simply state that to exhibit a Warner tape without permission is illegal. While lending tapes to patrons is permissible, exhibition anywhere except in the patron's home, without permission, is not.

You can, however, obtain a public performance license from Warner Brothers. This license will enable you to show these tapes within your library, which will increase the popularity of your library within your community. Your library can select from our enormous catalog, which includes drama, comedy, family entertainment, action and adventure.

Our video licensing program is easy and an economical way to provide motion picture entertainment in your library. The procedure is simple. Just write:

    Public Performance Licensing Department
    Attention: P. Ray Swank, President
    Swank Motion Pictures, Inc.
    201 South Jefferson Avenue
    St. Louis, Missouri 63166

They will send you full licensing information. The telephone number is 314/289-2100 or 314/289-2123. We want you to abide by the copyright laws and we fully intend to protect our rights under these laws.

I hope that this letter is informative and we will soon be able to count on you as a valued customer.

    Very truly yours,

    D. Barry Reardon

lmr

A Warner Communications Company

FIGURE 6.2 LETTER FROM WARNER BROS. DISTRIBUTING CONCERNING LIBRARY USE OF HOME-USE VIDEOCASSETTES. This letter implies that any in-house library use of prerecorded videocassettes, even individual, private, in-carrel use, infringes upon the copyright law.

3. Showings must be part of a systematic course of instruction and not for entertainment, recreation, or cultural value
4. Performance must be given by the instructor or pupils
5. Performance must be given in the classroom exclusively and not transmitted by broadcast or cable television
6. Showings must be part of the teaching activities of a nonprofit educational institution
7. Attendance at performances is limited to the instructor, pupils, and guest lecturers.[13]

The interpretation of the phrase "nonprofit educational institution," coupled with its lack of a legal definition, adds to the confusion of public librarians. Copyright lawyer Ivan R. Bender feels that a public library is not an educational institution; however, to date there has been no uniform definition established by the courts. Libraries should be able to meet five criteria if they intend to claim the educational use exemption as a defense:

1. Do students receive frequent reading, field, or laboratory assignments, for which they are held accountable?
2. Do instructors assign grades based on papers, examinations, oral reports, and other reliable measures of pupil performance?
3. Are grades reported to parents, guardians, employers, or other responsible parties?
4. Are transcripts of students' grades available to other educational institutions?
5. Does the course lead to a recognized degree, diploma, license, or certificate?[14]

Librarians must be careful to meet all the requirements of Section 110 if home-use videos are to be utilized for instruction in libraries. Performances in viewing rooms or carrels occupied by one person, a family, or a small group of friends do not necessarily meet the private showing requirements discussed earlier. The court decision involving *Columbia Pictures v. Redd Horne* (13 October 1983) found a video store in violation of the copyright law because videocassettes could be viewed on the premises for a fee.[15] Mary Hutchings Reed, ALA attorney, suggests that if library patrons are allowed to watch videos in-house, they should be "limited to private performances, i.e., one person, or no more than one family at a time."[16]

Ivan Bender feels that public libraries cannot show home-use videocassettes without obtaining performance rights, except in the rare instance involving educational exemption. He emphasizes that any other use, even by one person in a carrel, is a "public performance." The ALA does not agree and states that private performances in library carrels are not public and constitute "fair and ordinary use."[17] ALA Executive Director Thomas J. Galvin feels that "there is no qualitative difference between private home viewing and private library carrel-viewing."[18] Recently, ALA's guidelines were challenged by a New York law firm representing 12 film producers and distributors. The producers argued that "all performances in a library are public and therefore infringe on copyright."[19] The producers also maintain that libraries cannot insulate themselves from copyright infringement merely by displaying MPAA warning notices on videotapes. They also indicate that a student who misses a classroom performance of an instructional lesson should not be allowed to view the tape in the school library. The ALA's current position regarding this issue reflects the opposite viewpoint and upholds "ordinary use."

☐ POTENTIAL SOLUTIONS

If the *Redd Horne* decision is sustained by the courts within the context of the free public library, it will have serious ramifications upon libraries' rights to show videocassettes in-house under the auspices of "home use." Solutions that may be considered include:

Stop library video performances.

Continue the present policies until challenged by the courts.

Limit showings to those videos that display "public performance" rights or by label omission do not display the "home use only" restriction.

Obtain blanket clearances, lease agreements, or purchase only public performance programs. Currently, two distributors of low-cost public performance full-length motion pictures are Public Media Incorporated, 5547 North Ravenswood Avenue, Chicago, IL 60640-1199; and Tamarelle's International Films, 110 Cohasset Stage Road, Chico, CA 95926.

Seek to amend the copyright law to give libraries the right to free performances of copyrighted videocassettes.[20]

☐ THE MPAA WARNING LABEL AND LIBRARY USAGE

Despite the controversy over public or home viewing of videos, librarians need not be concerned about their rights to *circulate/loan* videocassettes to patrons. Sections 106(3) and 109(a) affirm that the owner (a library) who has acquired ownership of an authorized videocassette is entitled to lend it under any conditions it chooses to impose.

As mentioned, about 1978, several motion picture producers began displaying home-use warning labels (see Figure 6.1). Educators, school librarians, and public librarians are concerned about the videocassette warning label's legal implications for classroom and in-house library use. The label provides evidence of the proprietor's good faith efforts to inform viewers of the law and consequences of infringement. Dr. Jerome Miller stresses that

> libraries and/or librarians are not liable for copyright infringements on the part of individual patrons. A staff member can inform (and in the case of library-owned VCRs, should probably affix a copyright warning to the machine) a borrower about copyright laws—specifically, injunctions against duplicating and [home use]... but is under no obligation to challenge or cross examine a patron concerning intended use of the program.[21]

Off-Air Recording and the Law

The Copyright Act itself does not specifically address the issue of off-air taping. It allows a library or archive to tape "an audiovisual new program" (Section 108 [f] [3]). Currently, educational fair-use off-air taping guidelines do not carry the force of law because they are only part of legislative history. Listed below are the 1979 federal negotiating committee's consensus guidelines as to the application of the fair-use doctrine to the recording, retention, and use of television broadcast programs for educational purposes. They recommend specific retention time periods and use of recordings in nonprofit educational institutions.

1. A broadcast program may be recorded off-air simultaneously with broadcast transmission and retained by the institution for up to 45 consecutive calendar days after the recording date. After that time, all off-air recordings must be erased or destroyed immediately.
2. Such recordings may be used in a classroom once, and repeated once by individual teachers in the course of relevant teaching activities during the first 10 consecutive school days within the 45-day calendar retention period. They may not be used with students after that time. They may be used in classrooms and similar places devoted to instruction within a single building, cluster, or campus, as well as in the homes of students receiving

formalized home instruction. "School days" are school session days—not counting weekends, holidays, vacations, examination periods, or other scheduled interruptions within the 45-day retention period.
3. Off-air recordings may be made only upon individual teachers' requests; they must not be made in anticipation of such requests. No program may be recorded off-air more than once at the request of the same teacher, regardless of the number of times the program may be broadcast.
4. Copies may be reproduced from the original to meet legitimate needs of instructors; however, each copy is subject to all the provisions governing the original recording.
5. After the first 10 consecutive school days, recordings may be used up to the end of the 45-calendar-day retention period but only for determination of future curriculum usage. Recordings may not be used for student exhibition or any other nonevaluative purpose during this time period.
6. Recordings need not be used in their entirety, but they must not be altered from their original content. Contents may not be physically or electronically combined or merged.
7. All copies of off-air recordings must include the copyright notice displayed on the program as recorded.
8. Educational institutions are expected to establish appropriate control procedures to maintain the integrity of the above guidelines.[22]

☐ COURT DECISIONS

On 10 March 1983, a U.S. district court in New York handed down an interesting verdict relating to off-air videotaping rights. In the case of *Encyclopaedia Britannica Educational Corporation, et al. v. C. N. Crooks,* it was ruled that off-air taping and playback of copyrighted materials readily available by rental, lease, or license duplicating agreement is infringement and is not fair use.[23] The guidelines offered by the congressional committee do not apply in this case. The defendants were violating the 45-day use preview period and making illegal copies from copies. Joe Elliot, former president of MTI/Coronet, feels that "educational institutions" are exempt with regard to obtaining public performance rights as long as they meet the seven criteria set by the Congressional Committee Guidelines.[24] The ALA guidelines do not mention anything about prior determination of whether off-air taped programs are available through purchase or rental agreements. Because of this gray area, it would behoove librarians to try to obtain any program by purchase, rental, or license before taping of that program is done off-air. Many companies, such as National Geographic, permit their programs to be taped off-air, at no charge, and retained for the life of the tape. Librarians should contact the individual companies and the local PBS affiliate stations to inquire about upcoming programs and off-air duplication rights. If a source cannot readily be found, the program can be utilized within the 45-day period specified by the guidelines. Programs should not be kept after the 45-day retention period.

The New York court ruling mentions that a showing of an illegally made copy, even in a classroom, constitutes a public performance and is therefore illegal. The copyright law directly contradicts this view, however, and specifically outlines the seven criteria needed for exemption by educational institutions for compliance under the law. The problem stems from the fact that the law does not specifically mention off-air duplication. The key term here is *illegal copy*.

☐ AT-HOME TAPING FOR INSTITUTIONAL USE

Until recently, the privilege for institutional taping was interpreted to mean that the recording actually had to take place on the institution's premises. It appears that it is legally possible to record programs at home and bring them into school, as long as all of the institutional off-air taping guidelines are followed. The programs may not be retained by the individual who taped them, since the individual is now operating under the educational taping guidelines and not the privilege for home-use videotaping. So far, there have been no court cases or legal guidelines indicating that home taping for school use is actually permissible.

☐ VIDEO USE GUIDELINES

Although these procedures will be scoffed at by many instructors, educational institutions should protect themselves from possible copyright infringement lawsuits by establishing a copyright guidelines policy. This policy should address classroom use of pre-recorded home-use programs and procedures for institutional off-air taping, as well as home taping used in the educational setting. The policy should be acknowledged by the school board and explicitly explained to instructors. An example of such a policy as formulated by the author of this book using a fictional school district, is contained in the following pages.

SMITH COMMUNITY UNIT SCHOOL DISTRICT #226
Use of Copyrighted Video Programs Guidelines

In order to comply with the revised Copyright Act of 1976 as it applies to the use of copyrighted audiovisual programs, it is the policy of the Smith Community Unit School District #226 to abide by the following guidelines.

INSTRUCTIONAL USE

Video programs displaying the "public performance" restriction can be used for any school function providing no profit is made from admission charges. The following guidelines apply only to those copyrighted video programs used in the classroom that display the "home use only" restriction.

1. They must be directly related to the instructional program.
2. They must be shown by teachers, students, or guest speakers in the course of systematic instruction.
3. They must be shown either in a classroom or similar place devoted to instruction such as a library, gymnasium, or auditorium.
4. They must be shown in a face-to-face setting and where the entire audience is in the same building or general area.
5. They must be shown only to teachers, students, and people directly involved in the instructional program.
6. They must be shown using a lawfully made copy with copyright notice included.

Copyrighted "home use only" video programs *may not* be used under the following conditions:

1. They are used for entertainment, recreation, or enrichment programming.
2. They are shown in a situation before an audience not confined to students and not directly a part of an instructional program, such as an awards banquet or a sporting event.
3. An admission fee is charged.

Instructors utilizing rented or personal "home use only" video programs in their classrooms must follow the guidelines stated above.

OFF-AIR VIDEOTAPING

The school library media center is the only entity authorized to produce off-air video copies. The instructor must contact the librarian at least one day in advance of the program time by submitting Form A (see attached). All off-air videotapes will be used according to the following guidelines:

1. Off-air recordings may be made only at the request of an individual teacher for systematic instructional purposes. No broadcast program may be recorded off-air more than once at the request of the same teacher, regardless of the number of times the program may be broadcast (during the 45-calendar-day retention period).
2. A broadcast program recorded off-air may be retained for 45 calendar days, after which time the tapes must be erased.
3. An off-air program is limited to two showings per class: it may be shown once to students for relevant classroom activities and once more for necessary instructional reinforcement during the first 10 consecutive school days over the 45-day retention period. (Consecutive school days are school session days—not counting weekends, holidays, vacations, examination periods, or other scheduled interruptions.)
4. After the first 10 consecutive school days, the recordings may be viewed only by teachers for evaluation purposes.
5. If several teachers request videotaping of the same program, duplicate copies may be made, but the use of all copies will follow the above restrictions.
6. Recordings need not be used in their entirety, but they must not be altered from their original content or combined (edited) with others to form anthologies.
7. All videotapes must include the original copyright notice.

SPECIAL PROBLEMS CONCERNING VIDEO

If the school library media center cannot record the program(s) for an instructor, that instructor may privately record the programs desired, provided Form A is filled out and submitted to the media center after recording. All privately recorded off-air programs aired for classroom use immediately become "educational use" and, as such, must follow the above guidelines.

FORM A
Request for Off-Air Program Taping
Smith Community Unit School District #226

Date submitted:

Title, channel, date, and time of program(s) requested:

Title	Date	Time(s)	Channel	Format

1.

2.

3.

4.

5.

Recorder's signature:

List classes, periods where programs will be used (numbers match titles above).

1.

2.

3.

4.

5.

_____ Instructor will be recording these programs.

Instructor's signature:

☐ SOURCE MATERIAL FOR COPYRIGHT INFORMATION

The videotape copyright issue is shrouded in shades of gray. It is this author's opinion that librarians should adhere as closely to the letter of the law as possible but continue to abide by the ALA's recommended guidelines, outlined in the Appendix. Libraries should try to acquire public performance videotapes whenever possible or when the material will be used for in-house, group showing or library programming. Recently, the Los Angeles County Public Library entered into a public performance licensing agreement with MGM/UA for in-house, individual as well as group use of some one hundred titles. Some additional sources that may help librarians concerning the issues of videotape copyright are listed below.

Copyright Policy Development: A Resource Book for Educators. Charles Vlcek. Friday Harbor, WA: Copyright Information Services, 1987. $17.95.

An excellent primer for educational institutions wanting to write or revise their copyright policy. Six policies serve as examples, addressing topics such as off-air recording and librarian responsibility for copyright patrol and regulation.

Copyright: What Every School, College and Public Library Should Know. Ivan R. Bender and Jerry Hazelmeier. Deerfield, IL: Association for Information Media and Equipment (AIME), 1987. $65, 16mm film; $25, videocassette.

The program covers five areas: what copyright is, fair use, the face-to-face teaching exemption, off-air videotaping guidelines, and situations and questions. This would be an excellent introduction for educational administrators.

Video/Copyright Seminar, 1987. Jerome K. Miller. Friday Harbor, WA: Copyright Information Services, 1987. $24.95. Audiocassette.

This tape covers the pros and cons of showing videos in public, school, and college libraries; loaning videos for home, school, and organizational showings; off-air and satellite videotaping; and preparing a school district video copyright policy. Also included in the package are a seminar outline, an educational video copyright policy outline, relevant texts of the Communications

Act, Fair-Use Guidelines, and information from the Television Licensing Center.

What Educators Should Know about Copyright. Virginia Helm. Bloomington, IN: Phi Delta Kappa Educational Foundation, 1986. $.90.

This pamphlet is an excellent "layman's overview" of the copyright law as it pertains to AV materials. The fair-use doctrine is covered as well as the law and its restrictions pertaining to educational institutions.

FEE-BASED VIDEOCASSETTE LOANS

The debate over charging fees for certain library services has been going on for years but has most recently been rekindled over nontraditional services such as videocassettes. It is interesting to note that, as with copyright, there is a wide discrepancy of opinions concerning this issue, especially among laywers. An ALA attorney, Mary Hutchings Reed, advises librarians that "a nominal user fee may be charged."[25] However, the attorney generals of Rhode Island and Wisconsin have stated that library fees for videocassette loans are prohibited. The Wisconsin attorney general's opinion is particularly interesting because it discusses and defines three core and nontraditional services, the interplay of technology and information, and the definition of the public library. The inherent argument that the Wisconsin attorney general uses is that certain information-providing services within a public library must be provided free, i.e., "core" services. He argues that videocassettes are "traditional" library services. However, he continues, "those ancillary services which are not unique to libraries and which can be just as effectively provided in a non-library setting" are not inherent information-providing services; therefore fees are permissible.[26] Although certainly not a legal opinion, this author feels that the ready availability of video rental stores provides fuel for the argument that videocassettes are not a traditional core service. Also, the fact that videocassettes are not standard acquirable items, inasmuch as not every library provides them, should help to give credence to the argument for videocassettes as nontraditional materials.

As with interpretation of the Copyright Act in regards to libraries, there are no right or wrong answers—only shades of gray. Until the law is contested and an opinion rendered by a court of law, librarians can only continue to operate within the visible constraints of the law while interpreting it with the best interests of the library and the community in mind. The best answer to this question lies in the practice of accountability and developing traceable policies. As emphasized throughout this text, every library should have a variety of well-considered policies covering selection/collection development, copyright, and cardholder/circulation issues. Librarians considering videocassette loan fees should address the following questions:

- Is there a need for the service?
- Would the library be providing this service more equitably and to more people than could be provided through local business channels?
- Can the service be provided using existing funds without additional fees?
- What are the fee charges at the local rental stores?
- What will be the impact upon service in terms of patron attitudes, return of overdues/damaged materials, materials availability, and circulation?
- Has the state attorney general issued an opinion concerning this matter?

It is important to remember two facts when contemplating charging fees for video loans: (1) Public libraries were formed to give patrons within designated tax-supported areas free access to the facilities and materials traditionally associated with a library. Although not specifically stated, this definition implies across-the-board equitability based on tax paid—not additional fees charged on top of taxes. (2) Tax dollars are used to purchase collection materials—fee charging in effect is income that supplements those dollars. The revenue-collecting board may decide that library-generated revenue is a substitute for tax-provided funds and decrease future budgets accordingly.

Libraries that loan video recorders to patrons should not feel constrained concerning equipment loan fees or copyright law. Equipment loans are termed "tangential to a library's inherent information-providing function."[27]—fees are therefore permissible. Video recorders may also be loaned to patrons without fear of liability even if the patron uses the recorder to infringe upon copyright. However, warning notices like the following should be posted on all equipment: "Many videotaped materials are protected by copyright. Unauthorized copying is prohibited by law (17 U.S.C. Section 101–106)." Another, more efficient way to deter copyright infringement is to purchase/loan only video players.

Videocassette loans increase community visibility for libraries, provide them with a new approach to broaden their patron base, increase circulation, and promote positive public relations. Charging fees for videocassette loans does not necessarily adversely affect budgets or public relations, but the local community environment should be carefully considered before implementing fees. The fee should never exceed fees charged by local, private video rental stores and should be freely advertised. By planning for fee charging and taking certain precautions, fees can provide needed supplementary materials income while still maintaining a positive public image.

ACCESS BY MINORS

Another hotly debated video topic in library circles today is the access-to-minors issue. The U.S. Supreme Court has ruled that states may legally deny minors access to materials that are constitutionally available to adults. Most states have enacted access-to-minors statutes, and some prohibit libraries from loaning certain motion pictures and videos to minors. However, the great majority of states specifically exempt libraries and other educational institutions from this law. Librarians should contact their legal counsel and have the library board (or governing agency) approve a circulation and viewing policy that covers all the regulations and rules for video use. Otherwise, the library could face prosecution in a number of areas, including lending adult materials to minors.

Most librarians familiar with video are equally familiar with the MPAA film audience rating system. Those Ms, Gs, Rs, and most recently PG-13s are regarded by some people as a thoroughly accurate indicator of a film's content related to its intended viewing audience. In truth, the MPAA ratings are vague and indiscriminate and, in the eyes of the courts, totally unacceptable as intended audience content indicators. The legal counsel to the Ohio Library Association, Norton R. Webster, advised librarians to "continue to adhere to a policy of free access to minors, in keeping with their role as a forum of information and ideas." Librarians should have written materials selection policies and follow them. Webster also felt that library use of the MPAA rating system as a content indicator was inappropriate. Just as labeling of books is deemed an attempt to prejudice attitudes, so is the affixing of MPAA rating codes to videocassettes.[28] The MPAA system does not consider the range of attitudes from community to community, nor does it make a distinction concerning sex, violence, nudity, or obscenities in assigning ratings. In states such as Maryland, Illinois, and Mississippi, it is illegal to sell or rent videos unless the MPAA rating is affixed to them.

Of interest to librarians, particularly in Massachusetts, is a state bill entitled "An Act to Prohibit the Distribution of Video Movies Without Official Ratings." The bill (H.R. 5833) proposed to ban the sale or rental of movies produced after 1968 and now available on video that had not received an MPAA rating. The bill is fundamentally flawed because it prevents the sale or rental of nontheatrical releases, made-for-television movies, and even children's educational programs. Although the bill was tabled, it would have some serious implications for the entire video industry if other states take similar stands.[29]

Illinois Public Act 84–593, the Video Movie Sales and Rentals Act, effective 1 January 1986, states, "Anyone selling or renting video movies must display the MPAA official rating if the material has one." Libraries that do not charge for loans probably are not subject to the law because of the terms "selling or renting." The Intellectual Freedom Committee of the ALA felt that it might mount a constitutional attack in which the MPAA ratings would be termed labeling. The American Library Association endorses a "Statement on Labeling," which opposes any placement of labels on materials that indicate a particular audience preference or suitability, simply stating that it is the individual's right to decide what is suitable. The key to avoiding the Video Movie Sales and Rentals Act and remaining ethical regarding the "Statement on Labeling" (at least in Illinois) is not to charge a fee for loaning videocassettes.

Many libraries are avoiding the access-to-minors issue by giving video use and borrowing privileges only to adult cardholders or having parents of minors fill out consent cards for levels of video borrowing privileges. Some librarians might find it advantageous to decentralize their video collection and have two or more collections—possibly an adult collection, housed with adult materials, and a children's collection housed in the children's department. These suggestions, coupled with a sound collection development policy and circulation/viewing policy, will give the library a concrete foundation upon which to stand if challenged.

WEEDING

Most librarians are familiar with the concept of weeding in terms of book collections. Currently, video collections are enjoying immense popularity, and libraries have not had to do systematic weeding because the collections are essentially self-weeding; that is, collections are constantly ravaged by significant damages and losses. Also, the collection sizes, compared to materials budget allotments, have not reached a point where excess or superfluous items are being purchased rapidly. Having a well-developed collection development policy and keeping in tune with patron needs will reduce the chances for acquiring slow- and nonmoving titles, but some mistakes are bound to be made. Popularity shifts are bound to occur, and future advances in technology may diminish the overall popularity of the videocassette in our society. Today, librarians are in danger of treating videocassettes as fragile items to be kept under lock and key. Like other audiovisual items, librarians will keep them even though they contain outdated information or are in poor condition. Librarians need not be afraid of the videocassette medium; if a title contains outdated information, it should be withdrawn and put in an annual book sale. Weeding is an essential part of collection development that will ultimately contribute to building a strong, well-used collection.

Weeding is defined by G. Edward Evans as "the practice of discarding or transferring to storage excess copies, rarely used and non-used materials."[30] The term *purging* refers to withdrawing the item entirely, while *storage* refers to maintaining items in a second level of access, usually a warehouse. There are particular dangers in warehousing videocassettes for long periods of nonuse. The magnetic tape and cassette parts must be used every so often to keep them in proper working order.

Every collection development policy should contain a section that delineates an active, continuous weeding procedure. Unfortunately, there exist two natural weeding laws that every experienced librarian knows: (1) no matter how outdated or strange an item may seem, at least one person will find it valuable; and (2) no matter how long an item has remained unused, ten minutes after it has been discarded, one person will walk in and ask for it.[31] Lazy librarians, like lazy gardeners, will find that weeding only gets harder through neglect.

Today, most libraries possessing video collections have not really passed the level of a core collection or a collection most likely to be used by patrons. The basic assumption of weeding is that the value of an item to its patrons can be estimated from its past use in terms of circulation. Most of the controversy over the weeding process surfaces when discussing the most effective way of predicting future use.

Librarians weed for five reasons: (1) to make the collection more appealing in terms of look and interest, (2) to make space for more valuable items, (3) to make the collection more current and accurate, (4) to encourage patrons to respect the collection by reinforcing items in number 1, and (5) to assure that full shelves are not just an illusion of a good library.[32]

The CREW (Continuous Review, Evaluation, and Weeding) method provides excellent guidance for accomplishing the task. In order to weed effectively, certain objectives must be established. The collection should be broken down into small, workable subject/genre sections that can be easily evaluated. One major objective should be to determine weeding by use or content currency. Videocassettes pose a particular problem for determining currency; the librarian must actually view the cassette or rely on patron observations concerning content. One person should be in charge of the weeding program. Several people may be working on individual sections, but the process should be controlled by one person so as to ensure continuity.

It may be helpful to imagine that the library is a profit-making business. It is expensive to keep materials on the shelf and actually more expensive to keep unused materials shelved. Businesses cannot afford to keep unpopular inventory. Granted, in library situations, some items should be kept for historical and local significance, but the entire collection should not be considered "historical." Librarians must realize the future importance that weeding will play in developing videocassette collections. Weeding should be considered as a positive public relations tool that keeps the library's inventory current, popular, and responsive to patron demand.

NOTES

1. *Bowker Annual of Library and Booktrade Information,* 30th ed. (New York: Xerox, 1985), 41–42.
2. Jerome K. Miller, *Using Copyrighted Videocassettes in Classrooms and Libraries* (Salem, MA: Copyright Information Services, 1984), 12.

3. Ibid., 16.
4. Randy Pitman, "Update On Copyright," *Video Librarian* 2 (April 1987): 3.
5. *Explaining the New Copyright Law* (New York: Association of American Publishers, 1980).
6. Randy Pitman, "Room with a View: The In-Library Viewing Controversy," *Video Librarian* 1 (October 1986), 3.
7. Ibid.
8. D. Barry Reardon, Warner Bros. library copyright letter, 25 July 1986, quoted in Pitman, "Room with a View," 3.
9. Pitman, "Room with a View," 3.
10. Ibid., 2.
11. Carol A. Emmens, "Copyright Considerations," *School Library Journal* 32 (February 1986): 35.
12. Miller, *Using Copyrighted Videocassettes*, 21.
13. Ibid., 24.
14. Ibid., 28.
15. Ibid., 35.
16. Mary Hutchings Reed and Debra Stanek, "Library Use of Copyrighted Videotapes and Computer Software," *American Libraries* 17 (February 1986): special pull-out section.
17. Emmens, "Copyright," 35.
18. "Film Companies Challenge ALA Copyright Guidelines; Galvin Responds," *American Libraries* 18 (January 1987): 76.
19. Ibid.
20. Miller, *Using Copyrighted Videocassettes*, 48.
21. Ibid.
22. Esther Rita Sinofsky, *Off-Air Videotaping in Education* (New York: R. R. Bowker, 1984), 119–120.
23. "Recent Copyright Court Ruling: What it Means to You," in *Learning Corporation of America 1985 Film & Video Catalog* (Deerfield, IL: Learning Corporation of America, 1985), 156.
24. Telephone conversation with Joe Elliot, president of MTI/Coronet on 3 May 1987.
25. Reed and Stanek, "Library Use of Copyrighted Videotapes," B.
26. State of Wisconsin, Attorney General, *Opinions of the Attorney General's Office* (Madison: Wisconsin State Library, 17 August 1984), 89.
27. Ibid.
28. "Videocassette Circulation: A Legal Opinion from Ohio," *Library Journal* 110 (1 May 1985): 16.
29. David Wykoff, "Mass. Bill Banning Unrated Tapes Stalls," *Billboard*, 23 August 1986, 55.

30. G. Edward Evans, *Developing Library Collections* (Littleton, CO: Libraries Unlimited, 1979), 216.
31. Ibid.
32. Carol Mahon, "Weeding Is PR Too," *Library Insights Promotion & Programs* 1/2 (January/February 1987): 3.

7 EXPLORING OPTIONAL PURCHASE PLANS

In the current economic climate it is often difficult for libraries to maintain existing services while simultaneously developing new ones such as circulating videocassette collections. The purpose of this chapter is to explore the following options available to libraries wishing to start video collections: (1) consortium purchasing; (2) video leasing plans; and (3) rotating collections (video circuits).

CONSORTIUM PURCHASING

In almost every case involving library materials, purchasing volume dictates price/discount. Producers and vendors are very willing to negotiate substantial discounts for guaranteed volume business; therefore, if several libraries can band together in a cooperative purchasing arrangement, they can receive better discounts than if they were to purchase as single entities. The Monroe County Library System in Monroe, Michigan, established the River Raisin Library Video Purchasing Project. Seven libraries drew up lists of the videocassettes they wanted to purchase. These were merged into one master list that was distributed to vendors for bids. Bernard A. Margolis, director of the Monroe County Library System, says that the libraries saved substantially: "for example, *The Exorcist* retails for $60 and wholesales for $44, and our bid was 3 percent less than that."[1]

Academic libraries have long been involved in organized purchasing consortiums. One such organization is the Northern Illinois

Learning Resources Consortium (NILRC), which serves member colleges, universities, and community colleges in Northern Illinois. One of NILRC's functions is to seek out, develop, and negotiate discount purchasing agreements for audiovisual materials. Many states have regional purchasing organizations, called BOCES, that perform similar purchasing functions for public schools.

Joining an organized purchasing consortium is somewhat expensive, and many such organizations do not open membership to public libraries or schools. Public libraries should develop contacts with their local colleges and universities to explore what groups might be open to them. Developing a plan like the River Raisin Library Video Purchasing Project takes a considerable amount of effort, but it is probably one of the best ways to go because it does not involve membership and exists for that one purpose. However, one important item must be considered when developing a concept such as this: There should be one person or a single committee responsible for all paperwork, such as receiving the master lists, establishing deadlines, merging lists, accepting bids, and, finally, choosing a purchasing source. Logistics such as pooling funds, establishing payment, and distribution procedures must also be established.

VIDEO LEASING PLANS

Cooperative and consortium purchasing offer attractive options for libraries wishing to own videocassette collections, but another option, a lease program, also provides title access. Currently, two companies provide a videocassette leasing program: Eastin-Phelan Corporation, 1235 West 5th Street, Davenport, IA 52802, (800) 826-2295; and Videoplan, Inc., 1448 West Rosecrans Avenue, Gardena, CA 90249, (800) 223-7672.

☐ THE EASTIN-PHELAN PROGRAMS

The library can select any catalog titles (and multiple copies). These titles are leased for approximately 10 percent of the retail price of the cassette per month. At the end of six months, the library may exchange any or all of the titles for new and/or different ones. If they retain a title and rent it for one year, they may purchase it by paying a 13th month's rent. This program allows the library to offer the latest titles to their patrons and then to return slow movers at the end of six months. Two of the libraries in Illinois currently using this program are Lake Villa and Lake Bluff.

The second Eastin-Phelan plan packages videocassettes into groups of 20 or 30 per unit and rotates 13 units to subscribing libraries every two months. The library has no choice in the selection of titles, but each unit contains a good variety of children's titles, feature classics, and current popular features. No nonfiction titles are included. New titles are being added continually. Cost is $3 per title per month. Thus 20 times $3 equals $60 per month, times 12 months equals $720 per year. By rotating the collections every 2 months, libraries have use of at least 120 titles during the year. This is a very inexpensive way for small libraries to get started in video. This program does not restrict libraries from charging rental fees to patrons. Libraries currently using this plan in Illinois are East Moline, Shorewood, and Forrest.

☐ THE VIDEOPLAN OPTION

Videoplan Inc. is affiliated with Professional Media Service Corporation. Videoplan's program offers a wide range of services and options, but their plans are considerably more expensive than Eastin-Phelan's. Anyone familiar with Brodart's McNaughton lease plan for books will find many similarities in this service. The library chooses a plan size appropriate to its expected needs and available funds. The starting collection (Plan I) consists of 50 titles selected from a list. A library must maintain 55 titles minimum in its permanent inventory. An average of 60 titles per year or 5 per month must be ordered. A library may increase its inventory at any time during the 12-month service period; however, it must be done in increments of Plan I size (50 titles in permanent inventory and a new allowance of 60 titles per year). Minimum contract time is one year, but each month the library will receive a listing of new titles. The library must return the same number of titles that it requests to keep the collection at the contracted size. Plan cost is determined by title list cost. Titles with a list price of more than $40 are charged at the rate of two for one; and those with a list price of more than $80 are charged at the rate of three to one. Starting yearly costs for the minimum plan (Videolease II, Plan I) is $2,999. Plan I provides access to 110 titles (50-title starting collection and 60 additional) for a cost of $2,999. An average purchase price for that many titles would be about $4,400 based on an average per title price of $40.

Libraries may select virtually any title available, inclusive of all subjects and genres. Titles may also be purchased for 50 percent of the original retail price after they have been held in the collection for six months. Full cataloging and processing are provided, with complete card sets available with each title and Library of Congress subject heading and name authority terms used. Labels, containing title and running time in minutes, are affixed to the spine of each case, and circulation cards are also available. MPAA ratings are affixed to the display boxes where available. Videoplan prepares each title in a durable, generic container with identifying labels, while coinciding commercial boxes are provided for display purposes. In utilizing this packaging procedure, Videoplan advocates the behind-the-counter security/circulation method. The Santa Monica Public Library (California) utilizes the Videoplan service.

Video lease plans have particular appeal to libraries because videocassettes are fairly expensive and establishing a sizable collection requires a substantial investment. Another reason is that popular items, which may have only a temporary appeal, can be returned if that appeal dwindles or dies, while slow-moving or nonmoving items can be easily eliminated from the collection. Lease programs allow librarians the ability to experiment with various titles, making the titles patrons want "now" available. This currency could not be economically performed in any other manner.

ROTATING COLLECTIONS: VIDEO CIRCUITS

All of the optional programs discussed have involved, and been limited by, a library's existing materials budget allocated for videocassettes. Discounts and leasing plans help but do not adequately increase title availability proportionally related to expended dollars. Several libraries have developed unique approaches to locally organized and controlled rotating video collections called video circuits. Essentially, a video circuit involves a centralized agency that controls selection, acquisition, processing, and distribution of a collection. This collection is broken down into segments and distributed among participating libraries on a rotating basis.

In the most basic video circuit, a large city, district, or county library may be the centralized agency, while each branch may have a video collection. In this case, there exists only one materials budget, that of the central agency.

The Morgantown Public Library (West Virginia) is offering a video circuit service to eight local libraries. Members pay a yearly $800 fee to receive circulating packets consisting of 20 assorted videocassettes. The membership fee pays for approximately 75 percent of the cost of purchasing the titles. The makeup of each packet is predetermined: 6 family favorites suitable for children; 5 classics;

EXPLORING OPTIONAL PURCHASE PLANS

3 contemporary popular videos; 1 each of fantasy, foreign, science fiction, and horror; 1 concert performance; and 1 how-to/self-help.[2] East Brunswick Public Library in New Jersey charges members a $1,000 yearly fee for access to packets containing 35 titles. Each packet is rotated at two-month intervals. In 1983 the collection budget totalled $13,366.[3]

Under the auspices of the California State Library, the California/Washington Video Circuit serves 26 members, primarily public libraries, but including prison, school, and community college libraries as well.[4] The Wisconsin Library Audiovisual Circuit, Inc., is unique. The administrative office is housed in the State Library in Madison, Wisconsin; however, it is a nonprofit corporation that receives no state funds. Originally established as a 16mm film circuit, it now has about 20 members, each of which pays a yearly subscription fee of $500.

The Connecticut Region One Cooperating Library Service is an example of how one regional library started a rotating video collection on a very limited budget. In August 1984, the library service started a video circuit. A videocassette collection of 90 titles, at a total cost of $4,800, was divided up into 12 packets, each containing 6 to 12 videos, circulated among 10 member libraries on a monthly, rotating basis. Each library paid a yearly membership fee of $300 or $600, depending upon whether they wanted 1 or 2 packets per month.[5] A buy-in fee of $150 was adopted for new members coming into the circuit, based on the fact that they would have the use of titles already owned by the present membership. The rules were kept to a minimum in order to reduce confusion. Each library agreed to several conditions: to loan cassettes only to its own library patrons; to send a representative to each monthly swap meeting; and to provide monthly title circulation statistics. Use limitations such as circulation periods, loan fees, overdue charges, and reserves were left to each library's discretion. The main processing center handles the physical acquisition and processing of the videos as well as preparation of yearly packet routing lists and statistics. The packets are exchanged in monthly swap meetings; there is no van or mail delivery. The videos are packaged in generic, black Amaray protective cases with full-sleeve display for the commercial box frontispiece. The titles are not cataloged or classified, only given an accession number for ease of location. Member libraries are free to display and shelve them in any fashion. Each library is responsible for all damages and for lost or stolen titles. The breakage and loss of titles was about 5 to 6 percent in 1985.

The monthly meetings also give members the opportunity to share publicity ideas, discuss ideas that do not work, and formulate new policies and procedures. Press releases and various other advertisements are printed for members to distribute. A member selection committee meets regularly to discuss purchase requests submitted by the members. Through the end of July 1985, the 90 videos had circulated approximately 7,123 times. Circulation breakdowns were 39 percent box-office hits; 34 percent children's films; 16 percent classic films; and 11 percent rock music, concerts, and how-to's. Title purchases were based on these circulation percentages, resulting in accurate demand-oriented purchasing.[6]

During the fiscal year 1986/1987 the makeup and guidelines of the group will increase to the following: 32 participating member libraries; $150 buy-in fee no longer applicable, $400 fee per packet for each library per year; 46 monthly rotating packets of 19 to 27 titles, some titles duplicated from packet to packet but no duplicates within each packet; and a materials budget of $16,650.[7] Success will probably mean decentralization, and in another year and a half the circuit will probably have to divide up into two circuits just to manage the logistical problems of monthly exchange. However, in just a few short years, a program started "on a shoestring" has flourished into a successful venture boasting more than 30 members with a collection of 600 to 1,000 titles.[8]

Video circuits, if well planned from the start, are an easy and sure way for the small library to begin circulating videocassettes. In this manner, the individual members reap the benefits of the cooperative whole, resulting in improved service to their respective patrons. In order for the program to work effectively, several rules must be followed.

1. One person should be designated the administrator of the program, responsible for signing all purchase orders, directing distribution routes, negotiating acquisitions, supervising materials processing, and hiring any needed personnel.
2. A board should be established, composed of an equitable representation of the membership, to regulate and guide the administrator's activities. This board should also be involved in the selection policy.
3. The distribution system should be kept as simple as possible to avoid confusion and mix-ups in delivery and rotations. A simple, one-step process involving packaged sets of titles, distrib-

uted for specified loan times upon a calendar basis, seems to work best.
4. As a rule of thumb, there must be at least as many packets in rotation as there are participating libraries; however, there can be more packets than participating libraries. It is also helpful to have one rotation schedule per packet, e.g., 20 packets rotating among 10 libraries for a 20-month period. In the above example, the rotation period is 1 month. Rotation periods of 1 to 2 months are recommended.
5. Packet size must be kept manageable. Optimum size is 50 titles; anything over 200 titles is like moving a small library from location to location. Optimum packet size depends upon the limits of the delivery system and the needs, wants, and space requirements of the participating libraries. Maintaining the same number of titles/copies in all packets throughout a rotation schedule simplifies the inventory process. New titles can be introduced into each packet at the swap meetings or added when each packet arrives at the centralized distribution point. A consortium consisting of many different-sized libraries may prefer to have a tiered system consisting of two packet sizes, one for the larger libraries (those with more shelf space) and one for smaller libraries.
6. It would be wise to have a centralized return center where all packets would be inventoried; titles cleaned, checked, and repaired; new titles added and replaced; and overdue/replacement charges cumulated. A staggered rotation schedule may be necessary in order to accomplish a smooth transition from pickup and inventory to next delivery because of the number of videotapes involved at any one time. Depending upon the method of delivery, a buffer time period of one day to one week should be included in order to accomplish this inventory phase.
7. Participating libraries should handle all overdues and nonreturned/lost titles, assessing fines and damages to their patrons. However, all titles not in a packet at the time of rotation should be tracked by library; otherwise the inventory will be totally meaningless. Upon delivery of a new packet, each library should receive a packing/checklist of packet titles to be checked against packet contents.
8. Several written policies should be initially established to protect the interests of the membership, guide the organizational

activities of the group, and serve as legal documents against any lawsuits.
  a. A set of bylaws should be adopted describing the organization's function, administration, membership fees, and general rules and regulations.
  b. A dissolution clause is imperative. It should cover the mechanics of the disbanding process, in particular the distribution of assets. It is not enough to make a general statement, "... upon the dissolution of this [organization], all assets will be distributed among the membership according to a formula drawn up by the administrative board and approved by a majority vote of the members in good standing on the date of dissolution."[9] A precise formula should be established at the outset.
  c. A collection development policy, or at least a selection policy, including procedures, should be developed.
  d. A set of membership rules, specifically addressing the care and use of the collection, should also be established. Member libraries should be expected to provide a secure area, with shelving, to accommodate and house the video collection. A standardized method of reporting circulation (evaluation) should be developed, as well as damage and lost item replacement procedures and a copyright use policy.

IMPLEMENTING A VIDEO PACKET ROTATION SYSTEM
by Randy Pitman, editor of *The Video Librarian*

Individual libraries are beset with a variety of problems, ranging from storage to in-house use concerns, but are spared the difficult decision of solving a geographical distribution problem. Regional library systems, county libraries, and college and public libraries with several branches may find that creating a packet rotation system is not only the most equitable means of serving community or regional needs, but also may be the most economically feasible approach. This section will discuss the pros and cons of such a system, processing packets, and staff training, and will examine specific cases of existing packet systems and how they operate. For the purpose of what follows, a *packet* is any set of selectively chosen videocassette titles of indeterminate number, and a *rotation system* refers to the administration (timetable, transportation, and tracking) of packets among branch or member libraries.

There are two options for libraries considering the packet rotation system. A single library can start a packet system for its branches; however, the library should be prepared to increase the video budget. In this case, supplemental funding such as grants and/or nominal charges should be considered. If the current budget is insufficient, a second option involves several libraries banding together to form a video consortium. Annual fees or collection sharing would provide the money pool or inventory needed to support such a system.

☐ SELECTION

Packets are like weeds—they proliferate with wild abandon unless some form of quality control is set up. The two major ongoing concerns in packet maintenance are (1) striving to keep a balance of the various interest levels (adult, children) and genres (comedy, drama, science fiction, etc.) of videocassettes distributed evenly across the packets, and (2) replacing or repairing damaged tapes. The individual titles and the respective packets as a whole must also be kept complete; they require constant maintenance and the addition of new titles.

Initially, the library system or governing body of a video consortium will need to draft a working blueprint, so to speak, of the requirements they will need to meet in building a packet rotation system. What exact criteria are used will depend largely on the philosophical orientation of the administrative body. Many public libraries choose to build their packets along lines similar to the local video store's—in other words, current popularity will be the governing factor in title selection. Other libraries will try to find a happy medium between the popular titles that abound in video stores and cultural, educational, or instructional videos. A small percentage will focus almost exclusively upon titles not readily available to the public through either video or department stores.

Another criterion for consideration when building packets is title duplication. Some libraries will want maximum diversity and will, therefore, seldom purchase multiple copies of specific titles. Others, especially those who lean toward a current, popular collection, will automatically buy several copies of video bestsellers. Specific collection development questions are addressed in Chapters 2, 3, and 4.

Individual title circulation statistics, when combined into subject/genre categories, can provide excellent measures of patron interest useful in the selection process. Regardless of which overall principle of selection is adopted, some method of categorization is necessary to monitor the content of packets. Elliott Swanson, the head of branch services at the Kitsap Regional Library in Bremerton, Washington, designed and utilizes a microcomputer relational database program that provides a trilevel category approach for tracking the current "health" of any given packet:

> **LEVEL 1: Audience:** Titles are separated into the categories of "Adult," "Family," and "Children."
>
> **LEVEL 2: Type:** Titles are arranged by length and/or type of film into the categories of "Feature," "Featurette," "Animated," "Instruction," and "Music."
>
> **LEVEL 3: Genre:** Titles are arranged by content into the following categories: "Action/Adventure" (AA); "Comedy" (CO); "Documentary" (DO); "Drama" (DR); "Exercise" (EX); "Fantasy" (FA); "Feature-length Animated Film" (FF); "Fine Arts" (FI); "Horror" (HO); "Inspirational" (IN); "Martial Arts" (MA); "Music/Musical" (MU); "Science Fiction" (SF); "Sports" (SP); "Suspense/Mystery" (SU); "Travelogue" (TR); "War" (WA); and "Western" (WE).

The above-mentioned categories have undergone numerous refinements since the system's inception in 1982. Although the levels and categories will certainly vary from system to system, they all serve the same end: a means of monitoring, and thereby ensuring, balanced video packets.

Processing a Packet

Basic processing procedures of videocassettes will vary widely from system to system; video packets, however, will require a few additional steps:

1. The number (or letter) of the packet needs to be affixed to each individual videocassette within that packet in three places: the videocassette, the tape case that holds the tape, and the display box or annotation card that patrons trade for the video in closed-access circulation arrangements. If catalog cards are provided with each packet, these must also carry the packet designator.

2. An inventory list containing the titles in each packet is necessary as a check-in device when rotating packets between participating libraries. Some libraries with online circulation systems have found that once packets reach a certain size—say 100 titles plus—it is no longer necessary to closely track either the movement of packets or even the content. For example, in a 25-title packet, 2 James Bond films would stand out, whereas in a 150-title packet they would not. Likewise, if 5 titles were overdue at the time the 25-title packet was set to rotate, one-fifth of the packet would not be forwarded to the next library. In the case of a 150-title packet, the late arrival of 5 titles would hardly be noticeable. Not many systems could afford the staff time. Rotation periods should be of equal length for all participating libraries; however, each library should have control over both the loan period and method of circulation.

3. Branch library size should determine the number of packets assigned on a regular basis. The Kitsap Regional Library, for example, has thirteen packets of approximately 125 titles each. Four packets (500 titles) are allocated to the main library, two packets to the largest branch, and one packet each to the remaining seven branches. In a video consortium composed of member libraries, the number of packets a given library receives would be based upon a step-increment fee per packet.

Rotating Packets

In dense metropolitan areas, a packet rotation system may fully operate in a 20-mile radius. In some regional video consortiums, on the other hand, packets may be rotated to member libraries sprinkled throughout a state. Both transportation and scheduling need to be considered when setting up packet systems. Many metropolitan libraries, library systems, and schools possess van delivery systems; however, courier services can be leased. United Parcel delivery may also be used, but delivery/return time is prolonged. Some systems use a monthly meeting for the exchange of packets by participating members. This meeting also serves as a selection, problem-solving, and information exchange forum among the members.

The trick in rotating packets is not so much in setting up transportation as in working out a schedule. Depending on the number of participating entities and the number of packets involved, creating a seamless schedule can be an exercise on the order of solving a Rubik's cube. Naturally, adding new packets and/or new sites will often require a complete rewrite of the schedule. Most schedules are arrived at by trial and error.

☐ STAFF SUPPORT

Large libraries with branches can increase staff morale by simply making sure that branches have a voice in as many different areas of administration, including materials selection and circulation procedures, as possible. Given both the rapidly changing nature of the video medium and its relatively recent appearance in libraries, it is unlikely that the initial implementation of a new packet rotation system will be automatically bug-free, even with prior planning. Staff input, however, will result in better communication and improved service, ensuring a smooth-running and flexible operation.

Video consortiums, on the other hand, have to work with a number of different libraries that have a wide range of policies and procedures. The Connecticut Library Service Unit (CLSU) has taken a laissez-faire approach: the consortium provides the tapes, and the member library sets the policies and procedures. In addition, the CLSU video consortium members meet on a monthly basis and take an active part in title selection.

Staff Training
The amount of training necessary for branch libraries will largely depend upon the degree of autonomy each branch has in handling videocassettes. At the Kitsap Regional Library, all videocassette problems are channelled through the audiovisual department at the main library, keeping the pressure on branch staff to a minimum. Other library systems have equipped each branch with a VCR and monitor, and branch staff are responsible for screening damage complaints before sending problem tapes on to the main library.

Staff should be given a basic workshop in VCR operation and maintenance. In addition, they should be shown the proper procedure for visually checking the condition of the videocassette to determine damage. Inspection before the tape is readied for each circulation is imperative. Much of the time, video damage is cumulative; therefore it is recommended that a problem/damage and repair log be kept so that recurrent problem tapes can be discarded. Videocassettes, like other forms of media, are subject to wear and tear, and will need to be either repaired or discarded on a fairly regular basis. At least one person on the AV staff should be acquainted with the basic skills necessary for making simple videocassette repairs. As the collection ages, the frequency of replacements may outweight the number of repairs. But initially, substantial amounts of money will be saved if newer tapes are repaired rather than replaced. During 1986, the Kitsap Regional Library discarded 131 damaged tapes from a collection numbering some 1,500 titles. During that year, 122 videotapes were repaired. Based upon an average cost of $50 per tape, $6,100 worth of tapes were put back into circulation. Of the 122 tapes repaired, 83 needed simple leader splices—a procedure that generally takes less than five minutes. *Video Tape Repair—Do It Yourself,* available from Multi-Video Inc., P.O. Box 35444, Charlotte, NC 28235, is an excellent training tape, illustrating repair techniques and visual examples of how different damage such as dropout appears on-screen. Familiarity with the medium and the ability to recognize and assess videocassette damage will give staff a measure of confidence that will offset some of the stress of adding a new service.

☐ PROS AND CONS

What are the advantages of using a video packet rotation system?

1. For libraries with several branches, the primary advantage in rotating video packets is optimum use of the collection: By rotating packets, branches are able to offer a wide variety of titles to their patrons since the collection turns over, in effect, on a regular, short-term basis.

2. Particularly for libraries with limited budgets and/or those libraries who are just beginning to build video collections, a packet rotation system has definite economic advantages. Rather than setting up core collections requiring unnecessary title duplication at considerable expense, precious budget dollars can be spent more efficiently in building a diverse rotating collection with little emphasis placed on title duplication.

3. For member libraries of a video consortium, there is the added advantage of having no administration. The actual purchasing, processing, and maintenance of the packet rotation system is handled by the consortium.

What are the disadvantages of the rotation concept?

1. Concurrent with the advantage of maximum collection usage is the disadvantage of administering the rotation system. Administering a packet rotation system means handling staff resistance, juggling schedules, providing balanced packets, and fielding complaints from libraries and patrons.

2. The primary disadvantage for member libraries in video consortiums is the absence of control over the collection. As more and more patrons request instructional videocassettes, libraries will need to develop their own collections and not be dependent upon packets whose rigid scheduling will rarely coincide with meeting a patron's immediate needs.

3. Packet rotation systems have a point of diminishing returns. Once an individual packet reaches the vicinity of 200 to 300 titles, it may be time to consider breaking up the packets and establishing core collections in the branches. Obviously, at some point a critical mass will be achieved, whereby administering and transporting huge collections of videocassettes will be the equivalent of moving a small branch library. Once small core collections are established, new title additions could still be rotated before they are permanently assigned, thereby keeping the branch collections fresh.

☐ A TALE OF TWO SYSTEMS

A Public Library with Branches

The Lake County Public Library System in Merrillville, Indiana, began loaning videocassettes in 1980. The main collection of 250 videos was housed at the main library, which reserved titles three months in advance and sent over 100 videos a day by courier to their 13 branches.

Dawn Mogle assumed the audiovisual directorship in 1983 and decided to build up the collection and create a packet rotation system. After a year, during which the collection had been expanded to approximately 600 titles, seven packets with 85 titles each were created. In addition to the main library, six branch sites were chosen to carry packets. A three-ring notebook containing annotation cards for each title accompanied the packets, which were rotated on the second Tuesday of each month. Educational/informational videos are housed in the main library and are the only videocassettes that can be reserved.

Although initially no one thought it would be successful, the results were phenomenal. Today, circulation has doubled, with 100 titles accounting for 1,000 circulations per month. At the Lake County Public Library System, video packets have made the branch staff and patrons very happy.

A Video Consortium

The Southeastern Connecticut Library Association's video cooperative program was started up in 1985, with member libraries paying an initial buy-in charge for packet creation, and a $500-per-packet annual fee. During 1986, the program received a tremendous budgetary boost from a Library Services and Construction Act (LSCA) grant, and it presently routes 20 packets among 13 member libraries. Although the annual packet fee is still $500 per packet, the system is financially stable enough to eliminate buy-in fees.

☐ SUMMARY

In conclusion, a video packet rotation system is particularly economical in the transitional stage for placing videocassettes into library systems. As more emphasis is placed on videocassettes as an integral part of library services, and as budgets and collection sizes increase, video packets may well outgrow their usefulness. Because of the low cost of video, as compared to 16mm film, even the video consortiums may eventually fold. This has already happened to the Washington Library Video circuit, for example. Member libraries found it more cost-effective, and more in keeping with long-range goals, to purchase their own collections rather than rent from the consortium. Nevertheless, until the day arrives when videocassette purchases account for a substantial amount of the materials budget, public libraries with branches and/or member libraries of video consortiums will find that video packets stretch dollars and allow for the wide variety of titles necessary to satisfy community needs.

NOTES

1. Carol Emmens, "Cooperative Purchasing," *School Library Journal* 29 (February 1983): 42.
2. "WVA Video Circuit Offers 200 Tapes/Year for $800," *Library Journal* 109 (1 October 1984): 1,800.
3. "New Jersey Video Circuit: A Fast Growing Co-op Venture," *Library Journal* 110 (15 October 1983): 1,412.
4. Lee N. Flanagan and Linda Hale, "A Videocassette Circuit on a Shoestring," *Library Journal* 110 (15 November 1985): 40–41.
5. Wisconsin Library Audiovisual Circuit, *Handbook for Members*, 1985, 7.
6. Flanagan and Hale, "A Videocassette Circuit," 41.
7. Telephone interview with Linda Hale, Region One Cooperating Library Service Unit, Waterbury, Connecticut, 3 May 1987.
8. Flanagan and Hale, "A Videocassette Circuit," 41.
9. Wisconsin Library Audiovisual Circuit, *Handbook*, 12.

8 PREDICTING THE FUTURE

Today, videocassettes are such a hot item it is difficult to look back upon that time when video technology was just beginning. It is even harder to predict what the future will hold for this dynamic medium. Predicting the future of videocassettes in terms of industry trends is particularly important so that librarians can tentatively plan for the future. The American Library Association survey referred to in Chapter 1 showed that, in libraries serving populations of 25,000 or more, about 67 to 69 percent had videocassette collections. About 70 percent of those libraries surveyed reported that they had feature films, and 68 percent reported that they had some educational titles.[1] This chapter will discuss the extended five-year outlook for video in terms of software and technology.

THE SOFTWARE OUTLOOK

The general industry trend is toward production and marketing of nonfiction titles or made-for-video features. At the August 1986 meeting of the Video Software Dealer's Association (VSDA), executives from the video giant Karl Lorimar announced a campaign to exclusively market "specialty programming" titles rather than feature films. The year 1987 will be remembered as the year specialty nonfiction video came into its own. The current interest is led by cooking, travel, sports, and how-to, and, by next year, will grow to represent fully 10 percent of the 1988 expected retail sales of 83 million prerecorded videocassettes. Conservative estimates place the production of special-interest videos around 5,000 to 6,000 titles next year, with prices ranging from $9.95 to $29.95.[2] However, libraries will have to be on guard because the quality may not be consistent. Also, there will be a profusion of similar-subject titles, making selection more difficult than ever before. Patrons will be demanding alternate programming more because of increased producer marketing and advertising.

Business sponsorship, association certification, celebrity actors/hosts, and endorsements will play important marketing roles in the future of video programming to establish program credibility. For example, today there are over 300 exercise/aerobic videocassettes on the market. Many of these programs contain exercises that could be harmful. The Aerobics and Fitness Association of America has now begun to certify programs that meet their standards.[3] Sports video programs will become increasingly popular as patrons discover the viability of learning by seeing rather than learning by reading about it. Some subjects, like sports, are better suited to a video learning presentation rather than still pictures and the written word. Sports video is so new that the future cannot be accurately predicted because the industry is just discovering its potential.

Many productions are now employing celebrities as hosts, and production costs are becoming increasingly expensive. The production costs for a 60-minute video can run as much as $2,000 per minute, and moving 2,000 units of any title is considered a good sale.[4]

The consumer target age is also shifting. Within the next 20 years, the 1950s baby boom generation will be 45 to 50 years old. Today's teens will be in their 30s. The largest percentage of the population will be 65 years old and over. The question that remains for movie popularity is, Will today's classics be the classics of tomorrow's generation?[5] The current target age for popular Top 40 music is 12 to 24 years of age. The industry predicts that music video will grow to account for as much as 25 percent of the market by 1988.[6] This author sees the decline of music television (MTV) within the next eight to ten years. However, this gap will be filled by other music-type videos including theater musicals, classical operas, symphony performances, as well as contemporary music. The purchase of MTV-type music videos by libraries is not advocated because of their cost ratio versus the ephemeral nature of their popularity.

PREDICTING THE FUTURE
181

A new genre is also just emerging and will continue to gain popularity through 1988 and beyond—the video romance novelette. Companies such as Video Romance, Ltd., Karl Lorimar Home Video, and Atlantic Video Ventures are producing Harlequin-type romance videos. Prism Entertainment recently acquired the rights to the syndicated series "Romance Theater" for home video release.[7]

Today, magazine-like videos are just starting to appear. Currently, library budgets are in no position to acquire these subscription-based programs, but their popularity will continue to increase. *Esquire* magazine has a career/business line, Karl Lorimar has *Playboy Video Magazine*, Pacific Arts has *Overview*, Videofashion has produced *Videofashion Monthly*, and there are even magazine videos for scuba diving enthusiasts or aviation buffs. There are a variety of other magazine-related programs, including *Black Belt Karate, Parent's, Weight Watcher's, Consumer Reports, Working Woman,* and *American Health.* These are more sponsor-oriented agency programs than actual magazines but, because of their high visibility, they will definitely be popular. As long as the producers of video magazines realize the implications and limitations of the format and do not try to emulate print material, they will succeed.[8]

Another software prediction is an increase in the number of large film/video producers such as MTI/Coronet, Encyclopaedia Britannica, and AIMS Media delving into home video marketing or drastically reducing the prices of their public performance programs to be in line with the home video market. Early in 1988, MTI/Coronet will also enter the home video market arena as a wholesale jobber similar to Baker & Taylor Sound Video Unlimited and Ingram. This will continue to muddle the lines between "home use only" and public performance rights.

Although there have been new advances in magnetic tape technology, the sales base for the VHS format is so large that it will not conceivably become obsolete. The 8mm format does not have a significant inventory of prerecorded titles available yet, and the 4mm format is just now surfacing. The 8mm and 4mm formats will become popular as lightweight home-recording formats, but with the advent of the full-sized VHS and Beta camcorders, they will not usurp a major portion of the market.

High quality (HQ) video is just coming into its own, and its popularity will continue to grow. The major stumbling block in its acceptance is the fact that the system requires an improved matrix-quality monitor, requiring consumers to upgrade not only their VCRs, but also their televisions. True stereo, high-fidelity sound and Super Video (VHS and Beta) are also available. Digital television is just around the corner and promises to open up new doors in terms of visual-point access and information retrieval. Five years ago RCA and Pioneer were marketing the video disc. They were not totally successful, but the compact laser video disc will enjoy a resurgence in 1989 and beyond. The disc offers only playback capabilities at present, but the playback quality and digital quick-point access are superior to the tape formats.

The following dialog could be possible in a library AV department within the next five years. A lady comes into the library and asks for *Back to the Future, Part II*. The librarian has to ask, Soundtrack version or movie version? Digital, analog, or analog hi-fi? Would you like it in 8mm, 4mm, VHS, Beta, Super Beta, S-VHS, or compact disc video?

The video software arena will change dramatically in terms of the types of titles offered for sale. This will prove to be both boon and bane to libraries. Video software review sources will probably become more prevalent, and this will aid in the selection and evaluation of materials. The rapid proliferation of titles combined with low materials budgets will place increased selection pressures upon libraries.

VENDORS AND LIBRARIES

The entrance of MTI/Coronet into the wholesale home video jobber market has already been mentioned. This author feels that, while the number of video jobbers and distributors will not grow significantly, it will not decrease either. Large jobbers are here to stay and offer libraries products at considerable discounts. (However, to date a few large producers such as MCA, Vestron, and RCA/Columbia have substantially reduced the number of exclusive distributors and will seek to sell their videos through direct distribution. This will continue as a trend but will not seriously affect the larger distributors' or jobbers' share of the market.) In 1987, the libraries accounted for about $22 million, or 1 percent, of the total $2.2 billion in video software sales. Today, distributors consider libraries viable markets but do not as yet actively court them with the same enthusiasm as book jobbers. As this percentage increases, libraries will be able to exert their purchasing-power leverage on issues such as price discounts, returns, and previews.

THE HARDWARE SCENE

The future shows a slowing of video hardware sales through 1990, at least in terms of the current VHS hardware scene. The growth of the home video industry is about to taper off just as the industry reaches maturity. During 1987, annual VCR sales revenues were expected to be $4.85 billion—a 29 percent increase from 1986 totals. In contrast, predicted 1988 revenues are $5.64 billion—a 16 percent gain. Subsequent yearly jumps will be 9 and 7 percent for 1989 and 1990, when the market will hit the $6.5 billion mark.[9] Some reasons for this leveling off are:

- A slower expansion of the VCR-owning population. The rate of growth from 1981 to 1986 was 1,200 percent. Between 1986 and 1990, a 70 percent increase is projected, resulting in a VCR universe of from 34 to 58 million homes.
- There will be fewer affluent homes; consumers will have less disposable income.
- There will be a fractionalization of viewing shares, as only a certain amount of viewing time is available to the viewer. Cable and satellite television, pay stations, and prerecorded videocassettes in libraries and video rental stores are all competing for a piece of the market pie.
- Lower prices for rental, e.g., $2.20 in 1990 compared to $2.40 today.
- For the first time, programming costs are escalating faster than market growth. Quality nontheatrical programming is opening up many new opportunities.[10]

The technology of hardware will continue to improve, bringing Super Beta and Super VHS formats to the market forefront. Coding with Macrovision will be eliminated, and in its place special computer antipiracy chips will be installed into VCRs and software, preventing unlawful duplication. This technological advance will probably increase the price of VCRs by 10 percent. The technological wave has hit video with full force and will have long-range implications.

SPECIAL OPTIONS AND COPYRIGHT

The legal ramifications of home use versus public performance will finally come to a head in a court case involving a major public library. This will serve to clarify the ambiguities of the copyright law concerning in-house private videocassette use by patrons.

Currently, two companies are offering umbrella licensing for feature films, permitting libraries to use certain producer home-use videos for in-house group showing and private purposes. The Motion Picture Licensing Corporation, P.O. Box 3838, 2777 Summer Street, Stamford, CT 06905–0838, (203) 353-1600 or (800) 338-3870, offers a blanket public performance license for any title from Walt Disney, Touchstone Pictures, Columbia Pictures, De Laurentiis Entertainment, Best Film & Video Corporation, Metro-Goldwyn-Mayer, United Artists, and Warner Brothers. Licensing prices are based upon five factors: (1) number of locations/branches, (2) number of cardholders, (3) number of VCRs in use, (4) number of videocassettes in the collection, and (5) population of the service area.

As an example of price, a town library serving about 15,000 people and having 4,000 cardholders might expect to pay about $300 per year. There are no limits on the number of showings per title or the number of titles that can be shown. The only restriction is that this is a building license—the subscription fee does not include the purchase of the individual video titles.[11] Films, Incorporated will also be offering a similar plan with companies not carried by MPLC. The address is Films, Inc., 5547 North Ravenswood, Chicago, IL 60640–1199, (312) 878-2600 or (800) 826-3456. The umbrella license will continue to become popular, and more companies will start offering this relatively inexpensive service.

SUMMARY

Industry experts say that the video market has reached maturity. This concept is hard to fathom, as the revolution occurred only about eight years ago. Today, technology is taking video in several directions simultaneously, and it is difficult to believe that a plateau has been reached. Libraries will have a hard time deciphering the various options open to them as the 1990s open new doors; but by developing a carefully thought out strategic plan, keeping track of current marketing and industry trends, exploring new purchasing and circulation alternatives, and maintaining an active video collection development policy responsive to institutional library goals, librarians can minimize software and hardware obsolescence. Librarians should not be afraid of new video media and formats; they should see them as exciting opportunities to develop new service alternatives that will help expand the concept of traditional library service in the eyes of the general public.

NOTES

1. Linda Wallace, "Video Tapes on Tap at the Public Library," (Chicago: Doremus Porter Novelli, 4 May 1987), Special Press Release for the American Library Association.
2. Peter P. Schillaci, "Video Trends: Past, Present, & Future," *Sightlines* 20 (Winter 1986/1987): 8–9.
3. "A Retailer's Guide to Special Interest Video," *Billboard*, 25 April 1987, 51–52.
4. Schillaci, "Video Trends," 9.
5. Alan Penchansky, "Midwest's Top 40 Formats Fading," *Billboard*, 7 June 1986, 1.
6. Jim McCullaugh, "Kagan Seminar Foresees Slowed Industry Growth," *Billboard*, 25 April 1987, 53.
7. Frank Lovece, "Magazine-Related Product Is Growing, Innovating," *Billboard*, 15 November 1986, 60.
8. Ibid.
9. McCullaugh, "Kagan Seminar," 53.
10. Ibid.
11. Sal A. Laudicina, licensing director, Motion Picture Licensing Corporation, Stamford, Connecticut, interview with author, 10 December 1987.

APPENDIX
FREEDOM TO VIEW

The following statement was adopted by the Intellectual Freedom Committee, American Library Association, June 1979:

The *Freedom to View*, along with the freedom to speak, to hear, and to read, is protected by the First Amendment to the Constitution of the United States. In a free society, there is no place for censorship of any medium of expression. Therefore, we affirm these principles:

1. It is in the public interest to provide the broadest possible access to films and other audiovisual materials because they have proven to be among the most effective means for the communication of ideas. Liberty of circulation is essential to ensure the constitutional guarantee of freedom of expression.
2. It is in the public interest to provide for our audiences films and other audiovisual materials which represent a diversity of views and expression. Selection of a work does not constitute or imply agreement with or approval of the content.
3. It is our professional responsibility to resist the constraint of labeling or pre-judging a film on the basis of the moral, religious, or political beliefs of the producer or filmmaker or on the basis of controversial content.
4. It is our professional responsibility to contest vigorously, by all lawful means, every encroachment upon the public's freedom to view.

This statement was originally drafted by the Educational Film Library Association's Freedom to View committee, and was adopted by the EFLA board of directors in February 1979. Libraries and educational institutions are encouraged to adopt this statement and display it in their catalogs or libraries. The text of the statement may be reprinted freely; permission is granted to all educational institutions to use it.[1]

---

[1] John W. Ellison, ed. *Media Librarianship.* New York: Neal-Schuman, 1985, p. 58.

INDEX

AACR II. *See* Anglo-American Cataloguing Rules
Academic libraries, 32, 163–164
Access, 14–15, 38–40
  behind-the-counter, 15, 38–39, 50
  by minors, 157–188
  open, 17, 40, 46, 50, 55
Acquisitions, 18, 21, 22, 55–57. *See also* Purchase plans; Selection
"Act to Prohibit the Distribution of Video Movies Without Official Ratings, An" (MA), 158
Adventureland, 15
Aerobics and Fitness Association of America, 180
Agency for Instructional Technology, 61
AIMS Media, 56, 181
ALA. *See* American Library Association
Alpha Video, 129
Alternative Video, 60
Amaray boxes, 44 (photo)
Ambico, 129
American Health, 181
American Library Association (ALA), 144, 147, 149
  Intellectual Freedom Committee, 158

Amplifiers, 125–126
Anglo-American Cataloguing Rules (AACR II), 62–63, 65
Annenberg/CPB Project, The, 61
Anti-theft systems, 14. *See also* Security
Apple Video, 59
Appropriateness, 83. *See also* Access, by minors; Audience rating system
Artec, Inc., 58
Asheim, Lester, 4
Atlantic Video Ventures, 181
At the Movies, 102
Audience rating system, 157–158, 166
Azimuth recording, 113 (fig.), 117

Baker & Taylor Sound Video Unlimited, 181
Baker & Taylor Video, 58
Baskerville, Tim, 10
Behind-the-counter access, 15, 38–39, 50
Bender, Ivan R., 146
Berelson, Bernard, 3
Beta format, 8, 9 (table), 112, 114–116, 122, 127, 128, 135–136, 181, 182
Billboard, 22, 95
  "Top Videocassettes," 103–108
Black Belt Karate, 181

189

"Black boxes," 126
Blackhawk Films and Video, 59
Black Video Guide, The, 96
BOCES, 164
Booklist, 74, 95, 99
Books in Print, 95
Broadcast equipment, 126–127
Brodart, 165
Brodart Video, 60, 102
Browsing, 87
Budgeting. *See* Materials budget
Business. *See* Specialty video
Buying guides, 94. *See also* Selection, tools

Cable-ready equipment, 122, 123
C.A.I. Software Inc., 59
California State Library, 167
California/Washington Video Circuit, 167
Camcorders, 181
Cameras, 127. *See also* In-house production
Camera switchers, 128
Car and Driver, 96
Castell, Ron, 15
Catalog cards, 21, 65
Cataloging, 21, 55, 61, 62–66
C. C. Studios, 56
CED, 9 (table)
Certification, 180
C format, 8
Checklists, 94. *See also* Selection, tools
Checkpoint system, 14, 40, 46, 50, 55
Chicago One Stop, Inc., 45–46
Children's titles, 11, 13 (table), 17, 76, 103
Chip Taylor Communications, 59
Choice, 95, 101
Circuits, 166–170
Circulation, 20–21, 88
  automated systems, 20, 34, 70, 85
  budgeting and, 34
  closed-stack systems, 20
  collection development and, 82, 85
  data collection, 85–87, 171–172

manual systems, 34, 70, 87
policies, 66–67
staffing, 54
Classical Video, 60
Classic features, 103
Classifying. *See* Cataloging
Clearview Media Corporation, 60, 102
Cleveland (OH) Public Library, 22
Closed-stack circulation system, 20
CLSU. *See* Connecticut Library Service Units
Collections, 18–22
  budgets, 18, 32–37, 56, 85
  composition of, 19, 20 (table), 83, 87–88
  development, 12–13, 19, 21, 25, 26, 32, 79–109
  development policy, 32, 69–78, 159
  evaluation of, 70, 72, 77, 79–80, 82–84, 89–91, 160
  goals of, 80–88
  management, 21, 69–70, 77–78, 79, 159–160
  planning, 25–67
  rotating, 166–173
Columbia Pictures v. Redd Horne, 146, 147
"Commitment to Cassettes, A," 17
Commtron Corporation, 58
Complete Home Video Directory, 95
Comsewogue (NY) Public Library, 22
Connecticut Library Service Units (CLSU), 174
Connecticut Region One Cooperating Library Service, 167–168
Connoisseur's Guide to the Movies, 96
Consortium purchasing, 163–164
Consultations, 31
Consumer Reports, 53, 181
Content indicators, 157–158
Cooperating Libraries of Central Maryland, 21
Copyguard, 126

INDEX

Copyright, 62, 139–157, 183–184
Copyright: What Every School, College and Public Library Should Know, 154
Copyright Act of 1976, 140, 141, 144, 147–148, 150, 155–156
Copyright Policy Development: A Resource Book for Educators, 154
Coronet Feature Video, 58
Crafts. *See* Specialty video
CREW method, 160
Cribbins, George, 130
Critchfield, Bill, 15

Decatur (IL) Public Library, 22, 43–47, 51 (fig.), 73
Demand, 10–12, 69, 80–84, 87, 88, 105
Demco, Inc., 40, 45, 46, 62
Dewey decimal classification system, 66
Digital television, 182
Directories, 95. *See also* Selection, tools
Discount schedules, 58. *See also* Prices
Dicount Video, 59
Display options, 38–53
Distributors, 21, 40, 56–61, 182
  catalogs, 101–102
Do-it-yourself tapes, 11, 13
Dolby stereo, 122
Donors, 77
Dropout, 117
Dubbing, 127
Dummy display, 38–39, 44–46
Duplication, 84

East Brunswick (NJ) Public Library, 166
Eastin-Phelan Corporation, 164–165
East Texas Distributing, 58–59
Editing equipment, 126–127
Educational Film Library Association (EFLA), 187–188
Educational use, 144, 146, 148–149

Educational video, 32, 61. *See also* Specialty video
EFLA. *See* Educational Film Library Association
8mm video, 8, 181
Elliot, Joe, 149
Ellis, Jim, 14
Encyclopaedia Britannica, 56, 181
Encyclopaedia Britannica Educational Corporation, et al. v. C. N. Crooks, 149
Encyclopedia of Film, 94
Enhancers, 126
Entertainment Tonight, 102
Ephemera, 69, 78, 82–83
EQ Beta, 115
Equipment
  broadcast, 126–127
  editing, 126–127
  loan of, 120, 156–157
  maintenance of, 111
  purchase of, 50, 53
  selection of, 118–121
  See also Cameras; Monitors; Television sets; Videocassette recorders
Erol's, 15
Evaluation. *See* Collections, evaluation of
Evaluative tools. *See* Selection, tools
Evans, G. Edward, 159
Evergreen Video Society, 59

Facets Video, 59
Fair-use doctrine, 143, 144. *See also* Copyright; Use guidelines
Feature videos, 10–12, 20, 65, 76, 88, 103
Fees, 19, 20, 67, 83, 155–157, 158
Fiction (book), 88
Film, 3, 112
Film and Video Finder, 95, 99
Film File 1984–1985, 101
Filmic Archives, 59
Films, Incorporated, 56, 184
Findlay-Handcock (OH) Public Library, 22
Fine Woodworking, 96

First-sale doctrine, 140
Fitness video. *See* Specialty video
500 Best American Films To Buy, Rent, or Videotape, 96
Fontaine, Dick, 90
Formats, 8, 9 (table), 77, 112–118, 120, 122, 127, 128, 135–136, 181–183
4mm video, 181
"Freedom to View," 72, 73, 187–188
Frequency response, 117–118
Fresnel screen, 125

Galvin, Thomas J., 147
Gaylord Brothers, 40, 42 (fig.), 45
Genre labels, 66
Gift materials, 77–78
Gitlin, Michael, 2
Godfrey, John, 129
GPN: Instructional Television Library, 61
Greenleaf Video, 60, 102
Guidance Associates, 61
Guidelines for Audiovisual Materials and Services for Large Public Libraries, 4

Halliwell's Film and Video Guide, 94, 96–97
Halliwell's Film Guide, 74
Halliwell's 100, 94
Hayworth, Tom, 11
Head cleaners, 135
Hi Fidelity, 53, 95, 111
Hi-fi systems, 122, 182. *See also* Stereo
High quality (HQ) video, 181–182
Highsmith Co., 40, 44, 62
Hobbies. *See* Specialty video
Home use, 141–144, 147, 150, 151, 183, 184
Home Viewer, 95, 99
Homevision, 56
HQ. *See* High quality video

Indexes, 94–95. *See also* Selection, tools
Ingram video, 58, 181
In-house production, 120, 126–128
In-print directories, 95

Jobbers, 21, 40, 56–59, 62, 182
Jones, John W., 2
JVC (Japan Victor Corporation), 112

Karl Lorimar Home Video, 181
Kidvid: A Parent's Guide to Children's Videos, 97
Kinma, 129
Kitsap (WA) Regional Library, 172–173, 174

Labeling, 62, 66, 158, 166
Lake County (IN) Public Library System, 176
Lander's Film Review, 101
Laser discs, 8, 9 (table)
Leasing plans, 164–166
Leonard Maltin's TV Movies and Video Guide, 97
Librarian's Video Review, 74, 100
Librarian's Video Service, 60, 102
Libraries in an Information Society: A Statistical Summary, 18
"Library Bill of Rights," 72, 73
Library Journal, 74, 95, 100
Library Literature, 94, 95
Library of Congress List of Subject Headings, The, 65
Library Services and Construction Act (LSCA), 176
Library Video Company, 60, 102
Licensing, 184
Lorimar, Karl, 179, 181
Los Angeles County (CA) Public Library, 154
LSCA. *See* Library Services and Construction Act

McGrath formula, 33–36
McNaughton lease plan, 165
Macrovision, 183
Magnetic discs, 8
Magnetic videotape, 117–118
Margolis, Bernard A., 163
Marketing, 180
Marketing materials, 62
Materials budget, 18, 32–37, 56, 85

INDEX

MCA, 182
Media Review, 94
Media Review Digest, 101
Media revolution, 2–4
Megamovies, 13, 17
Metro Video Distributors, 59
MGM/UA, 154
Miller, Jerome K., 143, 144, 148
Minors' access, 157–158
Mission statements, 71–72
Mr. Video, 40, 131
Mogle, Dawn, 176
Monitors, 123–124
Monroe County (MI) Library System, 163
Morgantown (WV) Public Library, 166–167
Motion Picture Association of America (MPAA), 141–144, 147, 157–158, 166
Motion Picture Guide, The, 74, 94, 97
Motion Picture Licensing Corporation, 143, 184
Movies Unlimited, 59, 102
MPAA. *See* Motion Picture Association of America
M. S. Distributing Company, 59
MTI/Coronet, 56, 181, 182
MTS. *See* Multichannel television sound
Multichannel television sound (MTS), 123
Multiple-output devices, 125–126
Multi-Video, Inc., 131
Music video, 103, 180
Music Video Guide, 97–98

National Audiovisual Center, 61
National Geographic, 150
Nebraska Video Company, 129
Needs assessment, 25–32, 79
  instrument, 30 (fig.)
  See also Physical needs
Neuse Regional (NC) Public Library, 19
Newsweek, 96
New Video, 15
New York Public Library, Donnel Film Library, 17
NICEM, 95, 99

NILRC. *See* Northern Illinois Learning Resources Consortium
Noise, 118
Nonfiction video. *See* Specialty video
Northern Illinois Learning Resources Consortium (NILRC), 163–164

OCLC cataloging, 65
Off-air recording, 148–149, 150, 152–153
Onondaga County (NY) Public Library, 22
Open access, 15, 17, 40, 46, 50, 55
Overview, 181

Packet rotation systems, 170–177
Parent's, 181
Patron access. *See* Access
Patron input, 80, 84, 87, 88, 105
Patron survey, 29–31, 32. *See also* Needs assessment
PBS Video, 61
People, 95
Philipp, Fred, 18
Philips/Grundig VCR system, 112
Phoenix (AZ) Public Library, 54
Physical needs, 37–50. *See also* Needs assessment
Plaks, 41–43
Playboy Video Magazine, 181
Playing Hard to Get, 60
Polo Video Sales Company, 60
Prices, 56–58, 87–88, 180
Prism Entertainment, 181
Processing, 55, 61–62, 67, 172–173. *See also* Cataloging
Processing amplifiers, 126
Processors, 126
Producer catalogs, 21, 57
Production, 120, 126–128
Professional Media Service Corporation, 59, 102, 165
Projection televisions, 124–125
Public access. *See* Access
Public libraries, 3, 4–5, 17–21, 32, 80–81, 156
  as educational institutions, 146
  packet systems for, 171

Public libraries *(continued)*
 patronage of, 21
"Public Libraries and
 Videocassettes," 17
Public Media Incorporated, 147
Public performance concept, 56,
 57, 141, 146–147, 151, 183, 184
Publisher's Central Bureau, 59
Purchase plans, 163–177
Purging, 159. *See also* Collections,
 management
Purpose statements, 69, 73
Pyramid Films, 56

Quadruplex recorders, 112
Quality. *See* Ephemera; Selection,
 criteria
Quality Life Video Publishing, 60

Rabbits, 125
Radio frequency (RF) input, 120,
 121, 123
RCA/Columbia, 182
*Reader's Guide to Periodical
 Literature*, 94
Rear projection, 125
Receiver/monitors, 123–125
Recording, 148–149, 150, 152–153.
 See also Production
Reed, Mary Hutchings, 146, 155
Reference tools, 94, 95–103. *See
 also* Selection, tools
Replacement, 77
Research Technology
 International (RTI), 128
Reshelving, 54
Resolution, 123
Revenues. *See* Fees
Reviews, 21, 56, 82, 83
 evaluation of, 92–93, 102
 sources of, 91–92, 99–103
RF. *See* Radio frequency (RF)
 input
River Raisin (MI) Library, 163,
 164
Road and Track, 96
*Roger Ebert's Movie Home
 Companion*, 98
Rolling Stone, 95
Romance videos, 181

Rotation systems, 166–177
Routing connectors, 125–126
Rowe, David, 10
RTI. *See* Research Technology
 International
Rutledge, John, 35

Santa Monica (CA) Public
 Library, 166
School Library Journal, 101
Science Books and Films, 95, 101
Screen sizes, 124–125
Sears List of Subject Headings, 65
Seattle (WA) Public Library, 73
Security, 14–15, 17, 40, 43, 46, 50,
 55
Selection, 18, 21, 22, 55–57, 106
 budget and, 35, 37
 criteria, 74–76, 78, 83, 103
 policy, 56, 70–71, 72, 74, 79,
 82–85, 157
 process, 56, 72, 74
 for rotation systems, 171–173
 strategies, 88–89
 tools, 21, 22, 53, 74, 84, 85,
 91–95
Sensormatic, 14
Shelf arrangement, 66. *See also*
 Cataloging
Shelving, 38–53
Shoot 'Em Ups, 94
Simulcasts, 122, 124
S. I. Video, 60, 102
Smith, Roy, 55
Sneak Previews, 102
Snow, 118
S/N ratio, 118
Southeast Connecticut Library
 Association, 176
Space allocations, 37–39. *See also*
 Physical needs
Special effects, 128
Specialty video, 11–13, 16–17, 19
 (table), 20 (table), 60–61, 66,
 76, 87–88, 103, 179–180
Spiller, David, 32
Sports video. *See* Specialty video
Stabilizers, 126
Staffing, 22, 54, 173–175
Stanek, Debra, 143

INDEX

Star Video Entertainment, 59
Stereo, 122–124, 182
Stereo Review, 53, 95, 111
Storage, 159
Subject lists, 65
Subscription programs, 181
Super Beta, 115, 183
Super VHS, 183
Super Video, 182, 183
S VHS system, 115
Swank Motion Pictures, 143
Swanson, Elliott, 172
Swindler, Luke, 35
Switching, 125–126

Tamarelle's International Films, 60, 147
Tapechek, 128–129
Tape life, 129–131
Tape speed, 115, 117, 122
Tattle-tape, 14, 40, 46, 55
Tax-provided funds, 156
Television sets, 123, 124–125
Theft, 15, 55. *See also* Security
3M, 14, 40, 46, 50, 55
Time, 96
Titling, 128
Tolliver, Barbara, 25
Tomorrow Today, 129
Track display system, 43 (fig.)
Tracking, 118
Tuners, 121
Tworek, Ronald J., 46

U-matic cassette system, 112
Unactivated needs, 29, 31
United Ad Label Company, 66
University of Illinois Film/Video Center, 60
Use guidelines, 150–153
Use policies, 66–67
User profiles, 21, 22, 32, 87, 180

V: The Mail-Order Magazine of Videocassettes, 61, 101
Van Orden, Phyllis J., 80
Variety, 95
Variety's Complete Home Video Directory, 98
VCR, 100

VCRs. *See* Videocassette recorders
Vendors, 21, 56–61, 182
Vestron, 182
VHS (Video Home System) format, 8, 9 (table), 112, 114–117, 120, 122, 127, 128, 136, 181–183
Video, 100
"Video and the Public Library," 17
Video Browser Paks, 39, 46
Videocassette recorders (VCRs), 5, 183
 in-house use, 120–121
 library functions of, 199–121
 maintenance of, 130–131
 portable, 121
 sales of, 9–10
 selection of, 50, 53, 118–121
 tabletop, 121
 as teaching tools, 16
 technology of, 112–114, 121–122
 use patterns, 7–8, 10
Videocassettes
 consumer preferences in, 10–12, 69
 feature, 10–12, 20, 65, 76, 88, 103
 maintenance of, 128–129
 rental of, 10–14
 repair of, 131–137
 sales of, 10, 12
 specialty, 11–13, 16–17, 19 (table), 20 (table), 60–61, 66, 76, 87–88, 103, 179–180
 stereo, 123, 124
"Videocassettes in Libraries," 17
Video/Copyright Seminar, 154–155
Videofashion Monthly, 181
Videoflats display, 15, 39–40, 45–46, 51–53 (fig.)
Video Home System. *See* VHS (Video Home System) format
Video Insider, 101
Video Librarian, The, 95, 100
Video Movie Guide, The, 98–99
Video Movie Sales and Rentals Act (IL), 158
Videoplan, Inc., 164, 165–166

Video processors, 126
Video recording, 112–114
Video Review, 53, 74, 94, 95, 101, 111
Video revolution, 7–24
Video Romance, Ltd., 181
Video Schoolhouse, The, 61, 102
Videotakes, 61
Video Tape Repair—Do It Yourself, 175
Video Shack, 102
Video Software Dealer, 101
Video Software Dealer's Association (VSDA), 12, 14, 31
Video Source Book, The, 11, 95, 99, 101–102
Video stores
 inventory control, 13–17
 patron access, 14–16
 security, 14–16
Video Store Services, 40
Video Store Shopper, The, 40, 43 (fig.), 131
Video Tape and Disc Guide to Home Entertainment, The, 99
Video Trend, 61

Viditek SSV440, 125
Vid Pro Video Plak, 41–43
VSDA. *See* Video Software Dealer's Association

Walden Video, 60
Warner Brothers Distributing, 143, 145 (fig.)
Washington Library Video Circuit, 177
Webster, Norton R., 157
Weeding, 77, 79, 159–160. *See also* Collections, management
Weight Watcher's, 181
Weston Woods, 56
What Educators Should Know About Copyright, 155
Whisper-tape, 14, 40, 46
Wholesalers. *See* Vendors
Wisconsin Library Audiovisual Circuit, Inc., 167
Workflow, 54
Working Woman, 181

Zenger Video, 60, 102

Designed by Maureen Lauran
Composed in Aster with Serif Gothic
Typeset by The TypeStudio of Santa Barbara, California
Printed and bound by Braun-Brumfield, Ann Arbor, Michigan

238570